Managing The Welfare State

Managing the Welfare State

Text and Sourcebook

Updated and Revised Second Edition

Tony Cutler and Barbara Waine

Oxford • New York

First published in 1997 by
Berg
Editorial offices:
150 Cowley Road, Oxford, OX4 1JJ, UK
70 Washington Square South, New York, NY 10012, USA

Reprinted and revised 1997

Berg is an imprint of Oxford International Publishers Ltd.

Library of Congress Cataloging-in-Publication Data

A catalogue record for this book is available from the Library of Congress.

British Library Cataloguing-in-Publication Data

A catalogue record for this book is available from the British Library.

ISBN 1 85973 932 6 (Paper)

Typeset by JS Typesetting, Wellingborough, Northants.
Printed in the United Kingdom by WBC Book Manufacturers, Bridgend,
Mid Glamorgan.

Contents

Acknowledgements   vii

List of Tables   ix

List of Abbreviations   xi

Preface   xiii

1   The Politics of Managerialism   1

2   Managing by Numbers: The Bogus Prospectus of
         Performance Measurement   29

3   Welfare Markets   54

4   Compulsory Competitive Tendering: The Case of the
         Vanishing Producers   87

5   Determining Public Sector Pay: Prescription
         and Practice   116

6   Conclusion: A Managerialist Future   141

Documents   168

Bibliography   260

Index   277

Acknowledgements

We would particularly like to thank Shereen Colvin and Ross Woollard of the British Government Publications section of Senate House Library, University of London for always being able to find the HMSO publications we required, even when they were only published a few days before. Without their expertise, this book would not have been completed as quickly as it has.

Thanks are also due to the library staff at the Enfield campus of Middlesex University; to Peter Fisher and Jon Sutcliffe of the Local Government Management Board for the valuable information and advice on the issue of compulsory competitive tendering – like the Seventh Cavalry, this information and advice came at a vital time in the writing of the book; to Malcolm Read of the School of Sociology and Social Policy for his technical help; and to Pauline Foley, who typed all the documents and substantial parts of the text and who kept on assuring us that, 'it is all falling into place'; and to David Phelps, our copy-editor who meticulously corrected and enhanced the text. We are grateful to the Audit Commission and the Association of London Government who have kindly given permission for the reproduction of copyright material. Crown copyright is reproduced with the permission of the Controller of Her Majesty's Stationery Office.

List of Tables

1.1 Average annual growth rates of final consumption expenditure per head, real government consumption expenditure and rates of unemployment in the OECD countries, 1960–73   12

1.2 British general election results, 1945–92, percentage share of votes and seats won   22

1.3 UK general government expenditure (X) as a percentage of gross domestic product 1979–80 to 1995–6   25

1.4 General government outlays as a percentage of gross domestic product (G7 countries)   26

2.1 Comparison of mortality rates in California and New York contrasting inpatient and 30-day mortality figures for four clinical conditions   42

2.2 Comparison of rank order of twelve schools using total GCSE points per pupil and GCSE points per entry per pupil   44

3.1 Percentage of the 17-year-old age group (England) with 2 or more 'A' level passes   79

3.2 Qualifications on entry for first degree: former polytechnics (England) 1992   80

3.3 Qualifications on entry for first degree: ex-University Funding Council Universities (Great Britain) 1992–3   80

4.1 'Anti-competitive' notices under the Local Government Act 1988: 1989–96   94

4.2 DSO success rate in compulsory competitive tendering under the Local Government Act 1988 (England and Wales), 1991–6   99

4.3 Average number of contractors active at each stage of the tendering process by activity (England and Wales), 1991–6   100

4.4 DSO success rate by region in refuse collection contracts, under the Local Government Act 1988 (England and Wales), 1991–6   101

4.5 DSO success rate by region in education and welfare catering contracts under the Local Government Act 1988 (England and Wales), 1991–6   101

List of Tables

4.6 Relationship between authorities awarding contracts to
     private sector contractors and political control of the
     authority   102
4.7 DSO success rate in voluntary and compulsory competitive
     tendering in legal services, construction and property-
     related services and housing management to November
     1996 (England, Scotland and Wales)   103
4.8 Measures of 'level of service' in public services   107
4.9 'Efficiency' comparisons: refuse collection, local
     authorities in England and Wales, 1984–5   110
4.10 Labour cost and privatisation in eight municipal services
      in the United States   111
4.11 Differences between employment practices between
      municipal agencies and contractors in a sample of cities in
      the United States   113

List of Abbreviations

ACC	Association of County Councils
AES	Alternative Economic Strategy
ALA	Association of London Authorities
ALIS	A-level Information System
AMA	Association of Metropolitan Authorities
BG	British Gas
BT	British Telecom
CABG	Coronary Artery By-pass Graft
CBI	Confederation of British Industry
CCT	Compulsory Competitive Tendering
CT	Competitive Tendering
CIPFA	Chartered Institute of Public Finance and Accountancy
CTC	City Technology College
DES	Department of Education and Science
DevR	Development-Related
DfEE	Department for Education and Employment
DHA	District Health Authority
DMU	District Managed Unit
DSO	Direct Service Organisation
DSS	Department of Social Security
ECJ	European Court of Justice
EOC	Equal Opportunities Commission
ERA	Education Reform Act
ERM	Exchange Rate Mechanism
FHSA	Family Health Service Authority
FMI	Financial Management Initiative
FTE	Full-Time Equivalent
GCSE	General Certificate of Secondary Education
GDP	Gross Domestic Product
GGE	General Government Expenditure
GM	Grant Maintained
GMS	General Medical Services
GP	General Practitioner
GPFH	General Practitioner Fundholder
GSB	General Schools Budget

HE	Higher Education
HEFCE	Higher Education Funding Council (England)
IT	Information Technology
KWS	Keynesian Welfare State
LEA	Local Education Authority
LMS	Local Management of Schools
NBPI	National Board for Prices and Incomes
NDPBs	Non-departmental Public Bodies
NHS	National Health Service
NHSE	National Health Service Executive
NHSME	National Health Service Management Executive
NHST	National Health Service Trust
NIESR	National Institute for Economic and Social Research
NMNC	Nursing and Midwifery Staff Negotiating Council
OECD	Organisation for Economic Co-operation and Development
OFSTED	Office for Standards in Education
PCFC	Polytechnics and Colleges Funding Council
PES	Public Expenditure Survey
PI	Performance Indicator
PRP	Performance Related Pay
PSB	Potential Schools Budget
PSBR	Public Sector Borrowing Requirement
QR	Quality-Related
RAE	Research Assessment Exercise
RAWP	Resource Allocation Working Party
SERPS	State Earnings Related Pension Scheme
SSA	Standard Spending Assessment
SSI	Social Services Inspectorate
STRB	School Teachers' Review Body
SWS	Schumpeterian Workfare State
TAPPI	Target Average Percentage Pay Increase
TQA	Teaching Quality Assessment
TUPE	Transfer of Undertakings (Protection of Employment) Regulations
UFC	Universities Funding Council
VFM	Value for Money
WTE	Whole-Time Equivalent

Preface

A crucial characteristic of discussions of social policy in the 1980s and 1990s has been the salience of management issues. In the National Health Service (NHS), in personal social services and in education, policy changes and legislation in the later 1980s and 1990s led to the creation of distinctions between purchaser and provider roles; such changes have been accompanied by shifts in organisational structure so that units providing services have been given a degree of financial and operational autonomy. In health, by 1995 98 per cent of hospital and community health providers were 'Self-Governing' Trusts (see Chapter 3) and 39 per cent of general practitioners were fundholders able to purchase a range of hospital and community-based services for their patients (Harrison and Choudry 1996: 332). In social security, as part of the 'Next Steps' measures in the civil service, the operational side of the Department of Social Security (DSS) has been broken down into the Benefits, Contributions, Information Technology, Resettlement, Child Support and War Pensions executive agencies.

In education the introduction of Local Management in Schools (LMS) under the 1988 Education Reform Act (ERA) has led to the majority of Local Education Authority budgets being devolved to individual schools, and there are proposals to extend the scope of this budgetary devolution (Department for Education and Employment 1996a). The same legislation allowed for individual schools (initially subject to various size constraints) to 'opt out' of LEA control to Grant Maintained (GM) status with funding coming directly from the Department. In higher education polytechnics (subsequently 'new' universities) were removed from local authority control and given 'corporate status'. In local government the policy of compulsory competitive tendering (CCT), introduced on a substantial scale in the Local Government Act (1988), led to the creation of Direct Service Organisations (DSOs) obliged to keep their own trading accounts and reach target rates of return on capital. This policy was initially applied to services predominantly provided by manual workers, but is currently being extended to white-collar staff linked to 'core' local authority functions in legal and financial services (Walsh 1995).

Two parallel features characterise these changes: the public sector is broken down into distinct organisational units, often operating in a form of market; and the expectation is that, to function in the new structure, the public units have to be 'managed'. Such changes have been reflected in the language used in the public sector and in conceptions of the occupational identity of staff. For example, a headteacher in a GM school, when interviewed about changes in the nature of his work following the ERA, gave the following response: 'I might describe this place as a "state school", but it's more like a limited company. I have a "board of directors" and I am a kind of "managing director". I am now . . . much more concerned with financial and personnel management' (Halpin *et al.* 1993: 12–13). Techniques associated with the private sector, such as the use of business planning or management accounting, have been introduced into the public sector (Basford and Downie 1991). New institutions congruent with these developments have also been created – in particular, the Audit Commission. Its role is the monitoring of practice and a quasi-consultancy function which, for example via 'value for money' reports, attempts to promote what the Commission sees as good management practice.

In general, and with respect to specific techniques, a concern with management in the public sector was not a novel phenomenon in British politics. The idea of introducing private sector management concepts was embodied in reports such as that of Fulton (1968) on the civil service. Equally, contracting out of services, such as cleaning and catering, occurred in central government departments and the NHS in the 1950s and 1960s. This was by no means a preserve of Conservative governments, as the initiative in introducing contracting out of cleaning in central government departments came from Labour in 1968 (Ascher 1987: 24–5). The Layfield Committee (1976), on the financing of local government, suggested an extension of the scope of local authority audit to address issues of how efficiently resources were being used (see Document **1.1** at the end of the text).

However, what was different about the 1980s and 1990s was the systematic introduction of managerialism, a process which drove the plethora of institutional changes referred to above. In a general sense, public sector managerialism is chararacterised by the belief that the objectives of social services, such as health, education, personal social services or social security, can be promoted at a lower cost when the appropriate management techniques are applied (see Pollitt 1990a: 2). This book is concerned with both the general link between managerialism and politics and with four distinct manifestations of managerialism. These four aspects are: (1) the emphasis on the measurement of 'performance' and the use of performance indicators, which is examined in Chapter 2; (2) the character of quasi-markets and the issues raised by their introduction, discussed in Chapter 3; (3) the use of Compulsory Competitive Tendering (CCT) in 'market testing' (Chapter 4); and (4) pay determination in the public sector, which is analysed in Chapter 5. Chapter 1 seeks to relate public sector managerialism to the central developments in British politics in the 1980s and 1990s.

Thus the outline of the book follows the structure of the 1994 edition. The book has been updated to take account of the considerable changes since that edition was published: it is accompanied by a selection of key documents. These are referenced by using the chapter number in which they occur and a document number, and are given in brackets and distinguished by being printed in bold (e.g. **1.1** refers to the first document of Chapter 1 and so on). The key documents can be found at the end of the text.

The 1994 edition was completed in 1992, and developments since that date have not led us to alter the framework of our own thinking on public sector managerialism. However, we are aware that there are alternative, and, in some cases, more positive views, which see management as potentially liberating or situate its development in an epochal shift to 'post-Fordism'. By the time this book is published the result of the 1997 General Election will be known. The bulk of the book is, naturally, concerned with initiatives stemming from Conservative governments of the 1980s and 1990s. Chapter 6 also examines the perspective of the Labour Party on public sector managerialism, and how far, if at all, the role of public sector managerialism might change should Labour become the party of government after the election. The focus of this book is an in-depth discussion of public sector managerialism as it has emerged and developed in the UK in the 1980s and 1990s: such a focus precludes engagement with similar developments elsewhere. Fortunately other texts are available (e.g. Flynn and Strehl (1996)) to address this issue.

The Politics of Managerialism

In this first chapter the aim is both to characterise contemporary managerialism as it has impinged on the social services in a general sense and
to situate this phenomenon politically. The latter objective is particularly
crucial, and is central to the whole thesis of this book. A striking feature
of managerialism has been that the key initiatives have not, in general,
emanated from public sector bodies providing services, such as schools,
universities or social service departments, from intermediary bodies like
Health Authorities, or from local government. Rather, these initiatives
have come from central government: the creation of the quasi-market in
primary and secondary education stemmed from the 1988 Education
Reform Act; that in higher education is structured by the provisions of
the 1992 Further and Higher Education Act; and those in community care
and health by the 1990 NHS and Community Care Act. The extension of
compulsory competitive tendering to a range of local authority services
was an effect of the 1988 Local Government Act, and central government
departments have engaged in numerous 'market testing' initiatives.

The impetus behind performance measurement has also, largely,
stemmed from the centre. The publication of school examination and test
results derived from powers conferred on the Secretary of State in the
1980 Education Act. Publication of performance measures across public
services has been substantially increased by the various Citizens' Charters.
The Audit Commission, itself created under the 1982 Local Government
Finance Act, is required, under the 1992 Local Government Act, to
determine appropriate indicators for the Citizens' Charter in local government services (Audit Commission 1994).

It is this very dominance of central government with respect to changes
in the management of public sector services that raises the key question:
How does managerialism relate to the politics of the Conservative administrations since 1979 and to the ideological framework within which policies
were justified, and, to some extent, formulated? It is this question that
this chapter addresses. The chapter is divided into three sections: the first
develops a more detailed characterisation of the central elements of public

sector managerialism; the second looks at the ideological shifts in Conservative politics, in particular the emergence of 'New Right' doctrines; and the third considers the relationship of Conservative political practice to New Right ideology, and seeks to locate managerialism with respect to this relationship. This discussion of the relationship between politics and managerialism is designed to underpin the specific critical analyses of particular features of managerialism in Chapters 2–5 and to provide a basis for the concluding argument in Chapter 6.

Contemporary Public Sector Managerialism

There are, necessarily, difficulties in attempting to characterise the managerialist approach to public sector services in the British case when the phenomenon is diverse and the sources are varied. The argument, therefore, takes as its focus two reports: the first, the 1983 Griffiths report on general management in the NHS, officially entitled *NHS Management Inquiry*, comes early in the process of establishing a substantial managerialist agenda in the British public sector; the second is contemporaneous with the major changes in health, education and community care in the late 1980s, the 'Efficiency Unit' report *Improving Management in Government: the Next Steps* (Jenkins 1988).

Both reports exemplify the pattern already identified, namely, the initiating role of central government. In the case of Griffiths, Norman Fowler, the Secretary of State for Health and Social Security, announced in February 1983 that he had asked 'four leading businessmen' to prepare a report on the 'effective use of manpower and related resources in the National Health Service'. The time-scale envisaged for the completion of the report was a short one and the report was brief, appearing in the form of a 24-page memorandum to the Secretary of State dated 6 October 1983, and subsequently published on the 25th of that month (Harrison 1988: 60). The Efficiency Unit report was part of a series of measures whereby central government sought to achieve what it saw as efficiency improvements in the civil service. It was preceded by scrutinies of department work by small teams under the overall control of Lord Rayner. Such scrutinies led to specific changes; but an attempt to create a more general shift in the framework of departmental practice was heralded by the Financial Management Initiative (FMI), launched in May 1982 (Greer 1994: 9). FMI prefigured many of the central themes of 'Next Steps', which was an attempt to realise the goals of the earlier policy.

In both cases the reports had an influence on policy in their respective fields. The major recommendations of Griffiths were accepted by government (Harrison 1988: 62). Central here was the proposal to appoint general managers at (what were then) Regional and District Health Authority and at Unit levels. 'Next Steps' advocated the creation of 'agencies', which would be responsible for executing government policy (**1.2**). Such agencies would have a specialised function and would be part of the break-up of the civil service into distinct units. By April 1995 71 per cent of civil servants were working in units operating on 'Next Steps' lines (Government Statistical Service 1996). In the field of social policy the most significant impact was the creation of the five specialist agencies in the DSS.

However, the significance of these reports goes beyond their individual practical impacts. They are of particular interest because the intellectual approach underlying them gives important insights into contemporary public sector managerialism. In both cases the reports draw their preferred form of organisational structure from the private sector: viz a multi-divisional organisation (M-form), where a relatively small head office at the apex of the corporation interacts with a series of operating divisions (for a classic statement of this approach, see Sloan 1986). The head office role is to formulate strategy: that is, to decide which businesses the corporation should be in, and whether growth should be pursued via organic development of existing businesses or via acquisitions, and to allocate capital between divisions. Head office also monitors the divisions by scrutinising their financial status. Such monitoring would, in turn, influence capital investment and decisions on whether particular businesses or divisions would be retained or divested. Consequently, while units are accorded a degree of *operational* autonomy, they are subject, ultimately, to control from the top.

In the Griffiths Report this distinction is made in the recommendations for the role of different levels of the organisation. Thus, Griffiths proposed that a Health Services Supervisory Board be established, whose role would be the 'determination of purpose, objectives and direction for the Health Service; approval of the overall budget and resource allocations; strategic decisions and receiving reports on performance and other evaluations from within the Health Service' (Griffiths 1983: 3). The NHS Management Board was to operate at the next level down, and its main role would be to 'plan implementation of policies', but also to monitor performance (ibid.).

The monitoring of operational performance thus called for general management at lower levels of the structure, since responsibility for operational performance had to be located: 'one of our most immediate observations from a business background is the lack of a clearly-defined

general management function throughout the NHS. By general management we mean the responsibility drawn together in one person, at different
levels of the organisation, for planning, implementation and control of
performance' (Griffiths 1983: 11).

The combination of distinguishing strategic and operational issues and
the precise location of managerial responsibility was also central to the
Efficiency Unit report. Responsibility for strategic decisions was to lie with
the Minister and Permanent Secretary; but, once such decisions had been
made, operational policy was to be devolved to agency managers (**1.2**).

A correlative feature of this approach was the need for a flow of
information (mainly upwards) on performance. Here Griffiths and the
Efficiency Unit claimed that both the availability and use of data on
performance were inadequate. On the NHS, Griffiths argued: 'it still lacks
any real continuous evaluation of its performance . . . rarely are precise
management objectives set; there is little measurement of health output;
clinical evaluation of particular practices is by no means common and
economic evaluation of those practices extremely rare' (Griffiths 1983:
10). And the Efficiency Unit claimed that, while civil servants might have
become more aware of costs, they were insufficiently concerned with the
outputs of services (**1.3**).

In classic versions of M-form, information on performance is related
to incentives, in particular, the allocation of additional capital to units
that perform well. Given cash-limited budgets and other policy constraints
this is a more problematic concept in public sector services. However,
both documents included examples of such incentives.

The resource allocation pattern in health at the time of the Griffiths
Report was designed to distribute resources according to a measure of
'need', determined by a formula devised by the Resource Allocation
Working Party (RAWP) in 1976 (for a description of the formula, see
Mays 1987: 47–8). Given this framework, there were obvious constraints
on a policy of selective rewards and punishments in accordance with
measures of performance. However, Griffiths did argue that, 'cost improvement programmes can and should be initiated within the NHS; these should
carry with them the incentive that a significant proportion of the savings
made can be used *locally* to bring about further change and improvement'
(Griffiths 1983: 13; our emphasis). In the case of Next Steps agencies
Chief Executives are employed on short-term contracts, and contract
renewal is connected to achieving targets, as is a proportion of annual
pay (Greer 1994: 60).

Griffiths and the Efficiency Unit found the multi-divisional form of
organisation appropriate to the public services of their investigation. Yet

this response raises further questions regarding the assumptions made in their arguments.

A striking feature of both reports is their abstraction. The reader would learn much more about the views of the authors on management, organisation structure and control than on substantive issues related to the services themselves. This is, in fact, a crucial feature of managerialism. The central issue is the form of management adopted; the activity being managed is at best a secondary matter.

Thus, whether this form of management is appropriate to the service concerned is barely addressed. Griffiths does acknowledge the issue: 'We have been told that the NHS is different from business in management terms, not least because the NHS is not concerned with the profit motive and must be judged by wider social standards which cannot be measured' (Griffiths 1983: 10).

The response to this objection is rather summary. Griffiths argues that, in the private sector, profit targets do 'not immediately impinge on large numbers of managers below board level' (ibid.). Consequently, if non-financial targets, such as attaining productivity or quality levels, are used in the private sector, what is to prevent their use in the public sector? Thus a second key assumption is that management information is relatively transparent: that is to say, that it is clear what constitutes a standard of performance and that such standards can be measured relatively unproblematically. This position, as we shall discuss in more detail in Chapter 2, does not address the complexity and ambiguity of measures of public sector performance.

A final key element in managerialism in public sector services is its implications for professional practice. A central feature of education, health and personal social services in particular is that important decisions involving the deployment of resources are made by professional staff. Equally, these groups do not fit easily into the multi-divisional structure because of its hierarchical character. Consequently, managerialism operates in a state of tension with professionalism. Since, in the field of social policy, Next Steps principally affects social security, a department engaged mainly in income transfers rather than service provision, this question looms less large there. However, it is interesting to observe that the idea that service targets are necessary to hold public servants to account is supported by the Head of the Civil Service, Sir Robin Butler, in a commentary on the Next Steps initiative. Thus, discussing the Citizens' Charter he argues 'it requires that services shift their attention towards aspirations of the public and away from the interests of themselves as providers' (R. Butler 1993: 402; see also Greer 1994: 13–17).

The approach to this question in Griffiths is rather *sotto voce*: clinicians are to be involved 'more closely in the management process, consistent with clinical freedom for clinical practice' (Griffiths 1983: 6).

However, it is difficult to see how the multi-divisional structure can operate without attempting to subordinate and control professional practice. The whole approach stresses that those mobilising and utilising resources at an operational level should be accountable to higher levels of the organisation. In this respect the Griffiths approach was unstable, since, if doctors are to be no more than *invited* to be involved in relating their workload to budgetary constraints then, quite clearly, they can choose not to do so. Furthermore, investigations of the impact of general management in the NHS have shown that where reviews of clinical activity have taken place, they have concentrated on concerns of professional practice rather than making explicit links to the costs of clinical decisions, as in the Griffiths prescriptions (Pollitt *et al.* 1991: 69). The harder line implicit in Sir Robin Butler's comments is, arguably, more consistent with a multi-divisional structure of devolved management.

Griffiths and the Efficiency Unit thus give a guide to the key inter-locking elements of contemporary managerialism as it has been applied to public sector social services. The approach is hierarchical in the sense that at least the superordinate targets are set at the top, and monitoring, while a pervasive feature of the organisation, is ultimately controlled from the top. It is assumed that the structure is universally valid, can cut across public and private sectors, and is applicable whatever public service is considered. Since performance monitoring is crucial, it is assumed that valid management information can be developed. Finally, the hier-archical characteristics of the structure create tensions with the role of professionals in public services. Thus professional practice, in so far as it involves making decisions that commit resources and is a significant resource cost itself, should be incorporated into the management process of accountability. This in turn can take place in various ways: professionals themselves can be turned into managers or subordinated to managers in an organisational hierarchy.

These elements of managerialism have clear links with a number of the developments that will be discussed later in the book. Since manage-ment information plays a central role in this structure, there is necessarily an emphasis on performance measurement. The link with 'quasi-markets' would seem to be somewhat more ambiguous. Such markets operate in health, personal social services and education. In some respects this mechanism appears to involve less central government control. Quasi-markets require 'providers' to bid for resources by contracting with 'purchasers'. This gives the provider unit greater freedom, in the sense that it can choose a mix of activities on which it may decide to concentrate, which may differ from the historical pattern of its activities.

However, it is important not to exaggerate the extent of the decentralisation implied in quasi-markets (this point will be developed in Chapter 3). In all cases the quasi-market works within a context of predetermined public policy objectives. These have implications for the operation of the 'market': for example, maintaining access to services, particularly in the case of health, means that the scope of the unit to choose the activities in which it will specialise is circumscribed. Similar considerations bear on the extent to which competitive pressures will operate to determine how many provider units stay in the market. Centralisation also operates with respect to purchasers, so that, for example, the Higher Education Funding Councils (cf. Chapter 3) have acted to implement central government policy of expanding higher education while sharply reducing unit costs in the sector.

A similar hybrid combination, involving elements of market mechanisms and central control, operates in the case of CCT (see Chapter 4). The compulsory element here extends not just to the obligation to tender for the services covered, but also to a regulatory framework that seeks to determine the criteria used in the evaluation of tenders. Similarly, implicit in many variants of managerialism is the adoption of incentives linked to 'performance'. This, in turn, has influenced attempts to change the pattern of public sector pay determination by the introduction of performance-related pay (PRP) and pressures to decentralise pay determination, an issue discussed in Chapter 5.

Public sector managerialism is thus directly linked to a hierarchical approach in which central government has operated as a prime mover. This means that, if we are to understand this development, it is essential to relate it to the political ideology and practice of the party that has been continuously in office since 1979: the Conservative Party.

Ideological Shift: The Impact of the 'New Right'

In this section we will examine the implications of a major ideological shift in the Conservative Party, which dates from the mid-1970s. This phenomenon is often characterised as the rise to prominence of a doctrine referred to as the 'New Right'. Before discussing this in detail, however, it is worth making the point that the influence of the New Right in general, and on conservative parties worldwide, has been varied. It has been most pronounced in Britain and the United States, particularly under the governments headed by Margaret Thatcher and Ronald Reagan. In contrast, in areas such as labour market deregulation (see p. 19 below) and privatisation the impact on other European Union members has been much more circumscribed.

To understand the distinctive character of the New Right it is necessary to set it in the context of the ideological stance that dominated British Conservative politics in the period from the end of the Second World War to the mid-1970s. A good example of this approach comes in the published writings of Harold Macmillan, Conservative Prime Minister from 1957 to 1963, and previously Foreign Secretary and Chancellor of the Exchequer. Throughout his political career Macmillan had supported a form of capitalist economy with substantial state intervention both to regulate the economy and to ensure minimum standards of social provision. In the 1920s he had advocated the development of employment protection legislation to extend individual rights (e.g. through limits on working hours) and to impose obligations on employers to engage in collective bargaining (Eccleshall 1990: 180). Later he became an enthusiastic advocate of Keynesian economic policies, and his overall political stance has strong affinities with a 'liberal collectivist' outlook, combining state intervention to ensure minimum standards with a capitalist economy free to operate with respect to provision above the minimum (Cutler *et al.* 1986: 27 and 41).

The ideological tenor of Macmillan's position can be captured from, perhaps, his most representative work, *The Middle Way*. In this book he argued: 'For as far ahead as we can see, it is both possible and desirable to find a solution of our economic difficulties in a mixed system which combines State ownership, regulation or control of certain aspects of economic activity with the drive and initiative of private enterprise . . .' (cited in Eccleshall 1990: 193). He went on to describe his ideal social and economic form of organisation as 'planned capitalism, or as it may be, a new synthesis of Capitalist and Socialist theory' (ibid.). Such a social order he saw as a precondition for preserving '. . . civic, democratic and cultural freedom' (ibid.).

During the inter-war period Macmillan was an oppositional figure on the left of the Conservative Party. However, the concept of the 'middle way' swiftly became an orthodoxy in the post-war period (Eccleshall 1990: 184–7). It was this position, as much as explicitly socialist arguments, that New Right thinkers took as the focus of their criticism.

The Hayekian Critique: Political Philosophy

The extent of New Right work poses problems of selection. However, because his work covers issues of both political philosophy and political economy, the argument here concentrates on the work of *Friedrich Hayek* as a reference point. During the 1980s and 1990s an interesting feature of the way in which right-wing policies have been presented is that they often drew on a political language formerly used by the political left. Thus, Conservative policies have often been described as 'radical'; Thatcher and Reagan were said to have effected 'revolutions', and, of course there is the 'New' Right. This tends to obscure the fact that such positions are often a re-presentation of well-worn positions. This is true, not just with respect to the nineteenth-century lineage of New Right thinking, but also of Hayek's own career. Thus, one of his most famous attacks on economic planning, *The Road to Serfdom*, was published in 1944, and he continued working for the next thirty years as a relatively marginal figure both intellectually and politically until his views gained increasing currency in the 1970s and 1980s.

The first major difference between Hayek's approach and the liberal collectivism of the 'middle way' is his conception of the proper role for the state. Macmillan's view of the role of the state in ensuring proper economic regulation and minimum social standards involved a capitalist market economy, but one with a substantial sector of nationalised industries operating as state monopolies, extensive employment protection legislation and a welfare state, with virtual state monopoly supply of services such as health and education. Hayek was consistently and trenchantly opposed to all these: his general commitment to competitive markets led him to oppose any state monopolies of economic activity (Hayek 1960: 224). Although not against the state provision of a minimum income, he argued for compulsory social insurance so that, as far as possible, individuals should not 'become a charge on the public'(ibid.: 280). Equally the role of the state in social insurance would rule out monopoly state provision; the state would mainly operate in social insurance on an analogy with car insurance, making the individual insurance obligatory but leaving provision to predominantly private (or voluntary) suppliers (ibid.: 292). This approach led Hayek to attack health care systems like the NHS, where provision free at the point of use is combined with tax finance (ibid.: 298). Finally, Hayek consistently repudiated Keynesian economic policy (see pp. 13–14 for further discussion).

Central to Hayek's argument for a highly restricted role for the state in social and economic policy is the 'anti-rationalist' aspect of his political thought. In particular he argues that planning, whether social or economic, assumes an ability consciously and rationally to understand and manipulate social and economic mechanisms. However, this involves a basic misunderstanding of the nature of social order: 'the case for individual freedom rests chiefly on the recognition of the inevitable ignorance of all of us concerning a great many of the factors on which the achievement of our ends and welfare depends' (Hayek 1960: 29).

It is such ignorance that underpins the value of reliance on market mechanisms. Markets work by the mutual adjustment of individuals to signals, and this unconscious and unplanned mechanism ensures that 'more knowledge is utilised than any one individual possesses or than it is possible to synthesise intellectually' (ibid.: 30). It is interesting to note how far this Hayekian language and form of argument had, by the mid-1970s, been assimilated by prominent British Conservative politicians. Thus, in his *Stranded on the Middle Ground*, the title itself redolent of a repudiation of the Macmillan approach, Sir Keith Joseph argued 'the market system is the greatest generator of national wealth known to mankind: coordinating and fulfilling the diverse needs of countless individuals in a way which no human mind or minds could ever comprehend, without coercion, without direction, without bureaucratic interference' (cited in Eccleshall 1990). In line with Hayek's advocacy of a restricted role for the state was his criticism of another central feature of social democratic thought and its accommodation by Conservative politicians of the Macmillan persuasion: the pursuit of social justice. This goal has often been seen as at least part of the rationale for universal welfare services, and certainly for a system of progressive direct taxation, where higher rates of tax are paid at higher income levels. It has already been pointed out that Hayek was a critic of a comprehensive state welfare system. He was also opposed to redistributive social and economic policies and progressive taxation, favouring proportional rates which would be invariant with increased income (Hayek 1960: Ch. 20).

Hayek's attack on redistributive policies and on the concept of social justice can be approached from two distinct but related angles: what he saw as the contradiction between such objectives and the conditions of individual freedom; and,what he saw as the confusions surrounding the concept itself.

For Hayek the pursuit of social justice meant that society should be organised in such a way that it becomes possible 'to assign particular shares of the product of society to different individuals or groups' (Hayek 1976: 64).

This objective is seen as a threat to freedom in two senses: Hayek argues that the state must intervene to ensure that 'particular people get particular things' (Hayek 1960: 259–60), which involves 'discrimination between and an unequal treatment of different people' (ibid.). However, not only is the pursuit of social justice discriminatory, it implies an inevitable expansion of the role of the state. Hayek argued that the attempt to combine the objective of social justice with a market economy is bound to fail. Social justice, in his view, requires an attempt to ensure that each individual obtains his or her 'just' reward. However, market economies are characterised by endless adjustments, which simultaneously change relative earnings. Market economies are thus continually operating to subvert and undercut the 'just' distribution of incomes. Consequently, the logic of the pursuit of social justice is to restrict the role of the market and move towards a command economy. Thus, he argues that social justice can 'be given a meaning only in a directed or "command" economy . . . in which the individuals are ordered what to do' (Hayek 1976: 69).

This argument has important political implications. Advocates of the 'middle way', whether in conservative or social democratic parties, while anti-communist, drew a clear distinction between 'mixed economies' with a substantial welfare state and the command economies of the former Eastern Bloc countries. For instance, the original edition of *The Middle Way* displayed the swastika and the hammer and sickle on the dust jacket; the middle way was the alternative to totalitarianism. In contrast, in Hayek, social democracy and collectivist conservatism were not benign alternatives to a command economy, but carried within themselves the seeds of just such a development.

The second line of Hayek's critique of the pursuit of social justice turns on what he saw as the confusions inherent in the concept. Debates on social justice have often referred to the effects of impersonal social forces magnified by the operation of market mechanisms. Thus, the various effects of unemployment or ill health, or changes in the economic structure, create a distribution of resources unrelated to the merits of individuals. Hayek fully accepted that such processes do operate and, in fact, he was critical of authors who 'have defended free enterprise on the grounds that it regularly rewards the deserving' (Hayek 1976: 74). He argued that it was understandable that 'people resent that their remuneration should in part depend on pure accident', but 'that is in fact what it must if the market is to adjust itself and the individual is to be allowed to decide what to do' (ibid.: 81).

Furthermore, such processes were not pertinent to concerns of 'justice', since what is 'just' or 'unjust' concerns relations between individuals, not the effects of impersonal forces: 'Justice requires that in the "treatment" of another person or persons certain uniform rules be observed' (ibid.: 70). Consequently, it is a misuse of terms to apply justice or injustice to 'the manner in which the impersonal process of the market allocates command over goods and services to particular people' (ibid.). Tomlinson (1990) neatly summarises Hayek's position as being that where the concept of social justice is used, a *double* error is made, since the concept is inappropriately applied to the distribution of rewards, which, being unintentional, can neither be just nor unjust; and the pursuit of social justice involves genuine injustice, since individuals must be treated in a discriminatory manner (Tomlinson 1990: 18).

The Hayekian Critique: Political Economy

A central element of Hayek's defence for a highly restricted role for the state lies in a specific political philosophy. However, this argument is also articulated with a distinctive approach to political economy, at whose centre was a consistent critique of Keynesian economic policy.

Keynesian 'demand management' exerted a substantial influence over political ideology and practice in the period between the end of the Second World War and the 1970s. Unemployment, it was argued, stems from a deficiency of aggregate demand and could be controlled and minimised by a variety of means at the disposal of government: increases in public spending, tax reductions, an expansionary monetary policy. This appeared to allow not just a solution to the problem of unemployment but also, by precluding the onset of depressions, promoted a higher and more consistent rate of economic growth. This in turn fuelled optimism on the viability of the 'middle way', since it allowed for both higher levels of private consumption and of public social welfare spending. As Table 1.1 shows, these objectives were attained consistently in the era of the 'long boom'.

It is important to stress that, while Keynes emphasised the importance

Table 1.1. Average annual growth rates of final consumption expenditure per head, real government consumption expenditure and rates of unemployment in the OECD countries, 1960–73

	1960–68 %	1968–73 %
Growth of real final consumption per head	3.7	4.0
Growth of real government expenditure	4.7	2.5
Unemployment as % of total labour force	3.1	3.4

Source: OECD (1987).

of deficiency of aggregate demand as the principal cause of mass unemployment, he did not exclude other causes. Thus, both Keynes and subsequent Keynesian commentators have accepted that there are structural causes of unemployment. For instance, particular levels of regional unemployment may be inflated by that region's having an unfavourable industrial structure dominated by declining industries. However, a feature of the Keynesian approach has been the argument that levels of structural employment are significantly influenced by the level of aggregate demand (Thirlwall 1981: 21). Thus, for instance, structural unemployment could be reduced in a context of higher growth, in part because it would promote a higher level of vacancies in areas with a more favourable industrial structure, which will encourage labour mobility.

Hayek was a consistent and long-run critic of both Keynesian economic theory and the broad political economy that accompanied its emergence as an orthodoxy. This is hardly surprising, since Keynesian demand management represents a form of 'rationalism', maintaining that a capitalist economy could be organised to achieve predictable goals. In contrast to Keynes and subsequent Keynesians, Hayek looked at unemployment as a predominantly structural problem. Thus, he argued 'the older, and to me convincing explanation of extensive unemployment ascribes it to a discrepancy between the distribution of labour (and other factors of production) between different industries (and localities) and the distribution of demand among their products' (Hayek 1978: 200).

Hayek not only treated structural unemployment as independent of the level of aggregate demand; he took the view that Keynesian policies exacerbated structural distortions. For example, he inverts the Keynesian view in arguing that labour mobility is encouraged by lower levels of aggregate demand (Hayek 1967: 274).

Consequently, Keynesian approaches both fail to recognise the underlying causes of unemployment and reinforce rigidities and lack of adaptation in the market. The result of such policies was a mechanism for increasing inflation, since the control of unemployment would depend on policies to expand demand that would involve spiralling inflation: 'the amount of expenditure which would have to be incurred before the demand for the kind of services which the unemployed offer may have to be of such a magnitude as to produce major inflationary effects before it substantially increases employment' (ibid.: 272).

The commitment to full employment is thus seen as involving a vicious circle, since maintaining high employment levels in the light of structural maladjustments means courting inflation, which, in turn, is an obstacle to adjustment: 'the chief harm which inflation causes . . . [is] that it gives the whole structure of the economy a distorted, lopsided character. It does so by drawing more and more workers into kinds of jobs which depend on continuing or even accelerating inflation' (Hayek 1978: 192).

The Hayekian attack on Keynesian macro-economic policy articulates a vital strand of his thought and of that of the New Right in general, the critique of 'producer groups'. From this standpoint, a crucial obstacle to the adjustments required in, and made possible by, a market economy is the action of organisations of producers who operate to promote their 'special interests' at the expense of the public interest.

In Hayek's case the principal manifestation of the attack on producer groups is his hostility to trade unions. This follows from the assumption that the market should optimally function as a self-adjusting mechanism. Trade unions intervene in this process by acting to limit the freedom of employers to control the means of production. As far as Hayek was concerned, these effects were wholly negative. He claimed that trade unions had depressed the overall level of real wages (Hayek 1960: 271); that they discourage investment levels because they are able to reduce significantly returns to capital (Hayek 1967: 285 and 286); and that they increase inequalities in wage levels between union and non-union labour by means of the exercise of 'monopoly' power, thus creating a wage gap that has 'no foundation' in efficiency differences (Hayek 1960: 271).

Given the negative role ascribed to trade unions, the critique of Keynesian economics is reinforced. Not only is a commitment to full employment seen as strengthening the hand of trade unions against employers, but it also insulates unions from the effects of their own restrictive practices. Thus, as there is a commitment to full employment, government is required to use monetary and fiscal policy to sustain employment, whatever the inefficiency of labour or the wage levels demanded (Hayek 1960: 281).

Professionals as Producer Groups

So far in this section the discussion of the critique of producer groups has concentrated on Hayek's arguments on trade unions. This broad approach has also been taken up by other New Right authors to analyse those key players in welfare services: professional groups. The attack on the professions is similar to that on trade unions: the professions are accused of seeking to establish a monopoly over service provision – to fix job territories so that they cannot be entered by non-professionals, thus boosting professional job security, increasing costs and rendering working practices rigid.

However, whereas the power of trade unions is seen to be located in a combination of special legal privileges (see p. 16 below) and the guarantee of full employment, the power of professional groups is seen to lie in the conditions of the provision of social services established by the state, namely, the dominant, although not monopoly role of the state since the end of the Second World War; and predominantly tax-financed services, where the character and extent of the service has been determined by government. For the New Right the extent of state provision and finance operates to reinforce the power of professional producer groups by insulating them from the effects of market competition and consumer choice. Thus, for example, Lewis and Glennester state that one of the objectives of the NHS and Community Care Act 1990 was to remake social work (Lewis and Glennester 1996: 74). Since the overall funding of the service is determined politically, consumer choice can only operate in the limited area of private provision. While the global pattern of provision is determined by funding and regulatory decisions made by government, professionals are, according to the New Right, able to determine service standards at the micro level. Thus, for example, in the case of health care in Britain, Green argues: 'The NHS provides a standard considered acceptable by doctors within the budgets available to them' (Green 1990: 11).

A preferred New Right stance, and one consistent with Hayekian precepts, is to use a 'voucher' system. This system operates by providing a public subsidy in the form of a voucher of a given value, which can be used to purchase a given service. Under such schemes public service suppliers are obliged to compete with private or voluntary sector alternatives, and voucher holders may purchase the service where they will.

New Right authors on social welfare also want to take supply-side deregulation further than total or partial privatisation of service provision. In particular, they are concerned that professionals operate what they see as unnecessary restrictive practices in defining entry qualifications and in the control of who does what job. Thus, Chubb and Moe have argued for a system of education allowing any group to set up schools and receive state funding provided they meet minimal standards of teacher certification (Chubb and Moe 1990: 219). Such schools would have complete freedom over issues such as admission requirements,and structure of government and organisational form, although they would be accountable to the state for pupil performance.

It is clear that New Right thought represents a radical break with the premises of both social and economic policy involved in post-war social democracy and the liberal collectivist conservatism of Macmillan's 'middle way'. Both these strands, in their different ways, envisaged a mixed economy with a substantial welfare state in which producers, whether trade unions or professionals, were partners. The New Right envisages a minimal state operating within a legal and regulatory framework that constrains the power of producer groups. However, if we are to attempt to situate where public sector managerialism fits in with respect to this ideological set it is necessary to look at the relationship between the New Right and Conservative political practice.

The Conservatives and the New Right: Tempering the Shift with Political Expediency

Reference has already been made to the extent to which Conservative politicians in the 1970s and 1980s assimilated the concepts and language of the New Right. In addition to Sir Keith Joseph's Hayekian paean to the market he made a clear break with 'full employment' in textbook New Right terms: 'the duty imposed on itself by the State to maintain full employment was partly fulfilled by subsidising inefficiency and tech- nological obsolescence' (cited in Eccleshall 1990: 236). Mrs Thatcher referred in a House of Commons debate in 1981 to Hayek's *Law, Liberty and Legislation* as 'absolutely supreme' (**1.4**). However, rhetoric and ideological adherence are not the same thing as political practice. In this section we shall demonstrate that, with respect to the New Right, Conservative policy in the 1980s and 1990s has followed an ambiguous course, and that it is in relation to such ambiguity that public sector managerialism must be situated.

To illustrate the character of this ambiguity two areas of policy will be considered: (1) the position of 'producer groups'; and (2) the role of the State with respect to social services and the policy of privatisation.

The Attack on the Trade Unions: the Gospel of Individualism

As we saw above, a central plank of New Right ideology is the attack on producer groups. This is one area, as Wedderburn (1989) has cogently demonstrated, where, at least as far as labour law is concerned, Hayekian prescriptions have been particularly influential.

To understand the nature of the transformation it is necessary to set the changes effected during the 1980s in the context of approaches to labour law that had previously occupied a dominant role in twentieth- century British politics. Central to this earlier view was a linked set of assumptions: that the contract of employment was qualitatively different from other contracts; and that it involved a fundamental asymmetry in the respective powers of employer and employees. The assumption was, therefore, that *unorganised* employees had unequal bargaining power relative to employers, and that it was incumbent on the state to redress this balance. This took the form of establishing the legal conditions within which trade unions could operate and establishing a floor of statutory employment rights on wage levels, hours of work, health and safety and so on. It is interesting to note that, even at the outset of Mrs Thatcher's first administration, this broad conception was still being advanced. In introducing the 1979 Employment Bill, the then Secretary of State for Employment, James Prior, stated: that the law should recognise the power imbalance between employer and employee and what he termed the 'exceptional liberties' unions would need to offset this imbalance (**1.5**) (on the politics of Prior's relation to Thatcher see Gilmour 1994: 264).

The reference to 'exceptional liberties' referred to the peculiar and specific character of the treatment of trade unions in British law. Continental European jurisdictions have tended to recognise various 'positive' rights associated with trade unionism, such as the rights to organise collectively, bargain and strike (Wedderburn 1989: 4–6). As a corollary, in these jurisdictions, where industrial action is either threatened or taken, this does not involve a breach of the contract of employment. In Britain the whole issue has been treated differently. The threat to strike is usually a threat to break the contract of employment. Consequently, unless legal protections were given, trade unions and their officials would have been vulnerable to civil actions for torts such as inducing a breach of a contract of employment. The particular form that these protections have taken has been to give what have been termed 'immunities' against common law liabilities.

Thus, in a strict sense, British immunities were designed to achieve the same objective as positive rights in the continental European jurisdictions. However, the very use of this term has unfortunate connotations, since it gives the impression that trade unions are given preferential treatment, a feature illustrated by Prior's reference to 'privileges'. This is a perennial theme in Hayek's arguments: 'unions have not achieved their present magnitude and power by merely achieving the right of association. They have become what they are largely in consequence of the grant, by legislation and jurisdiction, of unique privileges which no other associations or individuals enjoy' (Hayek 1967: 281).

It is, of course, important to stress that the idea of state intervention operating to achieve a 'balance' between employers and employees was susceptible to a variety of readings. On the political left, for example, collective bargaining and the related strengthening of individual employment rights was, not surprisingly, pursued more vigorously than on the right. However, these were arguments not about whether the state should intervene to offset the bargaining weaknesses of the individual employee, but rather about what the appropriate measures to strengthen the hand of labour should be.

To the New Right it is clear that such a concept is anathema. It involves directly intervening in the market by means of restrictions on conditions of employment and strengthening a key institution, the trade unions, which act collectively to limit the control of employers over the production process. Equally, it implicitly assumes the goal of social justice by refusing to accept the verdict of the market as a given.

As Wedderburn (1989) demonstrates,the 1980s saw Conservative governments embracing the Hayekian message in a series of legislative interventions with respect to both collective and individual labour law.

In the field of collective labour law what is striking is the pronounced individualist bias embodied in the legislation. For example, since 1984 trade unions have been required to undertake a ballot of their members before taking industrial action. The Employment Act 1988 states that a union is prohibited from expelling or penalising a member because the latter has worked in defiance of a *majority* decision to strike in a ballot (Wedderburn 1989: 24). This condition applies even though the dissident member is in breach of his or her obligations under contract in union rules (ibid.). In other words the legislation embodies a marked hostility to collectivism, even if the latter is underpinned by democratic decision-making and contractual relations.

A similar example is provided by the treatment of so-called 'secondary' industrial action. For example, in 1980 solidarity action and picketing away from the worker's place of work was prohibited. In 1982, this prohibition was extended to action to help workers obtain recognition for bargaining purposes or even consultation (Wedderburn 1989: 27). Wedderburn calls this 'enterprise confinement' an attempt to limit industrial action so that collective solidarity across firms and sectors is eliminated (ibid.).

Parallel developments have occurred in individual labour law. The Conservatives adopted a deregulationist labour approach to the labour market. This meant that a whole series of protections with respect to pay and conditions were removed. An example which gives the flavour of this ideological and political shift and its reflection in policy is the approach to unilateral arbitration. Under this mechanism it was possible to extend the terms of voluntary collective agreements to employers who had not been party to them (Wedderburn 1986: 344–5). This policy could operate when the collective agreement was established by an employers' organisation and workers representing the workforce in the employments concerned. Such legislation embodies a whole series of collectivist assumptions, including: that it is legitimate to override individual contracts, since the terms and conditions set by arbitration were incorporated into the contracts of employment if the original contract terms were less favourable than the 'recognised terms'; and a *de facto* encouragement to the recognition of trade unions. Not surprisingly, such measures were set aside in the 1980s labour market deregulation programme. Unilateral arbitration was abolished in 1980 (Wedderburn 1989: 17). It is also worth noting that while measures of labour market deregulation were introduced in a number of EC member countries in the 1980s, in Britain these were far more extreme. Here the pattern has been to remove the legal protections concerned. It has been much more common in other EC countries to redefine the legal protections rather than remove them all together (Wedderburn 1989: 20–1). While these policies were established under Conservative administrations led by Margaret Thatcher, the emphasis on labour market deregulation has continued under John Major. Thus, for example, the 1996 'Competitiveness' White Paper contrasts what it sees as the virtues of British deregulation with the 'inflexible' labour markets of other European Union countries (**1.6**).

Many of these measures are significant because they have strengthened the hand of employers; but they are equally significant in setting an agenda for debate. In particular, they have contributed to a climate in which New Right hostility to the interests of producers has been accepted as a given parameter, and this has been particularly true where these producers are working-class manual workers. This theme will be developed in Chapter 4.

Conservative initiatives in individual and collective labour law follow a New Right agenda. However, this is not a general phenomenon. In particular, the New Right agenda has been effectively repudiated in the social services.

Safe in Our Hands? The Absence of Privatisation in the Welfare State

The New Right agenda does not require complete privatisation of the social services. What it does demand is that state provision should operate in a market in which the state limits its role to either minimal regulation (as in the Hayekian model of compulsory insurance) or, at least, as in voucher schemes, allows for mechanisms to opt out of state provision. In both approaches what is envisaged is competition between providers, and that the overall distribution of resources in the service is, if not wholly determined, at least heavily influenced by consumer decisions.

This is not the programme the Conservatives have adopted with respect to the principal social services. In all cases the overall level of service financing has remained politically determined and is, in general, subject to cash limits. In health, personal social services and education quasi-markets have been established that involve divisions between a 'purchaser' and 'provider' role. In principle this increases the scope of competition between the providers. However, the purchasers are not, with the exception of primary and secondary education, service users, but rather professionals or managers in government agencies or local government. Equally, as we shall demonstrate in Chapter 3, such markets are controlled by very substantial regulations on the activities of purchasers and providers. The quasi-market is, *par excellence*, the managed market.

It is also worth bearing in mind that the compromise involved in the adoption of quasi-markets, in many respects, replicates analogous features in the programme of privatising formerly nationalised industries. From a New Right standpoint a change in the ownership of the assets concerned is in itself a secondary issue. What is crucial is that privatisation ensures that effective competition occurs. However, the privatisations of utilities were effectively privatisations of monopolies where, at least in principle, the consumer interest was to be protected by the appointment of regulators, working within a pre-set framework of price control. Yet such controls were rejected by Hayek as involving a slide towards further mechanisms of control over the enterprise (Hayek 1960: 222).

Managerialism and Conservative Politics

Conservative policy in the 1980s and 1990s thus involved a mixed legacy. There has been a very marked ideological shift to hostility to producer interests, and this has been reflected in labour market deregulation, anti-trade union legislation and policies that have significantly contributed to the creation and perpetuation of mass unemployment. On the other hand the New Right agenda has not been generally followed. Both in social welfare policy and on privatisation, policies antipathetic to the New Right have been adopted.

This raises the question, how does public sector managerialism relate to this contradictory politics? On the one hand, managerialism, as was argued earlier, is essentially consistent with the anti-producer group stance so characteristic of New Right ideology, which has also been a central feature of British Conservative politics in the 1980s and 1990s. On the other hand, there are crucial and significant differences between the managerialist and New Right projects. The central figure in the Hayekian world is the entrepreneur, whose role is to adjust flexibly to the demands and requirement of the market. The essence of this role is its opportunistic character. For Hayek there can be no rules of entrepreneurship; the market itself is simply a 'discovery process' (Hayek 1978: Ch. 12). Nothing could be further from the approach of managerialism. Reports such as Griffiths and the Efficiency Unit espouse a prescribed model of managerial practice, which embodies what are seen as appropriate structures and techniques. Similar managerialist presumptions pervade the activities of institutions such as the National Audit Office and the Audit Commission. What is assumed is a rule-governed diffusion of best practice.

The Griffiths and the Efficiency Unit prescriptions are thus based on a corporate capitalist conception – or at least the kind of organisational form that has prevailed in Anglo-American corporate capitalism. Yet Hayek's relation to the modern corporation is, in fact, an ambivalent one. For instance, in an essay on the 'The Corporation in a Democratic Society' he argued a marked anti-managerial case including, *inter alia*, the proposal that individual shareholders should be able to determine what share of net profits they wish to reinvest in the company, rather than receiving a dividend determined by management (Hayek 1967: 307–8).

A second area in which there are major contradictions between managerialist and New Right positions operates with respect to quasi-markets. These deeply offend many crucial New Right precepts. This is nicely illustrated in a critical attack by Green on the quasi-market introduced into the NHS.

Green (1990) argued that the quasi-market proposals only mention consumer choice as a presentational device and that, while competition between providers in the delivery of services has been introduced, it is restricted to what he calls a 'defence-industry procurement model'. This was characterised by a situation 'where a few suppliers tender to provide goods or services to a government specification' (Green 1990: 7). The 'consumer sovereignty' approach, which Green favours, is abandoned in favour of 'a managed market where purchasers act as proxies for consumers and their contractual arrangements reached by purchasers determine the service provided which is constrained by a politically determined budget' (ibid.: 9).

In contrast, the assumptions of the Griffiths report and the Efficiency Unit sit quite happily with such managed markets. Note, for example, how the features of determination of overall policy objectives for the managed quasi-market that New Right commentators find so antipathetic are already anticipated in the strategic determination of objectives by bodies such as the NHS supervisory board in Griffiths; and note the strategic role of the Minister and Permanent Secretary in the Next Steps programme.

Consequently, Conservative social policy of the 1980s and 1990s has been a policy where managerialism has emerged at the expense of the ideology of the New Right. However, given the stridency of the ideological shift in British Conservatism and its manifestation in certain areas of policy, it is worth asking why this political option was taken.

At least with respect to social policy two related determinants stand out: the general electoral constraints on the Conservative Party during the 1980s and the particular problems posed by the application of radical right policies to social policy.

It might seem, at one level, rather strange to mention electoral constraints when discussing the Conservative party in the 1980s and 1990s. After all, the party has won the last four British general elections and achieved parliamentary majorities of in excess of 100 seats in two of those elections (1983 and 1987). However, as Table 1.2 illustrates, the Conservatives' election victories have not been achieved with a dominance in terms of share of the total vote. Consequently, they have remained vulnerable to relatively small shifts in voting patterns.

Table 1.2. British general election results, 1945–92, percentage share of votes and seats won

	Conservative		Labour		Liberal*		Other	
	SV	S	SV	S	SV	S	SV	S
1945	39.8	213	48.3	393	9.1	12	2.7	22
1950	43.5	299	46.1	315	9.1	9	1.3	2
1951	48.0	321	48.8	295	2.5	6	0.7	3
1955	49.7	345	46.4	277	2.7	6	1.1	2
1959	49.4	365	43.8	258	5.9	6	1.0	1
1964	43.4	304	44.1	317	11.2	9	1.3	0
1966	41.9	253	47.9	363	8.5	12	1.6	2
1970	46.4	330	43.0	288	7.5	6	3.1	5
1974 (February)	37.8	297	37.1	301	19.3	14	5.8	23
1974 (October)	35.8	277	39.2	319	18.3	13	6.7	26
1979	43.9	339	37.0	269	13.8	11	5.3	16
1983	42.4	397	27.6	209	25.4	23	4.6	21
1987	42.3	376	30.8	229	22.6	22	4.3	23
1992	41.9	336	34.2	271	17.9	20	6.0	24

* Alliance 1983 and 1987; Liberal Democrat 1992
SV = share of the vote
S = seats
Sources: (D. Butler 1989; *Guardian* 14 April 1992)

Indeed, much of the hybrid and ambiguous character of Conservative politics reflects attempts to reconcile ideological objectives with electoral calculations. The confused character of privatisation policy was referred to earlier (pp. 19–20). In many respects this derived from a constellation of opportunistic concerns. Thus, it has been argued that at least one reason why utilities like British Telecom and British Gas were privatised as *monopolies* was that such an approach was the only acceptable one to the incumbent management, whose cooperation was vital if the privatisations were to be accomplished speedily (Marsh 1991: 467). In turn, the haste to accomplish privatisations related not so much to overarching ideological objectives (the term was not even included in the 1979 manifesto) as to the attractions of the policy as a means of raising revenue (ibid.: 460). Equally, many features of privatisation contained clear elements of electoral calculation – for instance, the element of underpricing of issues to guarantee take-up and profits to investors.

Thus ideology was often tempered by electoral calculation. There were, of course, exceptions to this rule, the poll tax being the most notorious case; but in the sphere of social policy a strong element of pragmatism was present. To understand this pragmatism we shall need to examine whether social policy presented any special obstacles to a hard New Right programme. To do this, it is necessary to look at the evidence on public attitudes to social welfare during the 1980s and 1990s.

Public Opinion and the Welfare State

Since 1983 the *British Social Attitudes* survey has collected data on attitudes to the welfare state – on issues such as levels of support for increases (or reductions) in spending on social welfare programmes and for the public or private provision of social services. Notwithstanding the Conservative electoral success at the time, the 1983 survey showed there was not 'an emerging strong majority determined to roll back the frontiers of the State' (Bosanquet 1984: 96); while the 1990 survey concluded that 'the 1980s have seen a strengthening of public endorsement of centralised tax-financed state welfare' (Taylor-Gooby 1991: 41). Similarly the 1993 survey found that only 4 per cent of those questioned wanted to reduce taxes and public spending, while 29 per cent wanted to keep taxes and expenditure at the current level: thus the vast majority of respondents wanted to increase both taxes and expenditure. There was also a consistent trend to increased support for higher spending and taxation. In 1983 24 per cent of Conservative supporters were in favour of higher taxes and spending; but by 1993 this had increased to 55 per cent (Lipsey 1994: 3).

However, care is needed in interpreting such survey evidence, which *prima facie* contradicts material presented by Ralph Harris and Arthur Seldon of the Institute of Economic Affairs. They undertook five surveys between 1963 and 1987. These showed a high level of public support for private forms of provision. In the 1987 survey they found that 68 per cent of their respondents would accept an education voucher at full value that would allow them to send their children to private schools, although this figure was reduced when the value of the voucher was reduced (Harris and Seldon 1987: 41). Seventy-five per cent of respondents were prepared to accept a full-value voucher for private health insurance (ibid.: 47).

In part, such differences in results are determined by the character of the questions being asked. A criticism of the *British Social Attitudes* surveys is that they ask their respondents, for example, whether they support increased taxes to pay for additional welfare spending; they do not ask whether the individual respondent is prepared to increase his or her tax burden. The most recent British Social Attitudes survey, published in 1996, attempts to meet these criticisms. Thus, when respondents were asked if they were in favour of increased spending on social services they were also informed that such spending would involve either an increase of income tax of 1p in the pound or a flat charge of £35 for each adult in the household. The result did show that knowledge of the tax implications of spending did lead to a reduction in support for spending increases. In the case of education support fell from 73 per cent to 52 per cent, and in the case of health from 87 per cent to 64 per cent. However, as the authors conclude, even with knowledge of such tax implications there was still 'a comfortable majority' in favour of increased spending in the core areas of health, education and universal welfare benefits (Brook *et al.* 1996: 200).

However, there is also a question mark regarding how far such stated attitudes translate into voting intentions. Thus, during the 1992 general election a survey for National Opinion Polls found that 75 per cent of respondents favoured paying increased tax to fund improved public services; but when respondents were asked to give their attitude to Labour and Conservative policies on tax there was a 50/50 split in support for each party (D. Butler and Kavanagh 1992: 147). Thus, while voters may be ambivalent on their attitude to the tax implications of increased public spending, this is not to suggest that even a significant minority have embraced substantial privatisation of social welfare.

Thus, the evidence on public opinion and the Welfare State suggested that there would be considerable political risks in attempting to pursue a New Right line (privatising both finance and provision) on welfare, Inevitably this had implications for another issue: public spending.

Public Spending: Parsimony not Disengagement

The logic of New Right arguments tends to favour consumerist forms of provision like vouchers rather than direct state provision, even when it operates in a quasi-market form. Of course, in such situations, state finance of the service continues to operate. However, another important dimension of the New Right is the argument for state disengagement from both finance and provision of welfare except in a residual form, as illustrated in the Hayekian argument for compulsory insurance with a minimum income discussed earlier (p. 9). The abandonment of such a New Right project had implications for public spending. If the state continued to finance and provide the major social services, then the scope for radical reductions in public spending was not present. Again, this led to New Right disenchantment with the Conservatives. Writing from this position Burton published a critique of the first Thatcher administration entitled *Why No Cuts?* (Burton 1984).

Evidence on the limited extent of disengagement can be seen in Table 1.3, which presents a series for the government's main favoured measure for public expenditure, General Government Expenditure (X) (GGE (X)).

Table 1.3. UK general government expenditure (GGE)(X) as a percentage of gross domestic product (GDP) 1979–80 to 1995–6

Year	GGE (X) as a % of GDP
1979–80	42.5
1980–81	44.75
1981–82	45.5
1982–83	45.5
1983–84	44.75
1984–85	45.25
1985–86	43.25
1986–87	42.25
1987–88	40.5
1988–89	38
1989–90	38.25
1990–91	39
1991–92	41
1992–93	43.5
1993–94	43.25
1994–95	42.5
1995–96	42.25

Source: Treasury (1996).

This measure *includes* central and local government expenditure, but *excludes* items financed through the national lottery and privatisation proceeds (which had been treated as negative expenditure in earlier definitions) (Flemming and Oppenheimer 1996: 58). What Table 1.3 shows is that GGE (X) as a share of Gross Domestic Product (GDP) in fiscal year 1995–6 was virtually identical to the figure in the first full fiscal year after the Conservatives came to power in 1979.

The Evidence for Parsimony

However, although radical disengagement from state finance and provision of social services meant that substantial cuts in government spending could not be delivered, a case can be made that Conservative governments, since 1979, have operated a policy of parsimony. Thus, comparative evidence can be used to support claims that the UK has experienced a relatively rigorous regime of expenditure control. Thus, Table 1.4 gives OECD figures for general government outlays as a percentage of GDP in the G7 countries. As the table indicates, the UK and Germany were the only G7 countries to have a lower ratio of government spending to GDP in 1989 than in 1979.

Of course, analysis of trends in public spending relative to national income requires attempts to control for cyclical effects. Thus, while upturns in economic activity both boost national income and reduce social security spending because of reductions in both unemployment-related and other means-tested benefits, in downturns the reverse is true (Convery 1995/6). This feature is salient in the UK case since 1979, as both the late 1970s and the late 1980s were periods of substantial economic recession. One way of adjusting for such cyclical effects is to compare trends between two years at similar cyclical points (Hibberd 1993). Thus, Hibberd looked at movements in GGE between two recession years (1980/1 and 1991/2).

Table 1.4. General government outlays as a percentage of gross domestic product (G7 countries)

	1979	1982	1984	1989
USA	31.7	36.5	35.8	36.5
Japan	31.6	33.7	33.2	32.9
Germany	47.6	49.4	48.0	45.1
France	45.0	50.4	52.0	49.3
Italy	45.5	47.4	49.3	51.7
UK	42.5	46.9	47.2	39.7
Canada	39.0	46.6	46.8	44.2

Source: Oxley *et al.* (1991).

Over this period total government programme spending increased 1.7 per cent per annum in real terms, while growth in real gross domestic product was 2.2 per cent per annum (ibid.: 22). Thus, comparing years at similar points in the cycle, there has been a pattern of restraint in programme spending designed to reduce the share of public spending in GDP.

Representations of Expenditure

The combination of lack of radical disengagement and parsimony has left Conservative governments in a rather ambivalent position. On the one hand government retention of ultimate responsibility for the service has meant that there has been a political imperative to suggest that service standards have been at least maintained, if not improved. Yet at the same time the emphasis on restraining the role of the state means that there has been a simultaneous emphasis on demonstrating success in controlling public spending.

One result of such political tensions has been the significance of representations of public spending and of decisions having an impact on public spending. A frequent topic of discussion in this respect has related to claims, by central government, to have maintained or increased public expenditure in 'real' terms. A key aspect of this controversy is the use of the term 'real'. The use of the term by central government (and that used in earlier discussions in this chapter) simply means that nominal expenditure figures have been adjusted in line with price changes. The implication is that a 'real' increase means that additional resources are being committed to the service. However, critics of such claims have pointed out that the services concerned are usually highly labour-intensive, and thus that much of the 'real' increase will simply reflect increases in wages or salaries of government employees so that they either stay in line with or do not fall too far behind those of other employees in the economy generally (Rowthorne 1992: 268).

In a broader context, Pierson has also pointed to the importance of how expenditure cuts or decisions that have implications for public expenditure appear to the public. For example, government policy has involved a sharp reduction in standards of public provision in the State Earnings Related Pension Scheme (SERPS). However, this policy has proved much less controversial than the treatment of health expenditure (where 'real' increases in spending have occurred). Pierson points out that a key difference is the lack of political 'visibility' of the former, since the reduction in benefit occurs incrementally over a long period (Pierson 1994: 134).

It is within this constellation of forces that one must situate public sector managerialism. The rejection of the New Right programme on social welfare meant that the state retained responsibility for running social services, and thus had to face the expenditure implications of this option. This called for control of public spending, which fitted in with the ideological and the political objectives of the Conservatives. On the other hand, control was a negative option, and managerialism offered a positive message: goals could be attained with the use of existing resources if only the appropriate management approach were adopted (**1.7**). To assess how far the promise of managerialism has been realised it is necessary to look at the substantive areas of policy where managerialism has had an impact. They make up the subjects of the next four chapters.

Managing by Numbers: The Bogus Prospectus of Performance Measurement

Attempts to measure the performance of public sector services are, in no sense, a new phenomenon. In a famous article, published in 1901, Sidney Webb called for an 'honorary competition' between local authorities, which would involve 'an annual investigation of municipal efficiency, working out their statistical marks for excellence' in such areas as 'drainage, water supply, cleansing . . . housing, hospital accommodation, sickness experience and mortality and publicly classifying them all according to the results of the examination' (Webb 1901: 378). The King was to present a 'shield of honour' to the authority which had made most progress with respect to these indicators, and civic dignitaries were to be recognised by awards, such as a knighthood for the mayor of the winning council. More recently, the 1952 report of the Chief Medical Officer included a comparison of 'bed turnover', i.e., number of patients discharged or who had died divided by bed numbers. Comparative data were presented for London and provincial teaching hospitals (**2.1**).

However, there are two distinctive features of performance measurements in public services in the 1980s and 1990s: one has been the scale and pervasiveness of such measurement; the other has been the significance attributed to measuring the performance of provider units. Thus, Sidney Webb's measures, while they were intended to compare local authorities, invoked many measures at a 'macro' level such as those for public health (for a discussion of contrasting definitions of 'efficiency' over time see Froud *et al.* 1997). It would be too strong to argue that current measures exclude such features; but there is a central emphasis on measures applied to units such as NHS Trusts, schools, universities and executive agencies.

The pervasiveness of measures is illustrated by central government departmental reports that, in addition to outlining government spending plans, include a plethora of measures that are claimed to be relevant to the performance of the service concerned (**2.2**). Similarly, ministers frequently make use of statistical data to seek to demonstrate what they see as improvements in service performance: for example, during her tenure as Secretary of State for Health, Virginia Bottomley, in a speech at the 1994 Conservative conference, cited data on NHS activity that she argued demonstrated 'efficiency' gains from the introduction of the quasi-market (Radical Statistics Health Group 1995).

A further crucial manifestation of performance measurement has stemmed from the work of 'evaluative' bodies such as the Audit Commission, the National Audit Office and the Social Services Inspectorate (SSI) of the Department of Health. As a central part of the remit of such bodies is to evaluate units providing services in the public sector, there is a correlative need for measures of performance. For example, the SSI has produced a set of measures for services for children under ten ranging from estimates of unit costs of residential care for children to user satisfaction with services (reprinted in London Region Social Services Research Group 1989: 11–14). Such measures are used as a framework for comparing public sector units: for example, the Audit Commission (1992) contrasted and sought to explain variations in length of stay of patients in acute hospitals across what were then District Health Authorities, and the National Audit Office used three financial ratios to assess the financial viability of higher education institutions (**2.3**).

A further major impetus to performance measurement has come from the various Citizens' Charters. Central to such initiatives has been the idea that establishing explicit targets for public services will improve their performance. These have included, in the case of health, ceilings for the length of time on a waiting list for certain treatments, maximum time-periods for which patients should wait for assessment in accident and emergency units; and guidelines on the time outpatients should wait beyond their appointment times (**2.4**). The use of such targets has been accompanied by publication of data on how providers performed in meeting them (**2.5**).

Extending Accountability

Performance measurement and review has often been justified on the grounds that it is vital to accountability. Such arguments have seen the process of electoral accountability as limited and partial. A good example is the case of the Audit Commission. Central to the work of the Commission is value for money (VFM) audit. This reflects the duties of the Commission under the 1982 Act to ensure that 'economy, efficiency and effectiveness' in resource use have been achieved (**2.6**). In turn, this involves a major extension in the role of audit, which, traditionally, had mainly been concerned with the accuracy of accounts and ensuring that public bodies were acting within their legal remit. VFM audit, however, involves an assessment of service performance (**2.7**), an area which, of course, intersects with professional judgements that were of limited or no relevance to the narrower financial and legal concerns of traditional audit practice.

An early publication of the Commission defended such activities in terms of the extension of 'accountability': it argued, with respect to local government, that, while councillors were politically accountable, the effect of this was limited by low turnouts in local elections. This meant that a more extensive form of audit was required to effect a broader form of accountability (**2.8**). Further, as was indicated in Chapter 1, this notion of performance measurement as a mechanism of accountability has been extended beyond elected representatives to civil servants and professionals.

Put in this way the virtues of performance measurement appear self-evident. After all, if the democratic process has involved checking that controls are exerted over 'inputs' (that money is being spent for the purposes intended by Parliament), why should review not be applied to the products of such public service activities? The object of this chapter is to examine such claims. The chapter is divided into four sections: the first deals with issues of definition and examines the range of variants of performance indicators and measures; the second looks at the political context in which performance measurement developed in the United Kingdom; the third considers some of the methodological and conceptual problems posed by the use of performance indicators; and the final section is an overall critical evaluation of how far performance measurement might advance accountability.

The Concept of Performance Indicator

Central to performance measurement in the public sector has been the development of Performance Indicators (PIs); thus any critical discussion of performance measurement involves an analysis of such indicators. What are the distinctive characteristics of performance indicators? One way to generate a working definition will be to look at the two terms 'performance' and 'indicator' and explore their ramifications. The term 'performance' implies a reference to the product of the organisation being assessed. This means that performance is not measured by looking at activities or expenditure on resources. Some indicator sets thus include measures that cannot be regarded as relating to performance. An example is the SSI set on children's services referred to above. This includes a number of measures referring to service expenditure or provision, for example on residential care for mentally handicapped children (per capita) or places in local authority day centres (London Region Social Services Group 1989: 11–12). Strictly speaking, such measures are of resource use, not of the product of the service.

The notion of an 'indicator' implies a norm, as Cuenin puts it: 'when an indicator shows a difference in one direction this means that the situation is better whereas if it shows a difference in the opposite direction, then this means that the situation is less favourable' (cited in Cave *et al.* 1991: 21). This definition should also be extended by adding a distinction made by Carter, Klein and Day. They make the point that indicators can be used as 'dials' or 'tin openers'. 'Dials' are characterised by their clarity and lack of ambiguity, 'providing a precise measure of inputs, outputs and outcomes based on a clear understanding of what good and bad performance entails' (N. Carter *et al.* 1992: 49). They argue that 'dials' are unusual in the public sector, and that, generally, PIs are 'tin openers' that operate by 'opening up a "can of worms"' thus prompting 'interrogation and inquiry' (ibid.). With 'tin openers' the eventual possibility of drawing a normative conclusion remains; but, unlike the 'dial', they do not 'give' such a conclusion.

Indicators and Users

Performance indicators involve deploying data to allow normative judgements of the 'product' of public sector service providers. However, this general definition must be supplemented by examining the plurality of variant forms that performance indicators may take. It was argued above (pp. 30–1) that one of the potential attractions of PIs was their apparent role in rendering public service providers more 'accountable'. However, the notion of accountability presupposes a user of the indicators. In fact, there are a number of possible users, a feature that has implications for how performance measurement operates.

Top-Down Accountability

Top-down accountability occurs, for example, when central government or agencies use indicators to monitor the performance of units. Thus, an area of political concern in the NHS has been over the question of 'continuing care' for long-stay (usually elderly) patients. This relates to the tendency for acute hospitals to cut the length of stay in hospitals, a policy encouraged by quasi-market mechanisms (Cutler and Waine 1997) and by evaluative bodies (Audit Commission 1992). Such discharges often mean that, while patients may not need acute treatment, they continue to require non-acute care. If, however, such care is provided in the community, by social services, it is likely to be means-tested and subject to eligibility criteria, a feature that led to cases of discharged patients being required to pay for private provision (Cutler and Waine 1997). The political fall-out from such cases led to the creation of guidelines designed to ensure that continuing health care needs were met equitably and provided for by health and local authorities (Department of Health 1995a).

In turn the NHS Executive and the SSI were given responsibility for monitoring the guidelines and, as part of this remit, devising performance indicators. These included the number of emergency admissions of people over 75, numbers of re-admissions and the numbers and reasons for over-75-year-olds awaiting discharge from hospital (Department of Health 1995b). In this case the indicators could suggest, for example, inadequate community-based provision, although it is interesting that the document qualifies such judgements by arguing that, for example, numbers of re-admissions 'may indicate gaps in or pressures on community-based services for rehabilitation or recovery' (ibid.). In this case indicators are to be used in a 'tin opener' form.

The above example is top-down in that it is clearly consistent with the distinction between strategic and operational responsibilities characteristic of the Griffiths and the Efficiency Unit reports.

Performance Assessment as 'Self-Regulation'

In many cases of top-down assessment judgements are made of the activities of professionals. In contrast, indicators may be determined by professionals and used in a context of 'self-regulation'. The *Confidential Enquiry on Perioperative Deaths* is an example of such a use of performance measures. The Enquiry covered deaths within 30 days of an operation in three NHS Regions (Northern, North East Thames, Southern Western). It found variations in the extent of 'avoidable deaths' between surgical specialists, anaesthetists, hospitals and regions. Equally it drew normative conclusions, identifying deficiencies in practice such as lapses of delegation, where trainees undertook work beyond their competence, or instances where inadequate pre-operative assessment took place (Roberts 1990: 22).

There are similar instances in education. Thus, a concept which has played a key role in this area, and is discussed in more detail below (p. 41), is 'value added'. Such measures examine the relationship between, for example, student attainment on reaching a particular 'stage' in the National Curriculum (see Chapter 3 for this concept) and subsequent performance in public examinations. Such calculations can be undertaken by staff in schools or in further education, and could reveal that student performance could vary with the mix of subjects taken (Fitz-Gibbon 1996b: 124). Thus, the Audit Commission (**2.9**) cites an instance of biology teachers at a school using such an analysis, which demonstrated inferior performance in biology amongst students not taking chemistry. In such cases the operation of performance assessment is an intra-professional process designed to draw conclusions on desirable practice standards and to diffuse such practice among professional staff.

Performance Measurement and Service Users

PIs can also be aimed at service users. This, as will be discussed in more detail in Chapter 3, was particularly the rationale for the use of powers to publish school examination and test results. It is also worth noting that such data can also be utilised by newspapers to provide performance guides to parents. These are commonly published in 'league table' form (see below p. 34), and have appeared not just in the papers themselves but incorporated in guides in book form. Thus, the *Sunday Times* published the *Sunday Times State Schools Book*, which is designed to help parents 'decide which school is best for your child' (cited in Morrison and Cowan 1996: 243).

Citizens' Charter indicators on features such as waiting lists and time taken to process benefit claims are also designed to reflect 'consumer interests'. However, in this case, as with national examination and test results, it is important to stress that there is still a strong top-down element, as users/consumers do not set or contribute to setting the targets chosen or the indicators used.

It is also worth stressing that the same indicator may assume a quite different significance depending on whether it is being looked at by a manager or a service user. In the United States PIs in higher education are designed for use by potential students. This also has implications for how particular measures are interpreted. Thus a managerial user in the UK is likely to interpret a high student–staff ratio as an indicator of low unit costs (because academic labour costs in particular account for around 60 per cent of total institution costs in higher education), and thus as a favourable 'efficiency' measure. In contrast, the same result might be treated by potential students as *unfavourable*, since it is seen as indicative of a poor resource endowment for the college concerned (Cave *et al.* 1991: 60).

What Should Be Measured?

If there are various potential users of PIs, equally there are correlative variations in what is measured in PI sets. In particular a good deal of discussion has centred on the broad dimensions of performance covered by what have come to be known as the 'three Es': economy, efficiency and effectiveness. 'Economy' refers to obtaining 'inputs', such as labour, bought-in goods or services, at the lowest cost consistent with a constant quality level. 'Efficiency' is an input–output relation measuring the output achieved with a given input. Finally, 'effectiveness' means providing a range of services that are appropriate to realising the overall goals of the institution concerned (**2.10**). Thus, for example, it is possible for a service in this sense to be 'efficient' (producing a large output from a given level of input) without being 'effective', i.e. achieving its object. An instance of what has been claimed to be a disjuncture between 'efficiency' and 'effectiveness' is higher education (HE). Thus critics of the substantial expansion of HE since the late 1980s argue that, while it might be claimed to be efficient in that unit costs have fallen (see Chapter 3), this has been at the expense of the quality of provision; and that the premisses of the policy, that significant economic benefits would result, are flawed (Keep and Mayhew 1996). If such criticisms are justified (for further discussion, see Chapters 3 and 6) expansion of HE can be regarded as 'ineffective'.

The Politics of Performance Indicators

The use of PIs is thus potentially diverse both in terms of the range of possible users and the dimensions of 'performance' that are encompassed. However, this diversity has not been reflected in the United Kingdom in the 1980s and 1990s. On the contrary, the dominant model adopted has been one where initiation, design and use have derived from government and/or government agencies. This does not mean the initiatives have flowed exclusively from the top. For example, some local authorities developed their own performance assessment schemes (Warburton 1993), and instances of intra-professional initiatives have been discussed above (p. 34). Furthermore, it should not be assumed that the project met with favour only among Conservative politicians; the potential for control can appeal to senior public service officials (Pollitt 1986: 157). However, whether in specific services or with respect to the creation of monitoring bodies like the Audit Commission or the National Audit Office, the main changes have emanated from the centre.

This raises the issue of how performance measurement should be situated politically. An obvious point of reference would appear to be the link with a decline in economic performance in the advanced capitalist countries in the period since the end of the 'long boom'. However, such accounts are inadequate in that, while poor economic performance certainly exerts pressure to restrain public spending, this engenders the imperative to exert budgetary controls, not necessarily to measure and review 'performance'. This point is reinforced by the fact that the Callaghan government espoused, and practised, rigorous expenditure control without performance measurement, while attempts to control spending have operated in tandem with performance measurement under the Thatcher and Major governments (Pollitt 1986: 159–60).

As was argued in Chapter 1, a crucial ingredient here has been managerialism. Not only does the use of performance measures allow governments to exert pressure for more activity, but it allows them to present their record in a more favourable light. Thus, Pollitt has argued that an agenda of pure spending control is negative, while the emphasis on performance 'exudes an aroma of action, dynamism, purposeful effort' (ibid.: 160).

Equally, the use of PIs allows the possibility of comparisons between organisations providing services, such as local government, hospitals and universities. Such comparisons permit the compilation of 'league tables' of physical measures (e.g. staff–student ratios, average lengths of patient stay) or financial measures (e.g. cost per graduate, cost per inpatient hospital case). Thus it can be argued that, if the 'lagging' providers could match the 'best practice', then an expansion of service provision could be achieved within the existing level of resource allocation (for an example see Audit Commission 1992). Equally there is a strong emphasis in PI sets on 'throughput' measures. Examples of such measures are number of students graduating from universities or cases treated in NHS units in a given period and so on. In turn, such measures can be related to 'inputs' (e.g. graduates per FTE lecturer). Such PIs encourage throughput, and thus stimulate at least the appearance of 'efficiency' gains, i.e. the impression that an increased level of service provision is being made with an unchanged volume of resources.

Performance Indicators: Conceptual and Methodological Issues

The development and use of PIs has generated considerable debate and a substantial critical literature, the latter pointing to a series of problems, both conceptual and operational.

A central issue concerns the difficulties involved in the measurement of *outputs* and the *outcomes* of public sector services. The distinction between output and outcome is significant in a number of contexts in the PI debate. Outputs are sometimes also termed 'throughputs' of the service, and are measured by the flow-through of service users. Thus, for example, outputs/throughputs would be quantified by the number of patients treated (in aggregate or in a particular category); pupils or students completing a course of study; numbers obtaining a degree; numbers of children placed for adoption. In contrast, outcomes refer to the *objectives* of the service *per se*. In the case of health care such an objective would be to improve life expectancy or to improve quality of life, by, for example, increasing mobility or reducing pain. In the case of personal social services they might be to provide the social support to allow, for example, an elderly frail person to live in their own home, if they so wish.

The intangible character of outcomes means that measures are always dependent on constructs that attempt to generate proxies or substitutes for the outcome. The central difficulty, therefore, lies in the fact that the proxy can be criticised for failing to capture the character of the outcome. A classic instance is provided by higher education. Here it has been argued that a means of measuring the impact of research is via the use of citations. The technique operates by looking at the number of times a piece of work is cited in a range of academic publications. The outcome that the citation is aiming to measure is that part of the goal of research is to contribute to the development of knowledge in a given subject-area. However, the outcome is necessarily qualitative, and the use of citations as a proxy is vulnerable to the criticism that it is 'a register of fashion and agreed wisdom; not necessarily of excellence' (Minogue 1986: 398–9).

Outcomes invariably involve a set of difficult conceptual or measurement issues. For example, negative health outcomes have numerous dimensions, such as disability or discomfort (Orchard 1994: 1493). This raises a question over how to compare interventions that have different effects on different dimensions: when, for instance, intervention A is ineffective at improving mobility but will significantly reduce discomfort, while intervention B has the reverse effect. Furthermore, there are significant measurement problems with qualitative outcomes such as pain or loss of mobility (ibid.).

It is also worth bearing in mind that, while this problem arises in a pointed form in the case of outcomes, it is not in fact irrelevant even to some output measures. For example, one dimension of research output in higher education is publications. However, aside from any qualitative issues, there is the immediate question that publications come in a variety of forms: books, articles, communications, reviews, reports; pamphlets/ occasional papers. A weighting system consequently must be devised; but there is no obvious reason why one weighting system is superior to another. A study of the publications of political science academics illustrates the point. The weighting system used *inter alia* gave 10 points for a published book and 2 for articles in a 'leading journal'. Yet this raises the question as to why, 'a book [should] be worth five times an article rather than four times or six' (Minogue 1986: 398).

One of the ways of attempting to avoid arbitrary weights is to incorporate 'expert' judgements into performance reviews. This, naturally, has a somewhat paradoxical effect. As we saw in Chapter 1, performance measurement relates to managerial forms that are concerned not just to render managers accountable but also to place professionals within the hierarchy of control. To this extent, it incorporates the ideological trend of treating professionals as suspect 'producer groups'. However, the incorporation of professional judgement into the review process means not a judgement on professional practice *per se* but a peer review in a hierarchical framework.

In turn, this option leaves the assessment open to a different form of arbitrariness, the reliance on reputational assumptions and professional biases, which impart a circularity to the whole exercise. For example, clinical reviews of the appropriateness of medical practice have found systematic variations that reflect pre-existing standards. Thus a study, published in 1989, recorded the judgements of UK and American clinicians on the appropriateness of coronary angiography and coronary artery bypass (CABG) operations. The UK panel applied more stringent standards than the US one. However, in turn, these judgements reflected the pattern of *existing medical practice* since, for example, CABG operations are performed roughly five times as often in the United States as in the United Kingdom (Roberts 1990: 37).

There are similar problems of circularity and reputationalism in rankings of educational institutions. The 1989 UFC university research ranking exercise did not involve the expert sub-committees reading all the submissions from universities, and the composition of the sub-committees involved a statistical over-representation of academics from universities that also received high rankings (University Funding Council 1989: 8 and 11; Cutler 1992a).

The Question of 'Efficiency'

The fact that there are formidable problems with 'outcome' measures has a number of important effects on performance measurement. Quite clearly, it renders the measurement of 'effectiveness' highly problematic. Measures of effectiveness involve attempting to assess how far the *goals* of services have been attained; but such goals require reference to the outcomes of the services concerned.

Equally, there are difficulties with the concept of 'efficiency'. As efficiency is an input–output relationship, it presupposes that the output measures are not merely accurate but also at least reasonably appropriate measures of throughput. However, while such measurement does not involve the more vexed questions posed by outcomes, official throughput data are often problematic. A much discussed instance of this is activity measurement in the NHS. The creation of the quasi-market has generated an incentive for government to show that, with limited increases in funding, major increases in activity are occurring; and reference was made above (p. 30) to claims made to this effect by Virginia Bottomley. A major confusion in this regard is that, while figures are cited as if they referred to patients treated, the key measure of NHS activity is 'finished consultant episodes'. This change, which was introduced in 1988/9, records completed contacts with consultants (Radical Statistics Health Group 1992: 305). Thus, for example, if a patient has been involved in an accident and is seen by an orthopaedic surgeon and a cardiologist, this counts as two consultant episodes (ibid.).

This measure has clear drawbacks as an output indicator, and has implications for conclusions regarding efficiency. Thus, for example, what might, arguably, be seen as a service weakness, such as shortage of beds, would encourage treatment via a *series* of admissions and an increase in the number of finished consultant episodes (Clarke and Mckee 1992: 1307). Also, an internal organisational shift to greater medical specialisation (which might or might not be desirable) will boost the activity measure with no increase in patients treated (ibid.).

Equally, the use of activity measures to suggest an efficiency increase following an organisational change, like the introduction of a quasi-market, must set such measures in the context of previous trends. Thus the NHS Executive claimed, in a publication entitled 'NHS Reforms: the First Six Months' (1992) that, *inter alia*, the increase in day cases of 13.6 per cent was an effect of such market mechanisms. However, in a critical discussion of such claims, the Radical Statistics Health Group (1992: 706) pointed out that such changes reflected longer-term shifts in medical practice, and that the increase for the first six months of the quasi-market was below the 14.4 per cent increase from 1988/9 to 1989/90 that pre-dated the introduction of the quasi-market.

It is also important to note that varying conclusions can be drawn on the extent of efficiency gains depending on whether physical or financial measures are used. Thus physical measures relate a given output to a physical input measure, for example graduates per full-time equivalent (FTE) member of staff, whereas financial measures relate outputs to a cost measure, for example the cost of 'producing' a graduate. As labour costs tend consistently to be a large proportion of total costs in the public sector, it might be expected that physical and financial efficiency measures ought to move together. However, this is not always the case. An interesting example is provided by reductions in the length of stay in acute hospitals, which are often cited as a physical measure of efficiency. Such reductions are not reflected in *pro rata* reductions in cost per case, because the cuts in length of stay usually occur after investigation and treatment have been provided and the patient requires cheaper non-acute care (Clarke 1996: 177). This means that costs per hospital day tend to go up under a rapid throughput regime as the (increasing number) of patients who are being treated are receiving more intensive staff input in the form of tests and treatment (ibid.). It is, of course, also important to bear in mind that unit cost measures refer to costs incurred by the organisation concerned. Thus, in the case of acute care, reduction in length of stay can pass nursing costs on to other public services like GPs or social services or to informal carers (ibid.: 177; Stott 1992).

Ensuring Comparability

As was indicated earlier, a feature of contemporary performance measurement has been the importance attributed to comparisons of public sector provider units. However, this raises the question of the extent to which such evaluations compare 'like with like'. This problem arises because services like health and primary and secondary education are virtually universal services. This means that the population served is highly diverse and the service is provided under a wide range of conditions (Froud *et al.* 1997). Schools will thus take in children with a wide range of attainment levels on entry and hospitals will treat patients of different age ranges, and the nature and severity of the conditions for which they are being treated will also vary considerably. What this means is that comparisons of 'raw' data, where no adjustment has been made for such variations, are likely to be misleading, since the relative performance of the units can only be judged if such variations in circumstances are taken into account.

The area in which this issue has been most pointedly debated is education, where (see Chapter 3) the government has used its legal powers, under the 1980 Education Act, to require publication of school test and examination results. Such results are 'raw' attainment scores: i.e. they show the performance of students in the tests or examinations concerned, but take no account of features such as the student's attainment on entering the school or his or her class background. This has led educational researchers to call for the use of 'value added' measures as a supplement or alternative to such raw data. For example, instead of simply comparing the A-level results of different schools, data would also be collected on prior attainment, for example at GCSE. If these two sets of data are compared then regression techniques can be used to explore the relationship between prior and subsequent attainment. In turn this allows expected final scores to be calculated for every given input level. Actual results could thus be similar to, better or worse than the predicted level. As value added calculations compare actual to expected performance rather than actual attainment, the relative performance of schools on a value added basis can be quite different from that given by attainment comparisons. A school with less good attainment might have better value added once the levels of attainment on entry are taken into account (for illustrations see McPherson 1992 and Jesson 1996).

Analogous problems also arise in connection with measures of health outcomes. Thus, there has recently been pressure to publish hospital mortality tables. Such tables in raw form are potentially misleading, because they taken no account of the age of patients treated or the severity of their condition on entry to the hospital. In addition, as the measure is one of *in-hospital* mortality it is highly sensitive to variations in patient length of stay (Mckee and Hunter 1994: 112). The significance of this feature can be seen from an American study that compared mortality rates for patients who had inpatient treatment in two states, California and New York State. The comparison was made for mortality rates for three conditions within thirty days of admission, whether the death occurred before or after discharge from hospital (Jencks *et al.* 1988: 2241). Table 2.1, drawn from this research, shows that inpatient mortality for all three conditions was higher in New York State; but this reflected longer hospital stays in New York. In contrast, when the comparison was made on the basis of thirty-day mortality New York rates were 1.6 per cent lower than the California rates (ibid.: 2240).

Where cost comparisons are used it is also important to take into

Table 2.1. Comparison of mortality rates in California and New York contrasting inpatient and 30-day mortality figures for four clinical conditions

	California	New York
Stroke		
Average Stay (Days)	8.6	24.5
Inpatient Mortality	16.1%	25.7%
30-Day Mortality	21.2%	22.2%
Bacterial Pneumonia		
Average Stay (Days)	9.1	15.4
Inpatient Mortality	15.4%	19.6%
30-Day Mortality	19.9%	18.8%
Myocardial Infarction		
Average Stay (Days)	8.1	12.4
Inpatient Mortality	21.0%	23.8%
30-day Mortality	15.3%	14.8%
Congestive Heart Failure		
Average Stay (Days)	6.7	13.0
Inpatient Mortality	9.9%	13.7%
30-Day Mortality	15.3%	14.8%
Weighted Average (four conditions)		
Average Stay (Days)	8.3	16.5
Inpatient Mortality	15.4%	19.3%
30-Day Mortality	20.4%	20.1%

Source: Jencks *et al.* (1988).

account the characteristics of service users and the character of provision. In personal social services a considerable amount of work has been undertaken on the relative costs of provision across sectors, in particular comparing public and voluntary sector providers. Early work using crude cost data concluded that voluntary sector providers operated at significantly lower unit costs. However, such conclusions have been criticised on the grounds that they use 'bald' expenditure figures that fail to take into account variations in the nature of the services provided or the groups served. For example, a study of day centres for the elderly attempted to standardise cost comparisons for 'dependency' characteristics of users and the activities of units. It found that, after such standardisation, cost variations were much smaller than those based on crude cost figures; and that cost differences between voluntary and public sectors varied with size, with large voluntary organisations having higher unit costs than comparable public sector units (Knapp and Missiakoulis 1982).

Comparisons of organisational performance have also involved the construction and publication of 'league tables' of providers. A distinction needs to be made between a performance table and a league table; in the case of the former a list of providers is given, and the performance measured in terms of the criteria selected; in a league table the data on performance are used to construct a rank order of providers. In general, league tables in the strict sense have been produced by newspapers, although they have also been constructed by evaluative bodies (for an example, see Audit Commission 1992). Controversy over league tables in part reflects the fact that they use raw data. However, there are other important respects in which they can be misleading.

A good illustration of these problems is provided in a critical discussion of the *Sunday Times* guide to the 'best' state schools by Morrison and Cowan (1996). They point out that a rank order requires reference to a single dimension (e.g. academic success), since if, for example, an additional dimension like 'pastoral care' is also mentioned, then schools can score high on one and low on the other, thus making it impossible to establish a ranking (ibid.: 245). In this respect, the dimension used in the guide is of academic success, since the ranking relates to examination performance. In this respect, of course, the claim to indicate the 'best' schools is contentious, since it presupposes that academic success is, unproblematically, the appropriate basis for making the choice.

However, even assuming the validity of ranking on criteria of academic success and using examination results as the basis of such a comparison, there is the further problem that there are a plurality of examinations at different levels and, within a given examination, different parts of the distribution can be considered. Thus, the *Sunday Times* guide uses the following criteria; GCSE pass rate (GCSE); percentage of A and B grades at A level (AB); percentage of A-E grades at A level (AE); and the percentage of students progressing to higher education (HE). The rank order was decided by GCSE pass rate; if two schools were equal in this respect then the one with the higher percentage of A and B grades was ranked higher; if the two schools were equal with respect to this measure, then the higher percentage of A to E grades was used (ibid.: 243). While information on the percentage entering HE was given in the guide, it was not used for purposes of ranking. Thus, the ranking criteria operate in a hierarchy where GCSE takes precedence over AB and AB over AE.

Morrison and Cowan point out that, while the rank order generated by these criteria is supposed to be a reliable guide, in fact it varies considerably depending on what order of precedence is given to the ranking criteria. They show that, if AB is made the main ranking criterion and GCSE the second then 36 schools change their place by over 200 positions in an overall list of 500 (ibid.: 247). In one case a school moved 312 places in the rank order (ibid.). They also give a crisp example of how potentially misleading the guide is to a parent attempting to use it as a 'consumer'. They show that the school that was 58th in the table had the following profile: GCSE 97 per cent pass rate, AB 17 per cent, AE 86 per cent, HE 75 per cent (ibid.). In contrast, the school ranked 60th achieved a lower GCSE pass rate (96 per cent), but was ahead on all the other criteria, arguably more relevant, for example, to progress into HE; its scores were AB 62 per cent, AE 99 per cent and HE 92 per cent (ibid.).

The potential for fluctuation in rank order positions can, for the same reasons, apply in value added measures. Thus, Table 2.2 is drawn from Jesson's exploratory study of value added measures. This study used test scores at stage 3 of the National Curriculum as the initial attainment measures and either total GCSE points scores (with a starred A counting for 8 points, a G grade 1, and a fail 0) or GCSE points *per entry* as the final attainment level. Results using the two measures varied considerably, because schools had significantly different policies on the number of subjects for which students were entered. Again the two criteria produced radically different results. Thus, for example, the 'leading' school on the value added measure for total points and the school ranked 10th of 12 on that criterion had an identical result when comparison was made in terms of points per entry (Jesson 1996: 7).

'Ownership' and Causality

Many of the issues already discussed with respect to comparability concern problems inherent in how far the institution whose 'performance' is being

Table 2.2. Comparison of rank order of twelve schools using total GCSE points per pupil and GCSE points per entry per pupil

School	Value Added GCSE Points Per Pupil Rank	Value Added GCSE Points Per Pupil Entry Rank	Average Number of GCSE Entries
1	1st	Joint 5th	10.8
2	2nd	2nd	9.6
3	3rd	4th	9.4
4	4th	1st	8.5
5	5th	10th	8.4
6	6th	11th	9.1
7	7th	2nd	7.9
8	8th	joint 5th	7.8
9	9th	joint 5th	7.9
10	10th	joint 5th	7.9
11	11th	12th	8.7
12	12th	9th	6.5

Source: adapted from Jesson (1996).

judged is responsible for its outputs/outcomes, how far they are 'owned'. Some of the issues encountered in the public sector have private sector parallels. Thus studies of variations in labour productivity between plants and companies make the point that realistic comparisons must adjust for levels of capacity utilisation (Nichols 1986; Williams *et al.* 1994). Thus, the closer a manufacturing plant is working to its capacity the higher labour productivity is likely to be, since labour requirements cannot simply be reduced *pro rata* with reductions in output, at least in the short run. Similar issues apply to public sector service providers like schools. Thus, a school with a rapidly falling roll will tend to have higher unit costs than one where the school population is more stable, because of the problems of adjusting to lower levels of utilisation (Flynn 1990: 106–7). Similarly, if the number of patients in a residential home is being reduced as a result of 'community care' policies, then this will have an effect on unit costs. Running the home will mean that certain fixed costs must be incurred; but they will be spread over fewer patients, thus pushing up cost per patient. Equally, costs may be further inflated because the case-mix has been changed, with the home retaining patients with the highest level of dependence, who find it more difficult or impossible to function in the community (Treasury 1992b: para. 5.8).

Performance will also be affected by the historical inheritance of the provider. Thus, for example, a local authority with a poor housing stock will find it more difficult to relet property, because additional repairs are needed or the property is less desirable anyway (**2.11**). Under the NHS 'capital charges' system, introduced with the 'reform' of the NHS (see Chapter 3), Trust prices were designed to include charges designed to reflect the costs of capital assets. However, such asset levels are not easily controllable by current management, since, *inter alia*, they reflect past asset acquisitions.

Public sector performance is also characterised by numerous instances of interdependence between agencies. Local authority rent arrears will be affected, for example, not just by the level of poverty in an area, but also by the take-up of social security benefits, which, in turn, will be related to the operations of the Benefits Agency. These examples illustrate some of the difficulties in attributing blame – or for that matter praise – to institutions in public services. It is also worth noting how government policy itself generates tensions. Thus public sector services have been encouraged to maximise throughput and to reduce unit costs. However, the vast majority of services are now cash-limited, so that increases in throughput run up against the ceiling imposed by cash limits, thus depressing certain measures of 'efficiency' (Flynn 1986: 401).

Manipulating Performance Measures

As was indicated above, (pp. 32–3) public sector performance measures have been characterised by the key role of top-down approaches. In addition such measures have the potential for a significantly negative effect on public sector providers. The combination of these two features means that measures may be regarded as inappropriate by those who are subject to them and that they may gain or lose by the measured performance of their organisations or, in some cases, themselves, and hence that there is a strong incentive to manipulate measured performance. In this respect Citizen's Charter indicators have included waiting times and numbers on waiting lists as targets against which service providers are judged. However, such measures depend on the ease or difficulty of application for the service (London Region Social Services Research Group 1989: 3). Thus, the service could reduce measured waiting time and numbers on waiting lists by creating obstacles to access to the service. Equally, the reverse can happen. Clapham reports a case of a local authority that increased repairs to its dwellings but thus engendered higher service expectations, leading to greater demand for repairs (Clapham 1992: 211).

Waiting times are also easy to manipulate, because they refer to the numbers waiting more than a given time-period. This makes no distinction between the needs of different individuals. Thus, in order to ensure that no individual is waiting more than a given period, a person with a less serious condition but who has waited for a longer period may be given preference over a person with, arguably, a greater need for treatment, but who has been waiting for a shorter time (Macfarlane 1994: 23).

Manipulation can also operate where published measures relate to a part of the score distribution. Secondary education examinations measures provide an instance. As data are published in 'raw' attainment form and one of the measures is the number of pupils attaining A–C grades at GCSE, there is naturally an inducement to concentrate resources on students currently likely to obtain a D, but whose performance might be boosted with additional teaching time (Fitz-Gibbon 1996a: 411). Other students could, arguably, be in greater need, but could be ignored on the grounds that they are unlikely to make sufficient improvement.

This example is one where scope for manipulation relates to unadjusted data. However, it is worth bearing in mind that manipulation can also operate where data are adjusted to allow for greater comparability. As was indicated above, performance measures, like those in the Citizen's Charter, often refer to means of access to the service (e.g. waiting or appointment times). This, in turn, means that such measures are, in addition to themselves being manipulable, vulnerable to the criticism that they are superficial and do not relate to the quality of service provision once access has been achieved. Such criticisms clearly cannot be levelled at proposed measures of hospital mortality.

However, as data of this kind raise major issues of comparability it follows that the publication of raw data is inappropriate, because it takes no account of the case-mix each hospital deals with. Proposals for the publication of such data in the UK have not involved disaggregation to the level of individual doctors, but there are such examples in the United States, and such practice is consistent with the idea that performance measures can operate as a 'discipline' on professionals, identifying 'good' and 'bad' practitioners. Thus, in New York State, a 'cardiac surgery reporting system' was developed which involved reporting in-hospital mortality rates for coronary artery bypass graft operations by individual surgeons. Such data were published and used by the *New York Times* to construct a hospital league table (Green and Wintfield 1995: 1230). The data were adjusted for five risk factors: renal failure, congestive heart disease, chronic obstructive pulmonary disease, unstable angina and low ejection fracture (ibid.).

Consequently, identification of a patient as falling into one of the risk categories would improve both the individual surgeon's and the hospital's risk-adjusted score. There was thus an incentive (given the publicity surrounding such measures) to manipulate the data by inflating the number of patients classified under the risk categories. In their critical study of this scheme Green and Wintfield (ibid.) found considerable evidence to support a claim that such manipulation was being practised. Thus, in addition to a sharp overall increase in the reporting of risk factors following the introduction of the scheme and its surrounding publicity (ibid.), there were huge increases in patients in risk categories in individual hospitals. They cite a case of an increase in reported prevalence of chronic obstructive disease from 1.8 per cent to 52.9 per cent at one hospital, and in unstable angina from 1.9 per cent to 20.8 per cent in another (ibid.). Given only a marginal increase in the average age of patients (ibid.: 1230), it seems highly likely that such increases are an attempt to make use of the pliability of diagnostic categories to produce an artificially good outcome result.

The Extension of Accountability?

Earlier in this chapter we cited an Audit Commission publication, which argued that performance measurement could function to complement accountability through the electoral process. In this final section we shall consider such arguments by examining the relationship of performance measurement to accountability.

Any discussion of this issue must start by defining the form of account-ability: what is accounted for and to whom. As has been demonstrated earlier in this chapter, the dominant form of accountability during the 1980s and 1990s in the United Kingdom has been a managerialist one.

Studies of indicator sets have regularly pointed to the limited repre-sentation of 'effectiveness' measures. For example, a classification of types of indicators in three sets of PIs, one used by a local authority, one designed to measure educational performance, and the then DHSS set for the NHS, was undertaken by Pollitt (1986: 162). In all three, efficiency concerns were dominant, accounting for 61 per cent, 54 per cent and 43 per cent of indicators respectively, while effectiveness measures were peripheral, accounting for 1 per cent, 12 per cent, and 5 per cent of indicators res-pectively.

If this pattern is representative, then the idea that performance measure-ment could *extend* the scope of accountability appears rather lame. Indeed, the reverse has been argued. The marginalisation of concerns with effectiveness can be seen as a consequence of the framework within which PIs operate. For example, a discussion of the role of the Audit Commission has argued that, while measures of effectiveness *do* involve difficult technical issues, there is also a powerful political dimension: 'a greater focus on effectiveness could weaken the Commission's attempts to change local authorities. Influencing acceptance of reduced funding and a red-uction in the scale of organisations also means cutting back on purpose. Identifying unfilled needs and demands would have the opposite effect' (McSweeney 1988: 42). On this reading, since PIs are developed within a framework where constraints over public spending are an *a priori* assumption, this fact imposes a consequential bias on which aspects of 'performance' are evaluated.

It could be argued that such positions do not come to terms with the fact that monitoring bodies such as the Audit Commission are not agencies of government pure and simple, since they have an independent status. This, for example, gives the Commission discretion to select the topics that it wishes to study; and it remains free to criticise government policy. Furthermore, both the Commission and the National Audit Office have exercised this power, either by criticising government policy or by advocat-ing policies that are at variance with the prevailing biases in government. For example, the Audit Commission was critical of the central government policy that restricted the limits on the discretion of local authorities to use revenues from council house sales to finance new capital housing projects (**2.12**).

However, what is striking is how far such monitoring bodies reflect the general assumptions of central government policy. The argument above has already shown how the Audit Commission supported the view that the local electoral process is of questionable legitimacy. Central government policy in the 1980s and 1990s has introduced a series of centralising powers that have been justified in similar terms. Equally, a context of constraints on public spending is implicitly regarded as legitimate by the Commission. In this respect, it has been argued that it 'seeks to encourage and facilitate recognition and acceptance of restraint and shrinkage; to focus attention on managing within that context; and to reduce attempts to ignore or resist central government funding reductions and their consequences' (McSweeney 1988: 39). The kinds of assumption to which Mcsweeney refers are a common feature of Audit Commission publications. Thus, in *The Competitive Council* (1988), it is argued that local authorities must accept constraints on public spending as a given, and that expansion in service provision must stem from 'value for money' savings in other areas (**2.13**).

Such positions also illustrate important tensions in the work of evaluative bodies like the Audit Commission. On the one hand their work is investigative, which should presuppose, for example, that whether there is scope for savings without reductions in service quality is an open question. On the other hand, as McSweeney (1988) points out, such bodies are agents of organisational change. In this latter role the object is to convince groups like local councillors or public sector professionals that there is substantial scope for VFM gains. However, this stance presupposes what is to be investigated, and means that evaluative bodies operate with tensions between their investigatory and organisational change roles (Cutler 1993).

This tension also manifests itself in one feature in particular of Audit Commission work. Thus many Commission reports, particularly in the early years of that body, portrayed the status quo as in a situation of crisis. An instance is provided by an Audit Commission study of 1987 *The Management of London's Authorities: Preventing the Breakdown of Services*. The title itself is redolent of crisis, and the publication points to what it sees as management problems in Inner London local authorities, which threaten to lead to 'the urban dereliction that now affects some large North American cities' (**2.14**). However, as is invariably the case with performance measures, those used were susceptible of various 'readings'. Thus, the Association of London Authorities (ALA) produced a response to this report that argued that the Commission's comparisons of three groups of local authorities in a *de facto* league table failed to make sufficient allowance for structural differences between such authorities; that what were seen as unique problems of local authority mismanagement leading to higher costs could also be seen in bodies like the Metropolitan Police, under Home Office control; and that the necessary interaction between services meant that problems like rent (and what was then) rate arrears were not 'owned' by local authorities (**2.15**).

There is thus an important contradiction in the accountability argument in its managerialist form. The multi-divisional form of management illustrated in the Griffiths, the Efficiency Unit and the Audit Commission reports presupposes the transparency of information on 'performance' in public sector organisations. This goes hand in hand with the imperative to introduce a performance-orientated 'culture' where managers (and professionals) respond to goal setting and performance review.

However, a reference back to the conceptual and methodological difficulties (discussed above, pp. 36–8) makes it clear that such transparency is simply not present. Genuine measures of performance might thus be said to involve certain conditions: that measures be sufficiently inclusive to show cases in which improvements in one aspect are being achieved at the expense of decline in other aspects; that it is possible clearly to designate responsibility for or 'ownership' of performance; and that rigorous conditions of comparability apply.

The discussion has shown the difficulties all these aspects present. The difficulty with outcome measures means that the trade-off of throughput for effectiveness is hard to determine. This is particularly pointed where direct contradictions between elements of performance can operate: for instance, closing down branch libraries (**2.16**) or advice centres might encourage throughput and cut unit costs at the remaining centres; but such policies compromise access, and thus, arguably, effectiveness.

Similarly issues around causality create difficulties in attributing praise or blame for 'performance'. Such problems are exacerbated where there is scope for transferring costs either on to other budgets or outside the scope of public spending altogether by loading care burdens on friends or relatives.

In other words, there is a marked disjuncture between the conditions a 'culture' of performance requires and what performance measurement can deliver. This raises the difficulty that performance measurement can become a form of theatre, where the 'measures' demonstrate adherence to 'managerialist' ideology – a feature which, as we shall see in Chapter 5, is also, arguably, a characteristic of performance-related pay.

Accountability to the Consumer?

The argument so far has looked at the scope for increasing accountability from performance measurement in its overtly managerialist form. A key element in the criticism of this form was that behind the claim of wider accountability was a narrow top-down agenda reflecting the concerns of central government and of the managers of government agencies.

Implicit in at least some of this criticism is the view that the narrow scope of indicator sets and in particular the absence of 'effectiveness' measures reflects patterns of use. Managers are concerned with staying within budget and with cutting unit costs. They are less concerned, in a context of limited resources, with whether service objectives are being met. Most sets are seen to fail as mechanisms of accountability not only because of the limit on the dimensions of performance considered, but also because of the *de facto* exclusion of a key participant: the consumer of the service. It is this group that is seen to be concerned with effectiveness, because they use the services.

Indeed, so salient is this argument that it can certainly be classed as one of the major criticisms of the practice of performance measurement in the United Kingdom. Consider, for example, the following extracts from some academic discussions of PI sets: a study of indicators in housing pointed out that, of seventy performance indicators in a set designed by the Audit Commission to assess the performance of local authority housing services, only half a dozen related to 'customer evaluation of service providers or activities undertaken' (Conway and Knox 1990: 257–8); an analysis of indicators in higher education argued 'the group whose interests are most strikingly ignored by current PI systems is the consumers. If they had a say one would expect indicators of access, or teaching quality and of "employability" to be prominent' (Pollitt 1990b: 79).

Such arguments are also reflected in politics. Thus, in its manifesto for the 1992 election, Labour sought to outflank the Conservatives by adopting a consumerist approach to public services. This included proposals for a Health Service Quality Commissioner, an Education Standards Commission and a proposal to make it obligatory for local authorities to carry out annual surveys of consumer satisfaction (Labour Party 1992: 16, 18, 20).

This raises the final question to be considered in this section. If managerialist accountability appears to offer a limited and biased agenda, can such defects be rectified by bringing in the consumer? There are reasons for arguing that this is another false road. The first problem refers back to the transparency issue. If performance indicators raise problems of opaqueness and ambiguity, then this will compromise accountability in whatever form, to management, government or 'consumers'.

In overtly managerialist forms of accountability this problem tends to be assumed away, as with the dogmatism implicit in the 'culture of performance'. Similar ploys are present in the work of commentators who seek to give a consumerist bent to performance measurement. For example, Pollitt argues, with respect to outcome measures, that 'it is increasingly possible to measure some outcomes or good proxies' (Pollitt 1990c: 172). In another publication he cites an example of such a proxy, the use of 'value added' measures, and criticises a higher education PI set for not citing such this measure on the grounds that, 'the absence of value-added measures seriously undercuts the validity of any attempt to use PIs as an aid to judging universities' contributions to the economy or society' (Pollitt 1990b: 72).

However, as has already been argued, value added measures are not a panacea. The problem of variations in rank orders with different outcome criteria has already been pointed to. Equally, summary value-added data are actually of little or no use from a 'consumerist' stance, since it cannot be assumed that schools improve the performance of pupils of different initial attainment levels at the same rate. Some schools may give a particular boost to students with high initial attainment levels, others to those with lower starting levels (McPherson 1992). Thus a comparable overall value added performance may have radically different implications for different children.

There is, finally, a political issue here. As McPherson points out, value added is not necessarily an effect of teacher performance, but can also capture various other aspects of the school (ibid.). These could include peer learning effects, so that a concentration of above-average attainment pupils might have the effect of improving final attainment levels independently of teaching skills in the school. This might make the school particularly attractive to a parent interested in their child's achieving academic success, but has potentially negative implications for the school as a social institution. Thus, bringing in the consumer has often been seen as a reform project in which concerns of effectiveness act as a counterweight to an efficiency-dominated agenda; but on the other hand, such consumerism could also be argued to be in line with a Conservative project of reducing citizenship to consumerism, where the wider implications of individual decisions are de-emphasised.

There is a symmetry between managerialism and consumerism. In both cases there is an *a priori* commitment to performance measurement that glosses over the real difficulties involved. Thus, while it is valid to argue that existing indicator sets lack effectiveness measures that would, in principle, be of value to consumers, the argument loses much of its force if such measures are in fact questionable and ambiguous.

Finally, 'bringing consumers in' raises another rather different problem. Advocates of this position see it operating in a context in which PIs address a multiplicity of 'stakeholders', including politicians, managers, professionals and 'customers' (Pollitt 1990c: 174–5). Such extension of the range of indicators and the range of potential users is seen as redressing the biases in existing sets.

According to the agenda that combines consumerism with a correlative extension of the range of indicators, it will now be possible, in indicator sets, to have information on all of the 'Es' and to encompass the interests of the various 'stakeholders'. Yet even if one believes that it is possible to crack the problem of measuring effectiveness, there is a fundamental sense in which extending the scope of performance measurement makes the problem *more* difficult. Central to this is the issue of incommensurability. Thus, crucial to performance measurement is the idea that it provides a basis for assessing institutional performance; schools, local authorities, etc. can be compared against each other. Yet the 'Es' represent distinct and incommensurable measures of 'performance': for instance, how does one compare an institution where throughput is high but goal attainment is questionable with another institution where the reverse is the case? This problem is rendered yet more intractable if the category of 'consumer' is considered. In fact, in many areas of the social services it is unclear who the 'consumer' actually is. Thus, in the case of health care, is the consumer the patient, the potential patient, or, in the case of preventive health, the community as a whole? In the case of personal social services, is the consumer the 'client' or the provider of informal care? Given such indeterminacy there is a case for a plurality of 'effectiveness' measures addressed to a plurality of 'consumers'.

The promise of performance measurement was that it could establish normative standards. PIs were thus not just there to give information, but to indicate how well public sector organisations were run and to show who was running them better and who worse. Yet perhaps the ultimate paradox of this project is that indicator sets can be judged inadequate because they are insufficiently inclusive, because dimensions of performance escape them. On the other hand, the project of encompassing all dimensions and all interests threatens to degenerate into an indeterminate series of measures that literally don't add up. Either way the message seems blurred.

–3–

Welfare Markets

Introduction

Quasi-markets have played a key role in the reform of the British Welfare State since the late 1980s (Le Grand 1990). While the political background to their introduction was different for each of the welfare services (Cutler and Waine 1994: 51–4) and there are differences in their mode of operation, all quasi-markets share common features. There is a distinction between the role of purchaser and provider. The former is, in effect, an agent of central or local government, and is publicly funded: provider units are drawn from statutory, private or voluntary sectors, and compete for contracts from purchasers. Various forms of the purchaser–provider split now operate in health and community care (National Health Service and Community Care Act 1990), further and higher education (Further and Higher Education Act 1992), primary and secondary education (Education Reform Act 1988) and a number of services provided by local government (Local Government Act 1988). The programme of change was justified on the grounds that the quasi-market would replicate all the supposed virtues of the market in general – competition would lead to greater efficiency, decentralisation, enhanced consumer choice, diversity of providers and high-quality services. However, quasi-markets continue to be publicly financed, and thus subjected to government intervention and regulatory frameworks. Inevitably, this leads to tensions and contradictions in their operation. The objective of this chapter is, via a discussion of health, community care, and secondary and higher education, to examine some of the contradictions of this hybrid mechanism of the quasi-market.

The Quasi-Market in the National Health Service

The origins of the 1990 NHS reforms have been extensively discussed in many publications (e.g. Waine 1991; J. Butler 1992; Paton 1992; Timmins 1995). The Working Party established by the then Prime Minister, Margaret Thatcher, reviewed alternative forms of funding the service (Paton 1992: Ch. 3), but quickly became convinced as to the merits – simplicity and cheapness – of retaining a predominantly tax-financed service (Timmins 1995: 461). The challenge for the Working Party was how to change the service in ways that would allay public and professional concern about its funding, while at the same time allowing the Prime Minister to claim that the service was being modernised (J. Butler 1992: 9). This was to be achieved by shifting the focus of the service from the input of resources to the output of services, that is, through a concern with the efficient use of resources. The Working Party believed that such efficiency would follow from competition, and there were a number of proposals for the introduction of an internal market (Waine 1991: 71–2; Paton 1992: Ch. 3). The version eventually adopted was that of the American health economist, Alain Enthoven (Enthoven 1985). For Enthoven the main problem of the NHS was the lack of real incentives for good performance (ibid.: 15). This required the creation of an internal market, with District Health Authorities (DHAs) being responsible for purchasing services, but consultants and GPs providing the services. Enthoven's arguments were clearly taken up in the 1989 White Paper, *Working for Patients* (Department of Health 1989a) where the central concept is the division between the purchasing and the providing of services, which was also to be extended to GPs, who could opt to have their own practice budgets (**3.1**).

The internal market in health was introduced by the NHS and Community Care Act 1990, and began operating in April 1991. DHAs were to be allocated funds on the basis of a weighted capitation formula: they would not have to compete for funds. They would become the major purchasers of health services for their resident population, offering contracts and buying services from competing providers – their own District Managed Units, self-governing trusts or the private sector. In addition, DHAs would identify and plan for the service needs of their resident populations. Initially *Working for Patients* envisaged that only acute hospitals would become Trusts; but following the legislation, the possibility of Trust status was extended to all hospitals and community health service units, so that by April 1995, 98 per cent of all health care was delivered by Trusts (Review Body for Nursing Staff, Midwives and Health Visitors 1996: para. 7).

It is important to understand the financial framework within which Trusts operate. Before the creation of the quasi-market, NHS units were not charged in any way for funds provided to finance capital assets. However, with the introduction of the quasi-market Trusts are expected to set aside funds to cover depreciation of assets and to pay a capital charge for the use of such assets. With respect to the latter, assets are treated as financed in part by Interest-Bearing Capital, which is equivalent to a loan to the Trust, on which it is expected to pay interest, and in part by Public Dividend Capital, which is analogous to shareholder funds in a private company (Shaoul 1996: 5).

The purchaser–provider split was extended to general practice, with fundholding GPs becoming purchasers of outpatient services and a defined range of inpatient services. Non-fundholding GPs would refer their patients to hospitals with which Districts had negotiated contracts, and a contingency fund would also be available for them to refer patients to hospitals with which Districts did not have contracts. Fundholding has developed over the years, with the required minimum number of patients on GP lists having decreased, while the range of services that can be purchased has increased. From April 1996, fundholding practices will be differentiated into three categories: community fundholders will have minimum list sizes of 3,000 and above and budgets to cover staff, drugs, diagnostic testing and most community services; standard fundholders will have a minimum list size of 5,000 and budgets to purchase staff, drugs, all elective surgery (except vary rare or expensive procedures), all outpatient attendances and a wide range of community services; and twenty to thirty pilot practices will undertake total purchasing, including Accident and Emergency Services, on behalf of their patients (NHS Executive 1995a: 4).

The reforms seemed to promise not merely choice for consumers, but autonomy for purchasers and providers. Thus many health authorities were somewhat disconcerted when in the first year of the reforms they were actively discouraged by the Department of Health (DoH) from using their budgets 'entrepreneurially' and were exhorted to maintain a steady state in placing their contracts. It quickly became apparent, though, that government intervention in the market was to extend beyond the first year. One key example of this, was in respect of 'the London Problem'.

'The London Problem'

The introduction of the purchaser–provider split meant that whether London hospitals obtained contracts would depend in considerable part on decisions made by purchasers outside London. Such hospitals were often highly dependent on treating patients from outside the capital, and, in part, this reflected their prestige as institutions with specialist skills. However, they were likely to be disadvantaged by the workings of capital charges. These charges were to be reflected in provider prices, and would be higher the greater the value of the capital assets. In the case of London hospitals such asset values would be inflated by land values, building costs and, in some cases, greater use of expensive high-tech equipment (Shaoul 1996: 12). This, at least if the system worked as it was designed to do, would mean that purchasers might avoid placing contracts with such high-cost providers. The market, then, which introduced competition between the more expensive London hospitals and lower-cost providers outside the capital, was set to introduce a period of instability. The government responded by establishing the Tomlinson Inquiry in 1991, to consider the balance of health needs and health provision in the capital. The Inquiry recommended a rationalisation of the acute sector, with a reduction of hospital beds, the closure of St Bartholomew's and Middlesex Hospitals, and the merger of Guy's and St Thomas's Hospitals and other specialist hospitals, together with a transfer of resources to primary care and community services (Department of Health 1992b).

Tomlinson, in proposing that changes in the NHS in London should be planned, was obviously antagonistic to the operation of the market. The Secretary of State for Health, Virginia Bottomley, responded to the Tomlinson Report in February 1993 with *Making London Better*. In this she accepted the broad outlines of Tomlinson, stating that 'the Government recognises the concern that hospital rationalisation will be forced by the decisions of purchasing authorities . . . We intend to guard against this . . . by setting up an implementation group to drive forward and monitor the changes' (Department of Health 1993a: para. 11). The terms of reference for this London Implementation Group, which would analyse policy options and follow through the Tomlinson recommendations, were 'to advise . . . on the implementation of decisions on the future development of London's health service . . . to secure agreement among interested parties on the detailed way forward; to oversee implementation of the changes' (ibid.: 21). In effect it would regulate the market. Its work in the first year was primarily concerned with improving primary health care in the capital; the realignment of acute hospital provision; and assessment of specialist services (Kings Fund 1994: 15). This last task was to be undertaken by the establishment of the London Speciality Reviews for the six specialist services (cardiac, cancer, neurosciences, renal, plastics and children's specialist services) with the aim of achieving 'a more rational disposition . . . and avoiding unwarranted duplication' (Department of Health 1993a: 25). Subsequent to these reports there have been some changes in hospital provision in London (James 1995: 202–3). These changes are less important, though, than the key point that the government was not prepared to allow the purchasing authorities to determine which hospitals would close. It chose to manage the London problem itself by traditional interventionist measures.

Of course, intervention to 'solve' the London problem should not have caused surprise. A careful consideration of the NHS reforms pointed to a framework of regulation and centralised control.

Centralisation versus Decentralisation

Two original features of the NHS reforms were the introduction of NHS Contracts and NHS Trusts, referred to by Hughes as, respectively, the key legal relationship and legal entity of the 1990 Act (Hughes 1991: 90).

Three forms of contractual relationship were distinguished in the reformed NHS: that between DHAs (known as Health Authorities from 1 April 1996) and private sector providers; that between DHAs and their Directly Managed Units (DMUs); and finally that between DHAs and NHSTs and GPFHs (ibid.). The first of these would take a conventional legal form and would be legally enforceable. The second would be enforced through management processes (given the effective demise of DMUs, this contractual form is virtually redundant). The third form of contractual relationship was/is the most complex.

The key issue is whether this NHS contract conforms to the concept of contract in English law, with its defining characteristics of being an agreement voluntarily entered into by both parties that is enforceable at law (Hughes 1991: 90; Allen 1995: 5). Clearly this is not the case with the NHS contracts, which have been imposed, by legislation, upon both purchasers and providers. Further, the Act refers to an 'NHS contract' as an *arrangement* between health service bodies (Section 4 (1)) (our italics). The Act specifically states that the contract shall not be regarded for any purpose as giving rise to contractual rights or liabilities (Section 4 (3)). Instead, any disputes that arise between the parties may be referred to the Secretary of State, or his appointee, for determination (Section 4 (4)) and the parties involved will be required to comply with any directions (Section 4(6)). In addition, the Secretary of State 'may by his determination in relation to an arrangement constituting an NHS contract vary the terms of the arrangement or bring it to an end' (Section 4(8)). NHS contracts bear little resemblance to contracts *per se*. The key point here is that the contracting parties have no autonomous rights. The Secretary of State has, ultimately, the power to vary the terms of any NHS contract or terminate it.

NHS Trusts were to be given 'a range of powers which are not, and will not be, available to health authorities generally' (Department of Health

1989a, para. 3.10). These powers were outlined in the 'Working Paper on Self Governing Hospitals' (**3.2**). At the same time these powers and autonomy were to be heavily circumscribed by the 1990 Act. While every Trust will have a Board of Directors, the chair is to be appointed by the Secretary of State, who, in addition, will determine the numbers of those on the Board, their qualifications and tenure, and the persons who will appoint the other directors (Section 5(7)). The Secretary of State will be able to confer on a Trust such functions as she/he 'considers appropriate' (Section 5 (5)(b)). The Secretary of State will decide the amount of the originating capital debt to be transferred to the Trust (Section 9(1)). Every NHS Trust will be obliged 'to achieve such financial objectives as may from time to time be set by the Secretary of State with the consent of the Treasury' (Section 10(1)). In addition, Trusts will 'prepare and send to the Secretary of State an annual report in such form as may be determined by the Secretary of State' (Schedule 2 7 (1)) and furnish 'such reports, returns and other information as to its forward planning, as, and in such form as, he may require' (Schedule 2, 8). The Treasury will determine the methods, principles and information to be included in the annual audited accounts (Schedule 2, 24 (2)). Limits on the borrowing of Trusts – sources and extent of borrowing – will be agreed by the Secretary of State and the Treasury (Schedule 3). Ultimately, the Secretary of State may order the dissolution of a Trust (Schedule 2, 29(1)).

Decentralisation and Control?

Equally, elsewhere in the NHS, the autonomy of the devolved units is to be exercised within a structure of accountability to the centre. Three documents will be used to illustrate this point: *Managing the New NHS* (Department of Health 1993b); *An Accountability Framework for GP Fundholding* (NHS Executive 1995b); and *Priorities and Planning Guidance for the NHS: 1997/98* (NHS Executive 1996a).

The focus of *Managing the New NHS* was the development of central management functions following the implementation of the reforms. Although these changes are justified in terms of supporting 'the continued drive towards decentralisation in the NHS, with responsibility and decision making devolved as far as possible to local level' (Department of Health 1993b: para. 8), there is a considerable emphasis on central government involvement. The paper recommended that the NHS Management Executive (now the NHS Executive) should develop 'a clear identity as the HQ of the NHS' with its role being 'strategic rather than operational' (ibid.: para. 17). With a shift of responsibility to local purchasers and providers, Regional Health Authorities were deemed redundant, to be replaced by Regional Offices 'responsible for developing the purchasing function within the health service and also . . . the task of monitoring NHS trusts' (ibid.: para. 20). These offices would also 'provide a link between strategic and local management – a link which ensures that agreed national policy is implemented and which provides the information necessary for the NHS Management Executive and Ministers to carry out their functions' (ibid.: para. 21). The general principle underlying the allocation of functions to different management levels was 'to minimise centralisation and maximise delegation of responsibility to local level while maintaining clear lines of accountability' (ibid.: para. 29). Among the functions to be performed by the NHS central management were performance management, development and regulation of the internal market and ensuring compliance with the regulatory framework for that market (**3.3**).

This paper also proposed the integration of the purchasers (DHAs and Family Health Services Authorities (FHSAs)), which came into effect on 1 April 1996. This, together with mergers of DHAs, creates fewer but larger purchasers, potentially reducing a competitive element of the reforms.

The rationale for the GP fundholding scheme was twofold: to encourage GPs to improve the quality of services on offer to their patients and to stimulate hospitals to be more responsive to their needs and those of their patients (Department of Health 1989a: para 6.1). At the same time it was recognised that, as alternative purchasers to DHAs within the newly reformed NHS, GPFH had the possibility of fragmenting strategic developments within the NHS (Paton 1992: 127).

A first acknowledgement that consideration should be given to aligning the purchasing intentions of GPFH with those of DHAs came in the Audit Commission report of 1993 (**3.4**).

Following the proposals to extend GPFH (see above), the NHSE issued guidance describing the requirements for GP fundholder accountability (NHS Executive 1995b). While GPFH 'are free to use NHS resources to achieve the most appropriate care for their patients', they need to recognise that they are working within a framework where 'Health authorities have statutory responsibility for leading the implementation of Government policy at local level . . . [this] includes advising and informing GP fundholders on the wider implications of their purchasing intentions' (ibid.: para. 2.4). Departure from the framework would be followed by closer monitoring by the health authorities and the regional offices. 'GP fundholders are accountable to the NHS for their use of public money' (ibid.: para. 4.1). The guidance groups their responsibilities into four areas: management accountability; accountability to patients and public; financial accountability; professional accountability. The first of these forms of accountability requires the production of an annual practice plan outlining how the practice intends to use the fund in the coming year and longer-term developments: the authority will ensure that these plans 'are consistent with national priorities and . . . meet national targets and objectives set out in the Annual Priorities and Planning Guidance' (ibid.: para. 5.1). GPFH must also announce major shifts in their purchasing intentions to prepare NHS Trusts for any changes. Finally, the performance of practices should be annually reviewed against the plan. Accountability to patients and the wider public requires GPFH to publish information on their plans and performance, involve patients in service planning and have appropriate arrangements in place for dealing with patient complaints (ibid.: para. 6.6). The key financial accountability requirements are the preparation of annual accounts to be audited by the Audit Commission, monthly monitoring of expenditure by the health authority, and agreement as to the use of savings, and as to how the practice plan will contribute to the local efficiency targets set by the NHS (ibid.: para. 7.1). Key to pro-fessional accountability is to be clinical audit (ibid.: para. 8) (**3.5**).

The introduction to the *Priorities and Planning Guidance* (an annual report) states that its purpose is 'to focus the NHS on the most important national priorities . . . to give broad direction' (NHS Executive 1996a: 4). While account must be taken of local needs and priorities, this must 'be within the framework of national policies and priorities', while 'spec-ific quantified objectives and targets will be agreed between each Health Authority and the appropriate Regional Office of the NHS Executive' (ibid.).

The guidance distinguishes baseline requirements and objectives from medium-term priorities. The former, which tend to carry on from year to year, are those 'which every NHS organisation knows that they are expected to meet by virtue of being part of the NHS' (ibid.: 8). Progressing towards the targets outlined in *The Health of the Nation* (e.g. reducing the death rates from Coronary Heart Disease and various forms of cancer) 'remains the central plank of government policy for the NHS and forms the main context for NHS planning' (ibid.: 7). The other key policies are Community Care, a primary-care-led NHS and the Patient's Charter 'providing services which meet clearly defined national and local standards' (ibid.: 8). Among the medium-term priorities are decision-making based upon clinical effectiveness and collaborative working to ensure the development of continuing care (ibid.: 5–6). 'Clear measures for evaluating progress . . . should be agreed between regional offices and the health authorities . . . the delivery towards these objectives will be monitored and reviewed through the performance management process' (ibid.:12).

The commitment to autonomy and decentralisation in the reformed NHS remained at the level of rhetoric: the reality, as anticipated, is government intervention (Waine 1991: Ch. 3; Cutler and Waine 1994: Ch. 3).

The Quasi-Market in Community Care

Community care for 'vulnerable groups' such as elderly people and people with a mental illness or handicap had been pursued by governments of different political persuasions since the 1950s (Audit Commission 1986: Appendix A). Policies were characterised by issuing guidance to the providers of community care services, in particular local authorities, and encouraging them to develop relevant services and setting targets for service provision. However, failure to achieve such targets did not call forth penalties.

Such a *laissez-faire* approach was to end in the 1980s. Although the key document on community care, the White Paper *Caring for People*, was not published until 1989, it was the culmination of a number of ideas and policy options discussed throughout the decade. Speeches to represent-atives of Social Services Departments by two successive Secretaries of State for Health and Social Security, Patrick Jenkin in 1980 and Norman Fowler in 1984, had advocated an enabling role for local authorities. Of course, local authorities had always bought in goods and services from the private sector, and pressures to contract out services increased with developments in competitive tendering in the early 1980s (see Chapter 4).

However, it was the 1986 Audit Commission report, *Making a Reality of Community Care*, that was crucial in crystallising the new thinking in this area. The report discussed the shortcomings in the then current provision (**3.6**) and inappropriate placements in residential care, which undermined the independence of clients and increased costs (Audit Com-mission 1986: para. 13). Comparing the costs of care in different settings, there was a clear assumption that care in the community was a cheaper option (**3.7**). The report was also critical of the funding arrangements for community care, whereby those in residential or nursing care who qualified for Supplementary Benefit could claim a weekly allowance for board and lodging and personal expenses. In effect, this was a voucher system, whereby private choice was financed from public funds (see Lewis and Glennerster 1996: 2–4 for a full discussion of this). This whole process was referred to by the Audit Commission as creating a perverse effect by encouraging residential rather than community provision. The solution advocated by the Audit Commission was the use of a care manager with the responsibility for coordinating services to clients (**3.8**).

The main outlines of the Griffiths Report (1989) echoed those of the Audit Commission – an enabling role for local authorities, provision by the independent sector, access to publicly funded services only after a full assessment of the need for care, plus the transfer of social security money to local authorities (**3.9**).

Nearly all of Griffiths' proposals were accepted, the major exception being the ringfencing of central government funds for community care (but see below p. 65), and embodied in the White Paper, *Caring for People* (Department of Health 1989c) (**3.10**). The White Paper had several key objectives, which were to be achieved by the separation of the purchaser and provider roles and the introduction of assessment (**3.11**).

The reforms in community care were phased in: inspection units and complaints procedures were established in 1991; Community Care Plans were produced in 1992 (**3.12**); and the transfer of social security funding to Social Services Departments and the new assessment arrangements were introduced in 1993. Between 1990 and 1993 the local authorities were deluged with guidance from the Department of Health, management consultants and the Social Services Inspectorate (Lewis and Glennerster 1996: 10–11). The Social Services Inspectorate, together with the Audit Commission, also monitored the progress of local authorities in implementing the reforms. Again, such monitoring and guidance is not entirely unexpected if the 1989 White Paper is considered (**3.13**).

The support for the reforms was widespread: they were portrayed as creating needs-based services, with clients having the right to assessment and an enhancement of individual choice. However, Lewis and Glennerster, among others, make clear the reforms 'were driven by the need to stop the haemorrhage in the social security budget and to do so in such a way that would minimise political outcry and not give additional resources to the local authorities themselves' (Lewis and Glennerster 1996: 8). If the backdrop for the reforms was the capping of social security expenditure, then obviously constraints on budgets would remain a key feature in their implementation. How was this to be reconciled with a needs-led service that gave a right to assessment and promoted individual choice?

Choice versus Budgets equals Rationing

This was a particularly relevant question, as Mrs Bottomley's October 1992 speech to the Directors of Social Services reiterated the government's commitment to maintain client choice in respect of residential care (see **3.14** for the Department of Health Memorandum that accompanied Mrs Bottomley's speech).

A first formal attempt to tackle the issue of right to assessment and local authorities resources is to be found in a letter from Herbert Laming, Chief Inspector, Social Services Inspectorate, issued in December 1992. Referring to Section 47(i) of the NHS and Community Care Act, which imposed a duty on local authorities to carry out an assessment of a client who might be in need of services and to decide what services to provide (this could be taken as an open-ended financial commitment), the Chief Inspector noted two points:

- first, authorities do not have a duty to assess on request, but only where they think that the person may be in need of services they provide;
- second, the assessment of need and decisions about the services to be provided are separate stages in the process (Laming 1992: para. 5).

Local authorities must bear in mind that, once they have indicated that a service should be provided to meet an individual's need, the authority is under a legal obligation to provide it (ibid.: 13). If individual feedback is recorded, although it might not form part of the user's assessment, it may still be accessed by users. 'Practitioners will, therefore, have to be sensitive to the need not to raise unrealistic expectations on the part of users and carers' (ibid.: para. 25).

The advice of the Chief Inspector then, is to ration services. The need to ration, and the extent of that rationing, is inevitably linked to the adequacy of resources for community care; and it is to that issue that we now turn.

Before 1993, there were three major sources of public funding for community care: the revenue grant from central government to local authorities (included in money allocated for the Personal Social Services Standard Assessment), together with revenue raised by local taxes (rates/ poll tax/community charge); funds allocated by the DoH to Regional Health Authorities and DHAs for health-based community care services; and social security payments for individuals who qualified for supplementary benefit/income support and who went into residential or nursing homes. This last element grew from £10m in 1979 to £2.3bn by 1993 (Department of Social Security 1993: para. 135). Under the NHS and Community Care Act, 1990, local authorities would receive money transferred from the social security budget that would have been spent on new residents of residential and nursing homes if the system had remained unreformed. Initially, the government refused to ringfence that money for spending solely on community care (**3.15** and **3.16**), but then partially retreated, agreeing that the transferred money, together with a replacement for the Independent Living Fund and a grant for administrative costs, should be spent solely on community care. Two points about the ring-fencing should be noted: firstly, the social security transfer element would only be ringfenced in the year that it was paid, but in the subsequent year would be absorbed into the Standard Spending Assessment (SSA) for Personal Social Services, and thus was potentially available to be used to finance any service provided by the local authority. Secondly, the ring-fencing would end in 1995/6. Initially the transfer element was allocated by a formula whereby 50 per cent was based on the pattern of DSS spending (the amount of income support paid for independent residential and nursing home care in each local authority) and 50 per cent on the SSA formula for the local authority. This severely disadvantaged those authorities with little independent residential and nursing home care. In 1994/5 the government responded to their complaints and distributed all the transfer element according to the SSA formula. Finally, it should be noted that social security transfer is not new money, but merely reallocated from one budget to another and subsequently cash-limited. The social security transfer was conditional on local authorities' and health authorities' fulfilling certain conditions (**3.17**).

Once the government announced the financial settlement, the Local Authority Associations and Directors of Social Services expressed their concerns that the policy of community care, which they welcomed, was under-resourced, and underestimated future demands. In particular they argued that the publicity that had attended the changes would encourage more people to apply for services (e.g. Marchant 1992: 5; *Community Care* 1992: 14–15).

If resources for community care are underestimated in relation to demands, the obvious result is that some form of rationing will be introduced. Of course, local authorities (and indeed other public sector providers) have always been required to reconcile demand and supply; but the new dimension in the rationing debate is that it is now running parallel with the government aim to provide choice for the user. The likely restraint on consumer choice in the context of cash-limited services was noted in several government documents that accompanied *Caring for People* (Cutler and Waine 1994: 58). What was unclear was precisely how the inevitable process of rationing was to operate. Key to this process were to be the eligibility criteria. Social Services Departments were encouraged to develop criteria indicating who would be assessed as having a high, medium or low need, how these needs would be met and what resources would be allocated (Laming 1992: para. 14).

A number of surveys have examined the implementation of community care. While having somewhat different remits, all have discussed the operation of the eligibility criteria. Three surveys will be drawn upon to provide examples of findings in this area.

The Association of County Councils (ACC) and Association of Metropolitan Authorities (AMA) survey was undertaken 'in order to get a clear picture of who was, or was not, qualifying for services, given the financial pressures being experienced by local authorities' (ACC/AMA 1995: 15): 108 local authorities were surveyed, with a response rate of 68 per cent. Even in the initial year of implementation, which was the focus of the study, eligibility criteria were emerging as a key area: they were 'the passport to service provision' (ibid.:31) and were being used as a threshold for the receipt of service and for the allocation of differential levels of resources (ibid.: 5).

In March 1996, the Audit Commission published the third of its series of bulletins monitoring the implementation of community care, *Balancing the Care Equation: Progress with Community Care* (Audit Commission 1996). Unlike the ACC/AMA survey, that of the Audit Commission combines description of what is happening in the 17 local authorities surveyed with prescription of what should happen. Noting that most local authorities 'are under considerable financial pressure' (ibid.: para. 2), the Audit Commission discusses how needs can be met within the funds available. Obviously eligibility criteria are crucial, and the different approaches to establishing the criteria are outlined: for example, setting of priority levels, meeting all the needs of people in the top priority group and then meeting the needs of others within low-priority groups until all the resources run out. Such an approach obviously limits the flexibility to respond to risk in lower-priority groups. Some local authorities have dealt with this by allowing care managers to exercise discretion in the allocation of resources between priority groups. Still others specify a maximum amount that can be spent on each person in a particular category, and usually this is expressed as a percentage of residential care (ibid.: paras. 25–9). If that ceiling is exceeded because an expensive package of community care is required, then there may be no alternative to residential care. In addition, many local authorities are taking additional steps to keep within their budgets – waiting lists, resources panels to limit access to nursing home and residential care, and revising eligibility criteria in the course of the year (ibid.: paras. 30–1). To assist local authorities in this complex process of devising criteria, the Audit Commission outlines what should be their essential qualities – simplicity and ease of application, widely publicised, and both flexibility and precision (ibid.: para. 19). There is a recognition that these qualities may conflict or even be mutually exclusive. Whatever the criteria used, 'they should be set a level such that authorities can meet the needs of those who qualify and still keep within the budget' (ibid.).

In April 1993, the Local Government Management Board, the Associations of County Councils and Metropolitan Authorities commissioned the London Research Centre to undertake a project on the impact of changes in funding arrangements on local authorities. Two reports were published in 1994, and a third, undertaken with the cooperation of the Association of Directors of Social Services, in April 1996. This covered the period January to September 1995. A postal questionnaire was sent to 61 local authorities in England and Wales; 31 completed the questionnaire, representing one in four of all social services departments in England and Wales. There was also an interview sample drawn from the authorities used in the previous survey.

Nearly all the local authorities in the interview sample reported a reduced social services budget due to capping, adjustments to the SSA, and tighter local authority budgets generally. Although money for community care services continued to be notionally ringfenced, some authorities reported transfer to the general social services budget (Kenny and Edwards 1996: 6). Most local authorities surveyed had spent approximately 46 per cent of their annual budget in the first six months of 1995, with 7 out of 21 having spent over 50 per cent. As demand for services is usually higher in the last six months of the year, as this includes the winter period, the report notes that 'It seems therefore, that the majority of authorities will have had to rein in spending in the second half of the year, in order not to go over budget, leading to increased targeting of services' (ibid.: 8). Such targeting was already taking place in respect of domiciliary services, which were increasingly being concentrated on those requiring more complex packages of care (ibid.: 13), a development substantiated by the Department of Health's own statistics (ibid.: 16).

Local authorities had developed a number of strategies to prevent overspend. Among these were a general tightening up of eligibility criteria; a quota system for the number of placements to be made within a month; and panels to confirm care manager decisions (ibid.: 17). Of course, another strategy is that of charging for services. Clients have always had to pay for residential care; but this was not necessarily the case for domiciliary care. Although local authorities are now required to charge for the latter, the scale of charges is still at their discretion; but there are several indications that charging is becoming a more central issue for them (Audit Commission 1996: para. 55). Of course, charging can generate income; but it also reduces take-up for services, thereby assisting in the process of reconciling demand and resources.

Paradoxically, charging policies have raised questions about whether community care is a cheap option. Using powers under the 1948 National Assistance Act, local authorities have always charged for residential care, taking both capital and income into account. Thus it is conceivable, depending upon an individual's circumstances, that a high proportion of the cost of residential care could be recovered by the local authority. However, the powers to charge for domiciliary and day care services that derive from the Health and Social Services and Social Security Adjudications Act 1983 allow the local authorities considerable discretion both on charging and on the income and property to be taken into account when setting these charges. Section 17 of the Act states that 'the charge levied has to be no more than it appears to them that it is reasonably practicable . . . to pay'. But what is reasonable? As the Audit Commission states 'The financial incentive for authorities to use residential care remains strong. In nearly all situations it is substantially cheaper for local authorities to place people in residential care, even where there is no difference between the gross cost of residential care and care at home' (Audit Commission 1996: para. 70 and Appendix). The perverse incentive identified in its report a decade earlier thus persists.

Social services departments have always had limited resources and had to determine priorities. However, what has particularly exacerbated the situation post-1993 are increased expectations of service users, uncertainty as to funding (e.g. changes in the formula for distributing the transfer element, noted above), the reinvention of the role of the acute hospital, concerned only with short-term episodes of care (Wistow 1995: 1), and the implications of the moves towards a primary-care-led NHS. In addition, as community care is now covered more explicitly by legislation, this in turn has led to legal challenges. Thus, a judicial review in 1995 forced Gloucestershire social services to reassess 1,000 clients whose services had been withheld because of budgetary problems (*Community Care* 1996: 1). An Appeal Court decision in June 1996, also against Gloucestershire, means that local authorities cannot use lack of their resources as a reason for not providing services under the Chronically Sick and Disabled Persons Act 1970. The ruling, which as it stands can be applied to all community care clients, not merely the disabled, implies that eligibility criteria for determining need that have been drawn up after taking resources into account are unlawful, although it will still be lawful for such criteria to take account of resources when giving guidance about whether particular needs will be met (Cragg 1996: 19). The case has gone to the House of Lords.

Clearly, then, community care has moved rapidly from being the needs-led service that was a key feature of *Caring for People* to one where financial considerations have forced the implementation of rigorous rationing. Such a development has led the Audit Commission to ask in respect of rationing 'what are the limits? In a rationing environment how are the relatively low level needs of some carers to be balanced against the high costs of some users . . . Critically, how are future and growing expectations and needs, in the context of demographic change, to be met from limited resources?' (Audit Commission 1996: 34).

The Quasi-Market in Secondary Education

In effect, the creation of the quasi-market in secondary education dates from the 1988 Education Reform Act (ERA). Broadly, the Act had two sorts of effects: it transformed the relationship between Local Education Authorities (LEAs) and individual schools; and, via the imposition of a national curriculum, it allowed for a substantially increased influence of central government over the content of education.

The Local Education Authority and the Individual School

The change in the relationship between the LEA and the individual school came as a result of a series of linked measures in the ERA. It introduced 'open enrolment', which allowed parents to seek to place their children in state schools outside the boundary of their LEA. The idea of the education system's responding to the wishes of parents was not new. Section 76 of the 1944 Education Act (**3.18**) required that LEAs should 'have regard to the . . . principle' that pupils should be educated in the ways their parents wished, and this was reiterated in the 1980 Education Act (**3.19**). However, in both cases this injunction was qualified by the condition that the authorities had to ensure 'efficient' educational provision (**3.18** and **3.19**). The ERA removed this qualification (**3.20**), so that LEAs could not deny a child entry to a school on the grounds, for example, that the school was oversubscribed and the LEA needed to balance intakes between schools.

Of course, the ERA did not stipulate that no physical limits applied to school recruitment. However, the powers of the LEA were severely circumscribed. Section 26 (1) of the Act (**3.21**) stated that an education authority could not set an admission level to a school below the 'standard number' for that school. The significance of this requirement was that the standard number was defined as that applying at September 1979 or September 1988, whichever was the highest. Of central significance here is the former date, since this was a peak year for the secondary school population. For example, in England there were 3,872,000 state secondary school pupils in 1979, as against 2,992,000 in 1995 (Department for Education and Employment 1996b). LEAs can apply to the Secretary of State to reduce standard numbers; but the conditions are limited to the grounds that the standard number is incompatible with the physical capacity of the school.

The logic of these changes was that LEA powers to plan the allocation of pupils between schools were virtually negated. This was accompanied by a corresponding shift in funding and budgetary control. The Act envisaged that school funding would predominantly operate (**3.22**) via age-weighted pupil numbers. Thus, effectively, money followed pupils, and, given age-weighting, pupils who stayed on into the sixth form generated more revenue. A corollary of this shift was the introduction of Local Management of Schools (LMS). Under this system LEAs set a total spending figure, the General Schools Budget (GSB). From this budget funding for building projects, home-to-school transport, premature retirement costs and the educational psychology service is deducted. Once this has been done, the remaining figure is referred to as the Potential Schools Budget (PSB), and the current requirement is that 85 per cent of the PSB is devolved to individual schools, thus severely limiting LEA control over the education budget (Department for Education and Employment 1996b).

Grant Maintained Schools

A further reduction in LEA powers in the ERA related to the creation of Grant Maintained (GM) schools. An application for GM status can arise in one of two ways: via a majority vote of school governors at two meetings; or if a written request is made to the governors endorsed by parents of 20 per cent of registered pupils at the school (**3.23**). If this condition is met then a ballot of parents is held and, subject to voter turnout conditions, if there is a simple majority vote in favour an application can be made to the Secretary of State. If the application is approved the GM school is directly funded by the Department, and has 'opted out' of LEA control.

While, as will be argued below, it is questionable how far these changes have resulted in the effects anticipated by government, there is no doubt that the ERA involved a conceptual shift. Before this legislation it was clearly possible to speak of an educational system, in that LEAs could plan the allocation of pupils, schools and funding for their local area. However, the post-ERA structure is effectively one of a 'diverse set of enterprises' (Bowe and Ball 1992: 66). Schools compete against each other for pupils, and school funding is largely determined by success or failure in such competition. With respect to funding the Chartered Institute of Public Finance and Accountancy (CIPFA) has estimated that, on average, 65 per cent of secondary school budgets in England (1995–6) are accounted for by age-weighted pupil numbers (CIPFA 1995).

The National Curriculum and Publication of Performance Measures

Section 2 of the ERA introduced the National Curriculum (NC), and section 3 detailed the range of 'foundation subjects' to be included in it (**3.24**). The NC was divided into key stages at ages 7, 11 and 14 (**3.25**). At each of these stages tests are administered, and the results are published. A blanket power to publish such results was conferred on the Secretary of State by section 8 (5) of the 1980 Education Act (**3.26**). This power has been used to require publication of NC test results, GCSE and 'A' level examination results, results in vocational qualifications and school truancy rates.

The changes were justified by central government on grounds *both* of extending parental choice *and* increasing the efficiency of schools. With respect to choice, in the 1992 publication *Choice and Diversity* the Department argued that schools should give the 'maximum parental choice possible' (Department for Education 1992: 15). Clearly this objective can be linked to the combination of open enrolment and the short-circuiting of LEA powers to operate school quotas. Open enrolment extends, in principle, the range of state schools from which the parent can choose, and the operation of a high 'standard number' ceiling means that restrictions on recruitment to 'popular' schools will be less significant.

However, in addition, it has been argued that the changes will 'increase the quality of education by making more effective use of resources' (Department of Education and Science 1988), and thus improve efficiency. In this respect two aspects of the changes reflect prevailing themes of Conservative policy. The first is that competition will make schools more responsive. In this instance the combination of open enrolment with age-weighted pupil numbers as the basis of funding can be seen as operating a market discipline that is seen to reward the efficient/effective and penalise poor practice (**3.27**).

The second theme is that of devolved management. Thus, substantial budget devolution to the school level and the creation of GM schools can be seen as a means of enabling 'educational enterprises' to respond speedily to market pressures. Thus Bowe and Ball (1992: 24) argue that the theory behind the ERA is that the introduction of market forces 'changes the basis of the consumers' relationship with the school', while 'reform of school management . . . changes the means and medium of the producer's response'.

It is also important to emphasise the postulated links between the choice and efficiency/effectiveness objectives. Of central importance here is the obligation to publish information on school performance. This effectively operates as a key 'market signal'. For example, the latest version of the Parent's Charter stresses that, in addition to the publication of performance tables at a national level, each school prospectus 'must include examination results and National Curriculum test results for the school and compare the local and national results' (Department for Education 1994:7). The implication is that such results are a key indicator of 'good' and 'bad' schools, and hence ought to guide parents in choosing schools. In turn, the market will result in undersubscribed schools' suffering a financial penalty, and hence give them an incentive to improve their resource use and effectiveness.

Thus, choice objectives on one hand and efficiency/effectiveness on the other are seen to mesh unproblematically. However, there are, in particular, two central tensions in these arguments: one relates to the extent to which efficiency objectives are undercut by the pursuit of 'parental choice'; the other, conversely, the way in which efficiency objectives involve an incoherently prescriptive approach to parental choice.

As has been indicated on a number of occasions in this book, the term 'efficiency' has been regularly used to refer to increasing throughput, and hence reductions in institutional unit costs. However, this objective sits uneasily with the way government has sought to pursue the extension of parental choice. As was indicated in Chapter 1, central government has not adopted a full-blooded New Right approach like that advocated by Chubb and Moe (1990), where schools are privatised and a minimalist regulatory structure is adopted. The expected effect of such a policy is that it would radically change the supply side and would imply that the advantages and penalties of competition were now the responsibility of private and voluntary sector providers.

In contrast, changes to the supply side have been marginal to government policy in secondary education. The one example of a supply-side shift is the creation of City Technology Colleges (CTCs). This policy involved government financial support for CTCs as independent schools, run by educational trusts. These schools are thus private, and were to operate with a curriculum biased to technical subjects. The schools are non-fee-paying, and government anticipated that they would receive substantial support from private industry. This was not forthcoming (Walford 1990), and CTCs play a fringe role in secondary education: there were only fifteen CTCs in England in the academic year 1994/5 (Department for Education and Employment 1996b). Furthermore, although GM schools can opt out of local authority control, they are part of the public sector, in which there has been no significant privatisation of provision.

This has a crucial effect on the 'efficiency' of the sector. As was indicated above, the incentive to greater efficiency is seen to work through parents' moving children from school to school. In particular, the budgetary effects of such choices are seen as providing a spur to improved performance. However, the corollary of this postulated mechanism is that the school losing pupils will be undersubscribed, and hence operate with surplus places. Closure of such schools would be incoherent for two reasons: it would remove the claimed inducement to improved performance for the 'less efficient' schools; and it would reduce the competitive pressures on currently popular schools, and hence induce complacency. Thus, the logical corollary of the approach is that surplus places are a condition of 'parental choice'. However, this also means that, in a public sector service, the higher unit costs which are the effect of such a policy have to be absorbed by the *public* sector.

Unit efficiency is also an issue with respect to GM schools. Policy rhetoric suggests that opting out is driven by the desire to take advantage of the freedoms of devolved management. However, in the early phase of the policy quite different motives were salient. Thus Halpin *et al.* interviewed nineteen headteachers of GM schools: seven of them stated that the reason for opting for GM status was to challenge an existing proposal to close the school, and a further six stated that the aim was to frustrate such a proposal (Halpin *et al.* 1993: 7). Not only did the use of GM status to forestall closure push up costs, but they were also increased by inducements to seek GM status. Initially, in line with the notion of a level playing-field, the then DES stated (circular 21/89) that GM schools would be funded at the same level as if they had remained under LEA control. However, as a reaction to the slow take-up in applications, various financial privileges were given to GM schools. These included one-off payments on start-up as a GM school and privileged access to capital funding. The reversal of this 1989 policy was made explicit in a letter from John Major to Doug McAvoy of the National Union of Teachers, in which he stated: 'We have made no secret of the fact that grant-maintained schools get preferential treatment in the allocation of grants [for] capital expenditure. We look favourably at GM schools in order to encourage the growth of that sector . . .' (quoted in Rogers 1992: 113). Thus, again, the promotion of 'choice' involves a willingness to support higher costs at the unit level in favoured institutions.

Finally, it is worth bearing in mind that, even with the toleration of unit 'inefficiencies', which are so frowned upon in other areas, scope for choice varies enormously according to geographical location. This is illustrated by research in Scotland, where the opportunity for parental choice was greater throughout most of the 1980s because the Education (Scotland) Act 1980 was less restrictive than its English counterpart. Echols *et al.* (1990: 209) found that most 'placing requests' under the legislation occurred in the first year of secondary school, and in 1987/8 averaged 10.2 per cent of pupils for that year. However, there was substantial geographical variation in the incidence of such requests. They ranged from less than 1 per cent in sparsely populated areas, like the Borders, to 15 per cent in Lothian (including Edinburgh) (ibid.). Short of creating further surplus places in isolated areas, with further 'inefficiency' effects, such huge *de facto* differences in the range of choice must necessarily operate.

Choice, Responsiveness and Efficiency

As was indicated above, central government arguments on the ERA saw a link between the extension of choice and improvements in school efficiency and effectiveness. However, there is a major conceptual tension here. The extension of choice suggests that the shape of the educational system should be determined by whatever the preferences of parents happen to be. On the other hand, government arguments suggest a very clear-cut educational agenda, where 'parental choice' is a means of *realising* central government objectives. Thus, as has already been indicated, central government has worked on the assumption that parents should select the 'best' schools for their children, and that a key, if not the sole, criterion in this respect is measured performance in NC tests and public examinations (Bowe and Ball 1992: 27). Thus, for all the rhetoric of 'choice', the ERA framework involves a markedly prescriptive approach to how 'choice' should be exercised.

In addition, research has shown that, not surprisingly, criteria used in choosing schools vary considerably. For example, Gewirtz *et al*. group their respondents into 'privileged' or 'skilled' choosers; 'semi-skilled' choosers; and a group they term 'disconnected'. The first group combine the knowledge and resources to compare schools and act on the basis of the comparison. This group tend to combine concerns with both quantitative and qualitative aspects of school performance (Gewirtz *et al*. 1995: 25). The second believe the extension of choice is highly desirable, but are uneasy about how it should be exercised, finding it difficult to distinguish schools and, unlike the 'skilled/privileged', feeling they are outsiders with respect to the process (ibid.: 40–3). The third group are effectively outside the scope of the prescriptive approach to school choice embodied in Conservative policy. In this case the proximity of the school and the ease and safety with which a child can get to the school are the paramount criteria (ibid.: 47).

This diversity has a number of implications for the ERA framework. It means, for example, that, far from opening up 'choice' in a neutral way, the framework is designed to *preclude* certain choices. Thus, the prescriptive model aims to rule out locality and proximity as criteria: the neighbourhood comprehensive is a choice that ought *not* to be on the menu. Furthermore, case study research has shown how Conservative controlled LEAs, committed to marketisation, have sought to induce wholesale moves from comprehensive schools to selective forms (ibid.: 66).

It can also be argued that the prescriptive framework is likely to induce schools to be more responsive to *some* parents and to marginalise the concerns of others. Thus, there is research evidence to confirm that, in a regime where published performance measures loom large, considerable efforts are made to attract parents whose children are expected to perform well in tests and examinations (Gewirtz *et al*. 1995: 139–40; Bowe and Ball 1992: 53). However, these pressures can operate against attempts to cater for children with Special Educational Needs (SEN). For example, Gewirtz *et al*. (1995: 167) were told by a deputy head that 'SEN provision is expensive, so it's eating up your money, and if you're being asked to produce a good set of examination results, then you want as much of your resources to be directed at that.' It is also important to bear in mind that, with devolved management, specialist facilities for SEN pupils become dependent on the attitudes of staff, governors and parents at the level of individual schools. Thus, for example, Bowe and Ball (1992: 132) cite an example of successful pressure on an LEA to close a reading centre for SEN pupils and devolve the resources to the individual schools – a move which led to the end of this form of provision in the area. Thus, both the logic of the ERA and research findings suggest that the idea of a simple increase in responsiveness is facile. Gewirtz *et al.* (1995: 143) provide a more realistic account, arguing that 'it is only the preferences of particular groups of parents which effectively "count"'.

There is, finally, another major tension in the legislation that has often been the subject of comment. Naturally, choice over the content of education must now be circumscribed by the operation of the NC. Of course, it can be argued that schools retain a degree of freedom in how it is interpreted and implemented. However, case study research has shown that the combination of the NC with published attainment scores has engendered a tendency to *follow* the NC rather than adapt it to the conditions of the local school (Bowe and Ball 1992: 105).

The Quasi-Market in Higher Education

The quasi-market in higher education has operated in the context of two important policy developments: the formal unification of the sector via the abolition of the division between universities on the one hand and polytechnics and colleges of higher education on the other; and the massive expansion of student numbers in the sector.

The formal unification of the sector was proposed in the 1991 White Paper, *Higher Education: a New Framework* (Department of Education and Science 1991). The White Paper also contained a projection for the expansion of the system: the stated aim was to increase the percentage of 18–19-year-olds in higher education from 14.6 per cent in 1987 to 32.1 per cent by the year 2000 (ibid.: 41). However, with the government concerned with restraining increases in public spending, expansion had to operate in the context of falls in higher education unit costs.

The White Paper posits a link between unification of the sector and expansion without a *pro rata* increase in funding. 'The government believes that the real key to achieving cost effective expansion lies in greater competition for funds and students. That can best be achieved by breaking down the increasingly artificial and unhelpful barriers between the universities and the polytechnics and colleges' (ibid.: para. 17).

The White Paper proposals were carried into effect by the Further and Higher Education Act 1992. Unification operated in the three ways: the term 'university' became the norm across the sector, and thus all ex-polytechnics are now 'new' universities; the purchasing/regulatory body is also unified with three national funding councils; and all universities are subject to a common regulatory framework. The Higher Education Funding Council (England) (HEFCE) is substantially the largest of these bodies; an innovation of the legislation was the introduction of quality control *vis-à-vis* teaching, or what has become Teaching Quality Assessment (TQA), which is a responsibility of the funding body.

The funding councils operate as the purchasing bodies for the sector, with the universities as providers. Universities have two major types of activity: teaching and the undertaking of research and scholarship.

With respect to teaching, the aim of expanding the system while driving unit costs down meant that the national funding councils had to devise means to achieve this end. In the case of the largest, HEFCE, two tactics were used. With respect to government grants to institutions to cover teaching costs a distinction was made between 'core' and 'marginal' funding. 'Core' funding referred to a given level of funding for an agreed student intake. If, however, institutions wanted additional 'marginal' funding, this required a bid from the institution for the student numbers concerned. Such bids would, however, need to be pitched at below the unit cost level of core funding. Naturally this meant that expansion was connected with a cut in unit costs.

A second method was the incentive to take 'fees only' students. In the case of students entering under the core/marginal system outlined above, institutions received both teaching grant *and* tuition fees. However, universities were also free to take students for whom they just received tuition fees; again, institutions which admitted such students were allowing their unit costs to fall. Thus, the two purchasing body tactics were both designed to meet the government objective of expansion with substantial cuts in funding per student.

However, the quasi-market in higher education has undergone a major structural transformation. The underlying reason behind this was that the rate of expansion of the sector substantially exceeded government projections. Thus, for example, the 1991 White Paper projected a 30 per cent participation rate for 18–19-year-olds for 1996–7 (Department of Education and Science 1991: 41). In fact this level had already been reached by 1993–4 (Department for Education 1995: 83). Given that such an expansion triggered demands on public expenditure via, for example, student maintenance grants, central government acted to decelerate the expansion.

This involved unravelling the two mechanisms outlined above. Thus 'marginal' funding has virtually been abolished, as the current aim is to stabilise, not increase, student numbers. For example HEFCE teaching funding for 1995–6 was £2,270 million, of which virtually all, £2,210 million, was core funding (HEFCE 1995a). The inducement to take 'fees only' students was also removed, as tuition fees were sharply cut in 1993 (National Audit Office 1994: 28).

As far as research and scholarship are concerned, the pre-unification system in the 'old' universities was termed the 'dual funding' system. This meant that universities obtained research funding in two ways. Part of this funding was in the form of grants, which were designed to provide the pre-conditions for research and scholarship. Thus, for example, such pre-conditions might be sufficient funding to ensure that teaching time-tables were low enough to permit research, or that appropriate physical conditions were present, such as laboratory facilities; naturally the nature of the pre-conditions would vary with the subject concerned. An important change occurred with respect to research grant in 1986, when the Research Assessment Exercise (RAE) was introduced. This brought selective allo-cation of research grant, whereby the funding allocated was decided by reference to ranking in departmental submissions. In this process departments are judged by specialist subject panels by reference to the publications of 'research active' staff and a summary of the department's research/scholarly activity over the period for which the assessment runs (assessment exercises have taken place in 1986, 1989, 1992 and 1996). The number of research active staff entered is also crucial to funding, since it is used as a multiplicand: thus for example a department with a '3' ranking with 20 research active staff would receive double the funding of one with 10.

The other side of the 'dual funding' system is revenue obtained to undertake particular pieces of research. These funds are derived from government-funded research councils such as the Science Research Council; from charities like the Nuffield Foundation; or from industrial or commercial sources. Either publications deriving from such funding or even obtaining such funding *per se* can be a potential help to a depart-ment in achieving a higher ranking in the RAE.

Dual funding effectively did not apply to the old polytechnic and colleges sector. Thus, for example, before unification (in 1989/90) the then funding council for the 'old' universities, the University Funding Council (UFC), distributed £860 million in research grant; the corres-ponding figure for the funding council for the Polytechnics and Colleges Funding Council (PCFC) was £20m (Department of Education and Science 1991: 16). One of the effects of unification has been to bring the 'new' universities into the dual funding system, and the 1992 RAE was the first time they were included in the research ranking exercise.

As was pointed out above, the quasi-market in higher education oper-ated in the context of a massive expansion of the sector. Thus, no analysis of the arguments for the quasi-market in this sector can avoid discussing why this expansionary policy was adopted.

In this respect there is a fundamental difference between the quasi-market in higher education and that in secondary education. For those ages below the minimum school-leaving age, coverage is virtually universal, with the only exception being the small minority in public schools. However, even after the massive expansion, participation rates for 18–19-year-olds are still only just over 30 per cent. This expansion was fuelled by two features on the 'demand' side: firstly, at least in England, an increasing proportion of the age cohort are now qualified to enter as non-mature students (Keep and Mayhew 1996: 91). Thus, as Table 3.1 shows, the percentage of 17-year-olds with 2 or more 'A' levels virtually doubled over the period 1984/5 to 1994/5.

Secondly, it can be argued that having a degree might be seen, whether accurately or otherwise, as giving the holder an advantage in a labour market characterised by persistent mass unemployment (Keep and Mayhew 1996). Certainly, as was indicated above, the over-fulfillment of expansion targets suggests that there was a substantial demand for entry into higher education.

However, actual expansion requires that government should be willing to accommodate such demands, and they were, particularly as they took the view that the expansion of higher education was required to underpin the international competitiveness of the UK economy. Thus, for example, the 1996 White Paper on Competitiveness, issued by the Department of Trade, has argued that the expansion of higher education has contributed to strengthening the UK economy (**3.28**). However, a clear pre-condition for accepting central government's claims regarding the expansion of higher education would be that it had occurred without any fall in standards

Table 3.1. Percentage of the 17-year-old age group (England) with 2 or more 'A' level passes

Year	Percentage of Age Group
1984/5	15.5%
1987/8	16.6%
1988/9	17.3%
1989/90	20.0%
1990/91	21.7%
1991/2	24.4%
1992/3	26.5%
1993/4	27.9%
1994/5	29.1%

Source: Department of Employment (1996c).

or quality of provision. This follows from the stated objective that the larger system would expand the supply of 'highly qualified' men and women: the qualifications were not to change, just the numbers obtaining them. This argument will be examined with respect to two dimensions. The first concerns the pattern of expansion in higher education and, in particular, its impact on the 'old' and 'new' universities. This analysis will seek to show that there are reasons to be sceptical of claims of expansion's having had no negative 'quality' effects. The second aspect is related, since it appraises arguments advanced by the Department for Education and Employment to the effect that quality and standards have not fallen during the period of expansion.

The first key point to make regarding the unification of the sector is that formal unification, created by the 1992 Act, involved imposing a common structure on a heterogeneous range of institutions. This is illustrated by variations in qualifications on intake between the 'old' and 'new' sectors. Thus, Tables 3.2 and 3.3 show the 'A' level 'points' scores of entrants to the former polytechnics and the ex-UFC, 'old', universities and the percentage of entrants who came with 'standard' qualifications ('A' levels or the Scottish equivalent). This shows that students entering the 'old' sector with a standard entry had the equivalent of an additional 'A' level pass at grade 'B'. In addition the tables also show that the percentage of 'non-standard' entrants was much higher in the 'new' universities.

Any conclusions regarding such variations in entry standards have to be treated with caution. Thus, it cannot be concluded that lower 'A' level or equivalent entry standards mechanically translate into lower standards at work at undergraduate level. Equally, both motivation and analytical

Table 3.2. Qualifications on entry for first degree: former polytechnics (England) 1992

	Male	**Female**
Entry	62,381	43,019
% With 'A' Level/Scottish Higher	45.7%	60.4%
Mean 'A' Level Points	13.1	13.8

Source: Department of Education and Science (Undated).

Table 3.3. Qualifications on entry for first degree: ex-University Funding Council Universities (Great Britain 1992–3)

Entry	104,479
% With 'A' Level/Scottish Higher	75.8%
Mean 'A' Level Points	22.4

Source: Universities Statistical Record (1994).

skills developed in work situations can and do contribute to excellent work by mature, non-standard students. However, it would not be unreasonable to conclude that having a student population that has been less successful at 'standard' entry qualifications or is not as acquainted with academic conventions puts the new universities at something of a disadvantage.

As was indicated above, government policy, implemented through the funding councils, has been to drive down teaching unit costs. This has been a policy that is applied across the sector as a whole. However, it is important to bear in mind that, while funding council teaching money is a crucial source of university funding, there are other sources that can operate to provide a cushion against the rigours of teaching cost reduction. Two particular instances will be considered here: funding council research grant, and fee income from students outside the European Union.

As was indicated above, unification meant that the new universities were brought into the dual funding system. This is potentially significant because it represents 28 per cent of the HEFCE budget and because, as this is a subsidy to the institutional infrastructure, it can be seen as a potential condition of higher-level work.

However, the prior exclusion of polytechnics and colleges from dual funding put them at a disadvantage relative to the ex-UFC universities. For example, Halsey's 1989 survey of what were then university and polytechnic academic staff found that 77 per cent of polytechnic staff cited 'teaching commitments' as an obstacle to research, as against 57 per cent of university staff (Halsey 1995: 188), and while 27 per cent of university staff said they undertook 'substantial' research during term time (as against 13 per cent of polytechnic staff), only 24 per cent of university staff stated that the amount of research undertaken during term time was 'almost none', while the corresponding figure for the polytechnics was 44 per cent (ibid.). These figures also need to be interpreted in the light of apparent differences in expectations of the amount of time that academics thought ought to be devoted to research. Thus, Halsey also asked his respondents what percentage of working time they thought should be devoted to 'research and other creative activity': university staff put this figure at 43 per cent, polytechnic staff at 30 per cent (ibid.: 186).

The new framework did make some attempt to take this historic disadvantage into account. Thus, in the 1992 RAE a ringfenced part of research grant was Development Related (DevR), and this was exclusively allocated to the new universities. HEFCE argued that DevR 'aims to encourage the development of research activity in institutions which have demonstrated potential and which did not previously receive substantial research funds' (HEFCE 1995b: 18).

However, the effects of the creation of this part of the budget are nullified by the small scale of DevR. Thus, in the HEFCE allocations for 1995–6 the DevR figure is £16m, as against the Quality Related (QR) allocation, where funding is related to ranking and staff entered in the 1992 RAE, which is £600m (HEFCE 1995a: 5). This means that, effectively, research grant allocations are determined by RAE results. Thus, given the likely effects of earlier exclusion from dual funding, it would be expected that the new universities would do less well than the ex-UFC institutions. This has proved to be the case in both the 1992 and 1996 RAE, where both sets of institutions have competed for QR funding. For example, in 1996 (for a discussion of the 1992 experience, see Cutler *et al*. 1997) the *Times Higher Education Supplement* (20/12/96) published a 'league table' of average research ranking scores in that year's RAE. Listed in the table were 102 members of the Committee of Vice Chancellors and Principals. All the first 59 places in the rank order were occupied by ex-UFC institutions, and only one ex-UFC institution was (one place) below the highest ex-PCFC institution. In addition, the 1996 pattern confirmed that of 1992, where the ex-UFC institutions entered a much larger proportion of their staff as 'research active' in the exercise. Thus, given the role of research active staff as the multiplicand, outlined above, this amplified the dominant role of the ex-UFC institutions in obtaining access to this funding source.

The same pattern operates with respect to non-European Union student fees. The restraint on funding for domestic students relates to the desire to expand the system with minimal public expenditure increases, and such fees also apply to European Union students, as UK membership of the Union precludes discriminatory treatment of member-state nationals. However, naturally, these considerations do not apply outside the EU, and fees for the non-EU student group are substantially higher. However, again, access to this market is much greater in the case of the ex-UFC universities, where 11.3 per cent of students were non-EU in academic year 1992/3, as against 3.1 per cent in the ex-PCFC institutions (Higher Education Statistics Agency 1995).

These differences in access to sources of funding other than for the teaching of domestic/EU students have another important differential impact on old and new universities. In the case of the former it has generally been easier to defend their overall resource allocations because sources of funding other than for teaching EU students are more readily available. The converse is true for the new universities: to cover their costs they are much more dependent on funding council teaching allocations. This has a further important impact: they have been obliged to expand student numbers at a faster rate than the old universities, initially to obtain marginal funding and fees-only students. Thus, while student numbers in the ex-UFC institutions increased by 18 per cent over the period 1990–92, the corresponding figure for the ex-PCFC institutions was 34.5 per cent (Higher Education Statistics Agency 1995).

This is potentially significant for the issue of quality. The characteristic of the sector is that, broadly speaking, the 'production methods' are unchanged. Thus, it is not possible to identify an obvious means of boosting productivity through technical improvements. The increased throughput has been accommodated by a combination of intensifying work, larger classes and a reduction in contact time. Equally, as the above analysis indicates, the structure of the unified sector means that these forces have, broadly, been most marked in the ex-PCFC institutions, which, as was indicated, are taking a larger share of less formally well-qualified students. The combination of these factors suggests that it is difficult to sustain the claim that there are no negative quality implications of expansion. Indeed, it is worth noting that the logic of one of the commonest arguments for obtaining increased resources under the RAE is one that explicitly links quality to resources: thus it is argued that the most 'excellent' research and scholarship institutions need more funding to retain their standards. However, any decline in quality or standards has been explicitly denied by the DfEE; and it is to their arguments that we now turn.

In its 1996 report the Department for Education and Employment (DfEE) advanced various arguments in support of the claim that expansion with unit cost reductions had not damaged quality. It stated that: since expansion there had been no fall in the percentage of honours degree students obtaining upper second or first class degrees (in fact this proportion increased slightly over the period 1989/90 to 1992/3); that the average 'A' level points score of students admitted to UK universities has remained constant over the period 1990/1 to 1993/4; that, while drop-out rates have tended to rise since the mid-1980s they remain low by international standards; that the percentage of UK students finding employment has increased since 1991/2; and that quality inspections under TQA have resulted in only 1 per cent of departments inspected being classified as unsatisfactory (**3.29**).

However, all these criteria for a constant 'quality' level are problematic. The first is question-begging, since it presupposes what is to be demonstrated. Thus, the constant share of upper seconds and firsts could be an effect either of constant or of less exacting marking standards: the figures in themselves prove nothing. The second also runs into the same problem, and is of questionable relevance, since it refers to attainments on entry to universities. In addition, on the government's own figures, the measure is increasingly insignificant, since, whereas in 1990/1 76 per cent of home students entering full-time and sandwich degree courses in England were 'A' level entrants, this fell to 63 per cent by 1993/4 (**3.29**). The argument on drop-out rates also runs into the problem of circularity. As drop-out will obviously, although not solely, be related to assessment standards, a relaxation of such standards would lead to rates being kept at a fairly low level. Again, the Department assumes what is to be explained.

With respect to the use of employment criteria, there are two distinct problems. Firstly, graduate employment will, like other employment indicators, be highly sensitive to the economic cycle. This is implicitly recognised in both the Departmental reports of 1995 and 1996. In the former the increase in graduate unemployment since the late 1980s is seen as 'reflecting the business cycle' (Department for Education 1995). In the latter the improvement in graduate employment since 1991/2 is seen as relating to emergence out of recession. However, if this is the case, and hence graduate employment and unemployment are indicators not 'owned' by higher education institutions, it is difficult to see how they can be measures of the 'effectiveness' of such institutions.

A second problem relates to the fact that, even if adjustments are made for cyclical factors, any form of permanent employment is taken as an indicator of the effectiveness of higher education institutions. This gives an unargued privilege to the judgements of employers over quality issues in higher education. Furthermore, since any form of permanent employment is the indicator, it is clearly possible that a general inflation of qualifications means that degree-holders are displacing individuals with lesser qualifications.

The final point is perhaps particularly significant, since it relates to the mechanism of quality assessment established under the legislation. Under this system departments within the sector are visited by specialist panels predominantly composed of academics and, on the basis of prior documentation, documentation gathered during the visit, teaching observations and discussions with students, an assessment of 'teaching quality' is made.

There are two particular reasons why it is doubtful whether the results of these assessments can serve the purpose to which they are put by the DfEE. The first is that the implications of an 'unsatisfactory' finding are draconian for the institution concerned. Such a finding would involve the department's being re-inspected after a year, and a further unsatisfactory finding would result in a withdrawal of funding in the subject-area. Given these circumstances, it would hardly be surprising if teams were reluctant to give such an assessment.

Second, and arguably of greater significance, is the conceptual mis-understanding of TQA involved in the DfEE argument. The argument effectively assumes that assessment teams are applying an *absolute* stan-dard. However, the handbook provided by HEFCE to assessors (covering the period October 1996 to September 1998) makes it abundantly clear that this is *not* the case. As part of the TQA the department being assessed is required to produce a 'self assessment' document that details the aims and objectives of the 'subject provider' (HEFCE 1996: 7). The hand-book continually reiterates the central role played by the self-assessment document in the assessment. Thus, it is said to provide 'the framework for the assessment' (ibid.) and the 'purpose of the assessment visit is to gather, consider and verify the evidence of the quality of education *in the light of the subject provider's aims and objectives*' (ibid.: 8, our emphasis).

Clearly, then, what is envisaged is *not* absolute standards, but rather that the assessment is one that uses the aims and objectives of the depart-ment as the yardstick; and it is assumed that they can and will be different. Consequently, the arguments advanced for expansion with sharp unit cost reductions but no fall in quality cannot be sustained. The formally unified sector is not a level playing-field, because it superimposes a single quasi-market on a hugely heterogeneous set of institutions, some of which face intense cost pressures, while others have substantial cushions against the impact of cuts in grants and fees for European Union students. Similarly, the arguments that no quality penalty has been paid for the rapid and lower-cost expansion either involves question-begging measures or a basic misunderstanding of the assessment method used by the regulatory body.

Conclusion

Quasi-markets were introduced as an alternative to full-scale privatisation of welfare services. While the services would continue to be publicly funded, they would be provided by competing units, some within the public sector, but some also from the private and voluntary sectors. It was claimed that quasi-markets, via the introduction of competition, would generate efficiency, enhance consumer choice, deliver high-quality services and encourage diversity and decentralisation. However, such markets also generate contradictory pressures, and, this being the case, it is not possible to sustain all the claims that are made for them, as we have sought to demonstrate in this chapter. In particular it is difficult to reconcile con-sumer choice with budgetary constraints and efficiency; decentralisation and diversity with regulation; and maintenance of quality with 'value for money' and 'efficiency'.

In this chapter we have incorporated a particular critical perspective in analysing the quasi-markets: what we have referred to elsewhere as 'evaluative discourse' (Cutler and Waine 1997). Central to evaluative discourse is the implicit notion that quasi-markets are a technique to realise a set of goals – efficiency, quality, responsiveness, choice of service provision. The object of this discourse is to examine how far the technique has succeeded. Here we have used this framework to discuss why the quasi-markets have not succeeded, and to identify key tensions. However, quasi-markets are not to be understood only as techniques to realise pre-set objectives, but also as distributional mechanisms that, in their operation, can serve to reinforce differentiation by social class (for example, in education) or gender (in the impact of Compulsory Competitive Tendering; see Chapter 4). To open up such issues for analysis we need to develop a distributional politics of quasi-markets; and this will be pursued in the Conclusion.

—4—

Compulsory Competitive Tendering: The Case of the Vanishing Producers

An important development in the framework within which public sector services are managed in the United Kingdom has been the introduction of Compulsory Competitive Tendering (CCT). This policy has, from the outset, generated controversy; but it is important to stress that the debate is not just one about pros and cons, but also involves the question of how CCT is characterised. On the political left CCT has often been seen as an illegitimate and authoritarian policy, which has sought to impose an alien set of practices on democratically elected local government (see for example Shaw *et al*. 1994: 202). In contrast, CCT has also been seen as a neutral management technique that has no political implications. Thus, a *Financial Times* leader of 26 November 1986 refers to CCT as 'a micro-economic search for efficiency which has little to do with ideology' (cited in Cubbin *et al*. 1987: 56). In a similar vein the Audit Commission sees a simple parallel between decisions on contracting out in business and in local authorities, arguing that providing services in-house or buying them in is equivalent to commercial decisions to 'make or buy', and should be related solely to 'cost competitive' criteria (**4.1**).

The thesis developed in this chapter is that arguments of the latter form are untenable. It seeks to demonstrate that any evaluation of CCT cannot be divorced from the fact that it is a policy that necessarily involves fundamental political choices and reference to central political values. The argument is divided into four sections: the first examines the defining features of the policy and gives an outline history of its development in the British context; the second discusses the regulatory framework within which the policy has operated and its underlying rationale; the third looks at the impact of the policy in terms of whether it has generated 'savings' and its significance for conditions of employment in the areas covered — this section does not draw on just British experience alone, but also utilises evidence on the effects of parallel practices in the United States; and the final section discusses the political choices involved in the evaluation of CCT.

CCT and Privatisation

It has become a common practice to see CCT as part of a general trend towards privatisation. However, this runs the risk of obscuring certain distinctive features of the policy. Central to the UK privatisation programme has been the sale, in whole or in part, of major public assets such as British Telecom (BT), British Gas (BG) and the electricity and water industries. This has been a complex procedure, since it has usually involved the establishment by government of a regulatory framework within which the privatised industry operates. The regulatory framework means that in certain areas the companies concerned do not have a completely free hand in determining company policy. For example, in the case of BT and BG pricing policy is regulated and the government holds what is termed a 'golden share', which enables it to exert control over decisions such as disposal of assets and share issues (Marsh 1991: 464). Even so, there is a privatisation of both *provision*, as the service is now provided by a private sector firm, and *finance*, since, within the constraints imposed by regulation, the firm can set prices and raise capital in the form it regards as appropriate.

In contrast, competitive tendering (CT) is a process whereby services currently provided by public sector suppliers are put out to tender. This usually involves a bid by an in-house public sector supplier, which is compared to bids from outside contractors. With CT the planning and finance functions remain public (Ascher 1987: 7). Thus, a local authority that introduces CT will continue to decide what level of service it wishes to provide (e.g. the number of times refuse is collected per week) and specify features of how the service will be provided (e.g. whether refuse will be collected from the side of the road or the back of the house). The service continues to be publicly financed, being paid for predominantly out of a combination of central and local government taxation, although this does not exclude the use of direct charges.

The effect of CT *may* be that service provision moves from public to private sector. The public sector provider might be unsuccessful in its bid and hence lose the contract. However, the shift is not necessarily permanent. Contracts have been awarded for fixed periods to a contractor, but the contract has been returned 'in-house' in a subsequent round of bidding. (For an interesting case study, which is discussed later in this chapter, see Paton and Bach 1990.) Public sector providers under CCT are referred to as Direct Service Organisations (DSOs).

CT should be distinguished from contracting out. CT involves a regular competition between public and outside suppliers. In contrast, a policy of contracting out involves closing down the public sector provision and relying on outside contractors for the future provision of the service (Treasury 1986: 15). In such cases a genuine privatisation of *provision* operates, though planning and finance remain public. Finally, CT is distinct from procurement. All public sector bodies buy in goods and services on a substantial scale from outside suppliers, but procurement cases relate to goods or services that have never been produced in-house (purchase of motor vehicles is an obvious example). In contrast, the services covered by CT, like refuse collection or street cleaning, have usually been provided in-house; but the tendering process opens the possibility of a shift in provision (Ascher 1987: 136). CCT is sometimes treated as a form of quasi-market. This is perfectly legitimate in that it involves two defining features of such markets, public funding and the purchaser–provider split. However, we have opted to treat it as a distinct form for two reasons: because it involves conditions on the form of contract and criteria for tender assessment, imposed by central government, that are more detailed than those that apply in the quasi-markets discussed in Chapter 3 (as can be seen most recently in the case of 'white collar' services). In addition, it raises issues about the treatment of producer groups in a particularly pointed form. Both these questions are discussed in detail later in this chapter.

Compulsory Competitive Tendering: the Genesis of a Policy

Competitive tendering *per se* refers to a policy initiated by the public body involved. In contrast, CCT means that an *obligation* is being imposed to use competitive tendering for a range of services, and that such tendering operates within a regulatory framework. As will be argued later, the compulsory element has a number of crucial ramifications in assessment of this policy.

Throughout the 1980s CCT evolved in a series of developments at the level of central government departments (for a summary see Treasury 1991: Annexe) and in the NHS. With respect to the NHS the Conservative 1983 manifesto contained a commitment to introduce CCT for three ancillary services: catering, laundry services and cleaning. This policy was initiated in a DHSS circular HC (83) 18, issued in September 1983. The circular required that, from February 1984, what were then Regional Health Authorities (RHAs) should submit tendering programmes prepared by Districts to the Ministry within two months or furnish an explanation for the failure of Districts to provide such a programme. Similar obligations were imposed on special health authorities and teaching hospitals (Department of Health and Social Security 1983: 2).

However, arguably the most interesting developments have occurred in local government. The first major development came in the Local Government and Land Act 1980. This legislation imposed an obligation on local authorities to introduce tendering for building construction and maintenance of buildings and highways (Walsh 1989: 36). However, the impact of this legislation was limited, primarily because of the number of exceptions that were allowed: initially, tendering was not required for building work under £10,000 and work on highways under £100,000; and small providers were not covered (ibid.: 37). The effect of these restrictions meant that the impact on in-house providers, at least in terms of their share of contract work, was relatively small. Over the period 1982–3 to 1985–6 the DLO share of local authority construction and maintenance work in England and Wales fell only marginally, from 43.3 per cent to 42.6 per cent (ibid.).

A further and much more significant move to introduce CCT in local government came with the Local Government Act 1988. The Act requires that if 'defined authorities' (mainly local authorities, but also bodies like Urban Development Corporations) wish to retain a service in-house, then they must put the service out to tender (**4.2**). There is an additional requirement to advertise the offer of work in the local and trade press (**4.2**). Initially CCT, under the Act, applied to a set of activities that were predominantly provided by manual workers: refuse collection, cleaning (building and 'other'); catering (education and welfare and 'other'), grounds maintenance and vehicle maintenance (**4.3**). However, the legislation also gave the Secretary of State power to add additional activities (**4.3**). Thus, while the major impact of CCT has, so far, been with respect to these 'manual' services, the scope of CCT has been progressively expanded. The policy now covers sports and leisure management and 'white-collar' services such as information technology, legal services, construction and property-related services, housing management and financial services.

The Regulatory Framework

The imposition of CCT on local and health authorities was accompanied by an elaborate but ambiguous regulatory framework. CCT requires them to test in-house suppliers against external competition; but in itself this indicates nothing about the criteria that are to be used to select the winning tender. It is this that is revealed in the fine print of the regulatory framework.

The first striking feature is the dominance of cost criteria. In discussing tender appraisal in the services covered in the NHS, circular HC (83) 18 states: 'In no circumstances should a contractor not submitting the lowest tender be awarded the contract unless there are compelling reasons endorsed at District Authority level for taking such a decision.'

What counts as a 'good reason' for rejecting a lower bid is ambiguous. Circular HC (83) 18 states that the authority should only let the contract to the lowest bidder if it 'is satisfied about the ability of the contractor to deliver the service in accordance with contract terms' (Department of Health and Social Security 1983: Appendix ii). However, there is at least a strong *negative* injunction spelling out what is *not* to be taken into account, and that is the conditions under which workers are employed by the various bidders.

With respect to the NHS, HC (83) 18 advised that tender documents 'should detail the *service* requirements, frequencies and standards required. They should not stipulate detailed requirements for staffing, the length of time needed to undertake tasks, supervisors and equipment levels' (Department of Health and Social Security 1983: Appendix i; emphasis in the original).

A more systematic and comprehensive statement of this approach is in Section 17 (5) of the 1988 Local Government Act. This defines 'non-commercial' matters that ought not to be taken into account in evaluating tender bids. These include terms and conditions of employment, including policy on promotion or training and relations between contractors and sub-contractors (**4.4**).

There is an explicit political message here. As was argued in Chapter 1, a central feature of the New Right was the hostility to producer groups in general and trade unions in particular. Trade unions were attacked as key institutions that offended both the tenets of market economics and the dogma of individualism. A number of links exist between competitive tendering and the relative strength of trade unions. As will be demonstrated later, the process of competitive tendering is regularly associated with job loss. In such circumstances, even if a contract is won, there is the likelihood that job losses will mean a loss of membership for the trade unions involved.

Equally, where contracts are won by outside suppliers they are less likely to recognise trade unions. The 1995 Labour Force Survey includes evidence on relative levels of unionisation by economic sector: the overall level of union density (union members as a percentage of employees) in that year was 32 per cent, but the public sector included areas where levels of union density were much higher; in public administration density was 59 per cent, in education 56 per cent and in health 48 per cent (Cully and Woodland 1996: 216 and 220). In contrast, density in private services was low relative to the overall average, with, for example, density at 13 per cent in real estate and business services and 8 per cent in hotels and restaurants (ibid.: 220). This pattern is not unique to the United Kingdom. A study in the United States covering 1,256 cities each with a population in excess of 10,000 found that the 29 per cent of private sanitation employees working on public contracts were unionised as against a unionisation rate of 40 per cent for directly publicly employed staff (Chandler and Feuille 1991: 19).

In addition, the organisational separation involved in the creation of DSOs means that they can become effectively isolated from the impact of corporate local authority employment policies. For example, Walsh and Davies (1993: 75) found that many DSO managers they interviewed, from a panel of local authorities, were sympathetic to the idea of distinct DSO trading accounts. This went along with pressure from such managers to run their organisations as distinct businesses free from corporate supervision. As one of their respondents put it 'the principle over-riding the whole business planning process must be one of flexibility and the minimisation of . . . bureaucracy' (ibid.: 77).

Similar evidence of DSO managers' support for operational autonomy is provided by Shaw *et al.*'s study of CCT in twenty-three local authorities in the North of England. They reported a 'sizeable number' of DSO managers who wanted greater powers to reduce wages in line with competitive pressures and to match DSO employment contracts to service contracts, thus effectively moving towards fixed-term employment relations (Shaw *et al.* 1994: 211).

This process of reduced accountability to the authority was also reinforced by DSOs citing concerns of commercial confidentiality as a justification for less detailed reporting of their activities (Walsh and Davies 1993: 85).

The fact that a particular set of political values was being imposed by CCT is also reflected in the Local Government Act's provisions to prevent local authorities engaging in practices that have the effect of 'restricting, distorting or preventing competition' (Local Government Act 1988 section 7 (7)). An instance of such a practice relates to the 'packaging' of contracts. Thus, if contracts are sufficiently large, they can restrict competition, since the number of private sector bidders may be circumscribed, because few have the capacity to undertake such a volume of work.

These prohibitions are underpinned by sanctions. Under section 13 of the 1988 Act those authorities covered can be required to rebut claims that they have infringed the various prohibitions of the Act; and under section 14, if the Secretary of State finds the response unsatisfactory, the power is available to specify conditions attached to the work, i.e. to order the authority to re-tender, or even to prohibit the (in-house) supplier from carrying out the work.

The Acquired Rights Directive and the Transfer of Undertakings (Protection of Employment) Regulations 1981

While the regulatory framework established by the government embodied assumptions favourable to the promotion of labour market 'flexibility', there is also a significant countervailing aspect relating to questions thrown up by the Transfer of Undertakings (Protection of Employment) Regulations (TUPE). These regulations were introduced to conform with the 1977 European Community Acquired Rights Directive. That Directive was designed to ensure that, where an undertaking was transferred, existing employees retained their current conditions of service. Originally this was not seen as applicable to areas like CCT where, for example, staff might transfer to an outside contractor that had won contracts from the in-house provider. This was because of a restriction on the type of undertaking initially covered by TUPE. Thus, section 2 excluded from the scope of TUPE undertakings that were 'non commercial' (**4.5**)

This seeming lack of applicability of TUPE to CCT was transformed by decisions of the European Court of Justice (ECJ) and a report, critical of TUPE, by the European Commission (Napier 1994). In the *Sophie Redmond* case (1992) the ECJ ruled that the transfer of a body subsidised by a public authority fell under the directive; and in the *Rask* case of the same year it held that the contracting out of a service was covered by the directive (ibid.: 131).

Also, in the same year the European Commission produced a report on the way in which different Member States had sought to implement the Acquired Rights Directive (ibid.: 134). This contained criticisms of TUPE as inconsistent with the Directive in various respects. These included the claim that the exclusion of non-commercial undertakings was unsatisfactory, and that the requirement that a transfer of undertaking involved a property transfer was too restrictive (ibid.: 135). In response the UK government was obliged to meet such criticisms, and Section 33 of the 1993 Trade Union Reform and Employment Rights Act embodied important changes. These included the removal of the condition that a property transfer was necessary for a transfer of undertaking, and widened the scope of TUPE to encompass non-commercial ventures (**4.6**). Such changes have their limits: for example, they do not stop contractors seeking to vary conditions of employment of staff taken on by agreement, although they do impose legal limits on the degree of duress that an employer can exert. However, they are an important instance of an obstacle to the use of CCT to encourage labour market flexibility stemming from European Union law.

The Operation of the Regulatory Framework

As has already been argued, the emphasis on cost reduction and the pronounced bias against the interests of employees embodied in the legislation on CCT meant that Labour authorities in particular could be expected to resist it. For example, Kerley and Wynn point out that, after the 1988 Act was passed, the Convention of Scottish Local Authorities and the Scottish TUC formed a joint committee to 'formulate joint ground rules by which Scottish Local Authorities and the trade unions could cooperate to minimise the loss of employment and direct services arising from commercial tendering' (Kerley and Wynn 1991: 33).

The whole process of CCT is thus firmly inserted in the conflictual relationship between central government and local authorities that has been a central issue in British politics in the 1980s and 1990s.

As in all cases of this kind, it is difficult to assess the effects of the regulatory powers contained in the 1988 Act. Table 4.1 shows that the powers under sections 13 and 14 have been used relatively sparingly.

The limited use of sanctions does not, of course, imply that the regulatory framework is of no significance. Sanctions may not only be designed *pour encourager les autres*, but may actually do so.

In such a politically polarised context a relevant consideration is not just the content of the regulatory framework, but also its clarity and coherence. The regulation of CCT in both health and local authorities requires the authority to *disregard* conditions of employment in evaluating tenders.

Table 4.1. 'Anti-competitive' notices under the Local Government Act 1988: 1989–96

Year	Number of Section 13 Notices	Number of Section 14 Notices
1996	17	7
1995	10	5
1994	0	1
1993	16	9
1992	6	5
1991	11	3
1990	10	6
1989	5	2

Source: Local Government Management Board (1996a).

However, there is a fine line between this condition and the requirement that the viability of the contractor's bid should be evaluated. This tension is revealed in a report of a multi-departmental review of competitive tendering and contracting for services in central government departments, published in 1986. On the one hand, the document argues that savings from contracting out derived from contractors offering inferior conditions of employment (Treasury 1986: 33). On the other hand, it repudiates the notion that viability can be assessed without reference to conditions of employment: 'service contracts have to be conducted on the basis of mutual trust because although detailed specification and monitoring are necessary it is difficult to make such contracts entirely comprehensive. It is essential, therefore, to check that the contractor *plans to recruit enough staff and to pay them enough*' (ibid.; our emphasis).

It is also clear that, even amongst authorities that have not resisted CCT, staffing levels have been regarded as a pertinent consideration. A detailed case study by Paton and Bach (1990) discusses two rounds of CCT in a new District General Hospital. In this case senior management were sympathetic to CT, a fact that was indicated by an outside contractor's winning the contract in the first round of tendering. Five bids were short-listed, including the in-house bid, but the lowest bid, which proposed to undertake the contract with a staffing level of 29.37 Whole Time Equivalent (WTE) staff, was rejected in favour of an outside contractor bid with a staffing level of 45.68 WTE, on the grounds that the lowest bid was regarded as unviable by management (ibid.: 277).

A Level Playing-Field?

Discussions of CCT have regularly emphasised the pertinence of *competition* in analysing the underlying rationale behind the policy. This is reflected in official documents. The Local Government Act 1988 states that its aim is 'to secure that local and other public authorities undertake certain activities only if they can do so competitively'; similarly circular HC (83) 18 involves the objective of obliging authorities to 'test the cost of their support services' (Department of Health and Social Security 1983: 1). Furthermore, academic commentators have seen the policy as having the object of creating 'contestable markets'. This concept refers to a reorientation of the economic theory of competition during the 1980s (Walsh 1989: 46; Milne 1993: 204). According to this position the effects of competition are achieved, not by the number of actual competitors, but rather by the possibility of competitors' entering (and thus 'contesting') the markets concerned. In such circumstances, it is argued, economic enterprises will operate *as if* they were facing actual competition.

At first sight this argument seems to supply a *raison d'être* for CCT. Thus, what it can be claimed to achieve is the break-up of monopoly provision, exposing the in-house supplier to the effects of competitive pressures. In turn it is possible to argue that many key elements of the regulatory framework are consistent with such arguments. For instance, the Local Government Act 1988 obliges authorities to advertise the contracts in the local and trade press and make available detailed specifications of the work required (**4-2**). Equally, the prohibitions on such practices as contract packaging to deter entrants can be seen as part of the object of rendering the sector 'contestable'.

This, also, seems to imply that the legislation and regulatory framework is designed to create a 'level playing-field' on which private and public sector suppliers can compete on equal terms. In many fundamental respects, however, this reading of CCT is misleading.

The first significant difference between public and private sector providers is their ability to bid for contracts in the sector in which CCT operates. A private sector supplier is able to bid for any contract put out to tender. In contrast, public sector providers are much more circumscribed in the range of work for which they can tender.

The issue involves a number of complexities, and is governed by the Local Authorities (Goods and Services) Act 1970. Under this legislation local authorities were allowed to cooperate with each other to promote 'economy and efficiency'. The Act allows a local authority to supply services to another, and does not impose restrictions on the size or financial value of the contracts concerned nor the geographical area in which they may operate. What *is* precluded by the legislation is a situation where the Authority 'engages in trade' by providing services to other authorities that are incidental to their functions as authorities. This might be argued to cover a local authority DSO operating as a specialised contractor analogous to a private sector operator (Macgregor 1991: 61).

The Audit Commission has given a restrictive interpretation to this legislation. It has argued that a local authority may only supply its services to another authority if two conditions are met: it has surplus capacity; and the greater part of the work undertaken by the DSO is for its own authority. The evidence on the outcome of tendering discussed below indicates that successful cross-boundary tendering is relatively rare.

The issue may have significance for two reasons: the limitations on public sector bidders mean that there is an asymmetry between the effects of losing a contract for private and public sector suppliers. In the former case the loss is likely to *reduce* the volume of business for the enterprise, but it remains free to bid for other public and private sector contracts. In the latter case the loss is potentially fatal for the DSO. Thus, a DSO manager told Walsh and Davies (1993: 80) 'if we are restricted to our own authority then we must fail eventually . . . Unless I can spread over-heads if I fail to win a contract then I will eventually go out of business.'

Another difference in the treatment of DSOs and private sector suppliers relates to the conditions that require that DSOs are treated as distinct accounting units and make a positive rate of return on the capital they employ. For example, under the Local Government Act 1988 services the requirement is a 6 per cent rate of return. It could be argued that the treatment is equitable, in that private sector suppliers would also be expected to make positive rates of return. The difference is that the time-span for the rate of return (annual) is prescribed for the public sector providers by regulation, whereas it is discretionary in the private sector. This means that private sector providers could, if they wished, absorb losses in the hope of staying in the market and increasing their chances of winning future contracts. Thus Milne (1993: 315), in research on the early period of CCT in the NHS (1983–6), found that the profits record of nine new entrants to the NHS domestic cleaning market was 'poor'. Two of these firms made 'very large losses'; but their parent companies were willing to absorb them, seeing the NHS market 'as a new opportunity and were willing to make a major investment' (ibid.).

A more blatant variation in treatment, and one that flatly contradicts 'competition' criteria, relates to the difference in the regulation of contracted-out services and of services provided in-house. The legislation on CCT refers exclusively to services where the authority concerned *wishes to retain the service in-house*. In such a case, if the service is covered by the legislation, the CT is obligatory. In contrast, no such obligations apply to a policy of *contracting out*. Should a local authority wish simply to terminate public provision and contract out the service to the private sector there is no requirement to test the private sector contractor against a public sector provider (Painter 1991: 193).

Dividing Up the Market

A central political issue with respect to CCT relates to how far it has resulted in the privatisation of provision. However,it is important to stress that it would be quite wrong to limit any assessment of its impact simply to this issue. The impact of CCT may involve other key changes, since, given the regulatory framework, important variations in the terms and conditions of employment may be required to ensure that the contract is retained in-house (this issue is explored later in this chapter).

The importance of the *compulsory* element in tendering can be understood if it is set in the context of the *voluntary* local authority initiatives in competitive tendering. These have been given a significant amount of publicity because of the activities of 'flagship' London councils such as Wandsworth and Westminster. This might give the impression that government legislation bringing in compulsion was simply following a trend that was already well established, at least in Conservative-controlled councils. However, initiatives of the Wandsworth type are the exception rather than the rule as far as voluntary moves to introduce CT are concerned. Thus a *Local Government Chronicle* survey of activities contracted out to the private sector over the period 1981–7 found that their total value was only £75 million (Fretwell 1988: 4). In contrast, a recent Local Government Management Board survey (1996b: 12) estimated that the value of local authority work under contract as of June 1996 was £2,408.7 million.

The same survey provides a valuable source on the distribution of contract wins between client authority DSOs, outside DSOs and private contractors. Table 4.2 shows that the majority of contracts so far have been won by DSOs, and that this advantage is magnified when account is taken of contract values, with DSOs tending to win higher-value contracts.

However, the more recent figures do show that, relative to the early experience of CCT, the market share of private contractors has increased in all areas with the exception of Sports and Leisure Management (for evidence on the earlier rounds see Local Government Management Board 1992 and Painter 1991). This could, in some respects, have been anticipated, since, for example, once outside contractors have won contracts, this can operate to increase their credibility as bidders in future rounds (Milne 1993: 315). Furthermore, in an area like refuse collection, it has been argued that local economies of scale operate. Thus, for example, McGuirk (1991) claims that a pattern of competitive advantage can be achieved by building up a nexus of contract wins in adjacent local authorities, a pattern that he argues operates in London and the South-East.

The differences in private and outsider contractor success rate are, in part, related to variation in the extent to which private contractors have demonstrated an interest in bidding in different areas. This is illustrated in the case of local government, in Table 4.3.

This variation in the pattern of interest by service reflects an important difficulty with CCT. The central (positive) role attributed to competition in the policy presupposes that private sector contractors will be enthusiastic to enter the market and that private business will willingly act as a *de*

Table 4.2. DSO success rate in compulsory competitive tendering under the Local Government Act 1988 (England and Wales), 1991–6

Activity	DSO Wins as a % of Contracts	DSO Wins as a % of Value of Contracts
Building Cleaning	46.0	72.7
of which:		
Client Authority	41.5	71.8
Outside DSO	1.1	0.1
School-based DSO	3.4	0.8
Refuse Collection	62.7	65.3
of which:		
Client Authority	62.2	64.8
Outside DSO	0.5	0.5
Other Cleaning	65.2	71.7
of which:		
Client Authority	62.6	71.2
Outside DSO	2.6	0.5
Vehicle Maintenance	75.4	74.1
of which:		
Client Authority	71.2	73.8
Outside DSO	4.2	0.3
Catering	71.5	78.1
(Education and Welfare)		
of which:		
Client Authority	69.6	N.A.
School-based	1.9	N.A.
Catering	60.5	75.1
(Other)		
of which:		
Client Authority	59.6	N.A.
Outside DSO	0.9	N.A.
Grounds Maintenance	56.2	72.3
of which:		
Client Authority	53.3	71.1
Outside DSO	2.9	1.2
Sports and Leisure	79.6	88.0
Management		
of which:		
Client Authority	79.4	N.A.
Outside DSO	0.2	N.A.

Source: Local Government Management Board (1996b).

facto agent of government policy in this respect (although a strict theorist of 'contestability' would only be concerned with the *possibility* of entry). However, there are a number of areas in which private contractors show relatively little interest in pursuing such business. For example, the relatively low level of bids in catering in part stems from a preference on the part of contractors for an arrangement where they are paid a management

Table 4.3. Average number of contractors active at each stage of the tendering process by activity (England and Wales), 1991–6

Activity	Applying	Completing Questionnaire	Invited	Tendering
Building Cleaning	25.4	17.1	8.5	4.9
Refuse Collection	12.8	10.9	6.1	3.6
Other Cleaning	12.4	10.3	6.5	3.5
Vehicle Maintenance	12.0	8.4	5.7	2.8
Catering (Education and Welfare)	7.6	5.8	4.6	2.2
Catering (Other)	11.0	8.1	5.8	2.4
Ground Maintenance	14.2	11.3	7.3	4.3
Sport and Leisure Management	6.8	5.1	3.9	1.8

Source: Local Government Management Board (1996b).

fee and use staff who continue to be employed by the public sector body. Such preferences have been reported in both local authorities and the NHS (Sherman 1985: 806; Walsh and Davies 1993: 71). Walsh and Davies (ibid.: 72) also found that private sector catering firms were unhappy with contract specifications in schools, which limited business to tightly defined periods over part of the year and constrained their discretion over ingredients as a function of 'healthy eating' policies.

Thus, while there is certainly substantial business support for competition and deregulation there is also resistance to this agenda. The preference for management fees in catering reflects, in part, a lack of desire to act as an agent of labour market flexibility. In a similar vein Milne (1993: 309) points out that the Health Care Services Section of the Cleaning and Support Services Association, a key domestic cleaning industry pressure group lobbied (unsuccessfully) for the *continuation* of the Fair Wages Resolution, which required contractors to match NHS terms and conditions of service.

In addition to the variations in DSO success by service area there is also marked regional variation in local government in the extent of DSO success. This is illustrated by reference to the two largest areas of contract work (Local Government Management Board 1996b: 12), refuse collection (Table 4.4) and education and welfare catering (Table 4.5).

Given political differences over CCT it can be anticipated that regional

Table 4.4. DSO success rate by region in refuse collection contracts, under the Local Government Act 1988 (England and Wales), 1991–6

Region	DSO Success Rate: % of Contracts	DSO Success Rate: % of Value of Contracts
Northern	78.6	88.0
Yorkshire and Humberside	83.3	83.1
North-West	68.8	67.2
East Midlands	67.5	74.6
West Midlands	74.5	81.0
East Anglia	63.2	55.1
South-East	40.2	43.3
South-West	45.2	58.7
Wales	97.1	96.0
London	53.1	47.5

Source: Local Government Management Board (1996b).

Table 4.5. DSO success rate by region in education and welfare catering contracts under the Local Government Act 1988 (England and Wales), 1991–6

Region	DSO Success Rate: % of Contracts	DSO Success Rate: % of Value of Contracts
Northern	47.6	68.3
Yorkshire and Humberside	65.5	72.8
North-West	88.9	94.4
East Midlands	64.7	99.5
West Midlands	92.0	96.6
East Anglia	100.0	100.0
South-East	56.4	41.0
South-West	50.0	66.8
Wales	100.0	100.0
London	60.0	75.1

Source: Local Government Management Board (1996b).

variations will to a considerable extent reflect variations in the political control of the authority. This can operate directly, via the authority giving its political support to the DSO, but also indirectly, via private contractors concentrating their bids on more 'sympathetic' authorities. Local Government Management Board data are broadly consistent with such an argument as, in both refuse collection and education and welfare catering private sector interest is higher in regions like South-East England and East Anglia, where authorities may be more inclined to embrace a pro-CCT stance.

The Local Government Management Board survey does not directly show the relationship between DSO or contractor wins and the political control of the local authorities concerned. However, in their survey Walsh and Davies found that, in all services other than Grounds Maintenance, Conservative-controlled authorities were significantly more likely to award contracts to the private sector (see Table 4.6). However, it would be wrong to conclude that Conservative local authorities unproblematically embrace a New Right agenda in this area. Thus, earlier analysis of the relationship between contract wins and political control have shown that regional variations have an independent effect. For example, McGuirk (1991) showed that London was an example of a much more politically polarised approach to CCT than is reflected overall nationally, with Conservative councils in that area adopting a much harder pro-CCT line.

'White-Collar' CCT

The Local Government Management Board survey evidence on CCT in 'white-collar' and professional services gives evidence for market shares of DSOs and outside contractors for *both* contracts covered by CCT and voluntary tendering initiatives by local authorities. Market share evidence is available from three services areas – legal services, construction and property-related services, and housing management – and covers rounds of bidding to November 1996. The results are given in Table 4.7.

Table 4.6. Relationship between authorities awarding contracts to private sector contractors and political control of the authority

Activity	Number of Authorities Surveyed	Authorities Awarding Contracts to Private Contractors	Political Control of Authorities Awarding to Private Sector	
Refuse Collection	29	7	Con.	5
			Lib. Dem.	1
			N.O.C.	1
Building Cleaning	27	7	Con.	4
			Lib. Dem.	1
			N.O.C.	2
Catering (Education and Welfare)	19	2	Con.	2
Catering (Other)	21	4	Con.	3
			Lab.	1
Vehicle Maintenance	25	4	Con.	4
Grounds Maintenance	25	17	Con.	5
			Lab.	6
			Lib. Dem.	3
			N.O.C.	3

Source: Walsh and Davies (1993).

Table 4.7. DSO success rate in voluntary and compulsory competitive tendering in legal services, construction and property-related services and housing management to November 1996 (England, Scotland and Wales)

Activity	DSO Wins as a % of Contracts	DSO Wins as a % of Value of Contracts
Legal Services	76.5%	88.9%
Construction and Property-Related Services	59.7%	64.1%
Housing Management	88.6%	90.2%

Source: Local Government Board (1996b).

The very high success rate of DSOs in housing management has also been confirmed in other survey evidence: thus the Chartered Institute of Housing and Coopers and Lybrand Housing Services found a DSO success rate of 95 per cent in early CCT contracts (Brown and Fraser 1996: 14). In part the variations in DSO success rates, as in the case of manual services, reflect different levels of private sector interest. Thus, whereas the average number of bids in housing management in the Local Government Management Board survey was 1.7 (with an average of 11.6 companies showing an interest), the comparable figures for construction and property-related services were 4.2 and 38.7 respectively (Local Government Management Board 1996b: 90 and 92).

However, it is worth bearing in mind that the early DSO success rate in the manual services area was much higher than that in subsequent rounds, and this pattern might be repeated in white-collar and professional services.

CCT and 'Savings'

Central to arguments in favour of CCT have been the claimed links between the introduction of competition for the services covered and the savings that are said to accrue. In this respect, according to 'contestable-market' justifications for CCT, it is immaterial whether the contract is won in-house or not, since the introduction of competition is seen as creating efficiency gains and thus lower costs. It will be necessary to examine the concept of efficiency later in the argument. However, in this section the aim will be to look at the evidence on 'savings'.

It is worth beginning by making the point that there is no necessary link between competition and lower costs. This is illustrated, in particular, by evidence from the United States on forms of service provision. This provides an interesting contrast, because refuse collection services are provided there in much more varied forms than are encountered in the United Kingdom. Not only are there in-house providers competing with outside contractors, but, in certain areas, there are direct contracts between householders and private collection firms. The latter is, of course, not only a 'competitive' variant, but also, in contrast to tendering, a 'consumerist' variant. A study of refuse collection by Stevens (1984) attempted to control for various features of service delivery such as frequency of collection and the point from which refuse is collected — features that are likely to influence collection costs. She found that 'competitive' arrangements (where householders contract directly with suppliers) were, varying with the size of the city, 26–48 per cent more costly than situations where a private contractor collected all the refuse in a given area. Two reasons were given for the increased cost of this type of provision. One was the fact that contracts were with *particular* customers: thus the collector would not have the franchise to collect from each household in the area, and any economy of scale advantages would thus be lost. The other concerns the transaction costs associated with markets. Thus, Stevens was told by her management respondents that the costs of billing customers and collecting charges accounted for as much as 15 per cent of revenue (ibid.).

If, however, competitive processes *per se* do not guarantee savings, because of the effects of technical problems and administrative costs, this is not a criticism of CT. Thus, it could be argued that CT involves the 'disciplining' effects of competition without the cost drawbacks associated with direct contact between consumers and contractors.

A recent study produces evidence for savings from CCT. Szykmanski's (1996) study of refuse collection compared net annual expenditure figures on this service before and after CCT, adjusting for changes in retail prices (ibid.: 8). Net expenditure was defined as total expenditure minus income generated from selling services such as collection of commercial waste, and included administrative costs as well as payments to contractors (ibid.). The study found that CCT was associated with a cost reduction of around 20 per cent when private contractors won the contract, and 10 per cent when the DSO was successful (ibid.: 10). A difficulty with such comparisons is that cost reductions could be due, in whole or in part, to changes in the service provided. Using CIPFA data Szykmanski found that, in around a quarter of authorities, a fall in service standards did occur, as there was a shift from collection from the back door to kerbside collection (ibid.: 15). However, in other respects, there was evidence of service improvements, with increases in the percentage of authorities providing containers and an increase in the number of authorities providing at least some free of charge (ibid.). However, claims for savings in other areas have proved more problematic.

Thus Paton and Bach point out that a study by Milne (1987) claims savings within the NHS due to greater efficiency as an effect of CCT (Paton and Bach 1990: 266). However, the same study concluded that in three (out of six) contracts studied, 'a major reduction in total expenditure resulted from a change in specification' (Milne 1987: 153).

A further difficulty in defining savings relates to the effects of CT on other service providers. Thus in the case of hospital cleaning it has been argued that the impact of CT is both to define the job more narrowly as an effect of contract specification and to increase the demands of the cleaning task, so that greater areas need to be cleaned in a given working period. As a consequence, tasks previously undertaken by domestic staff tend to be displaced on to nurses. Thus a formal cost saving could result in the transfer of activities to other staff not covered by the contract (Bragg 1988: 336).

Similar problems arise with respect to issues of service quality. Again, a peculiarity of many accounts is that savings are cited in abstraction from any discussion of the impact on service quality. Thus, a general review of the effects of competitive tendering argues that the evidence is 'supportive of the claim that large efficiency gains are possible in the provision of local services' (Parker and Hartley 1990: 14). Yet the same study goes on to argue that 'most of the relevant studies have focused on costs of production though a number have endeavoured to control for changes in the quality of service' (ibid.).

Elsewhere in this book reference has been made to the difficulties involved in assessing service 'quality' in the public sector. Usually, these difficulties have been related to relatively complex services involving elements of professional judgement and a plurality of diverse perspectives from which the services might be judged. It is also likely that such problems will be replicated in white collar/professional services covered by CCT (Walsh 1995: 14). However, 'manual service' CCT does not appear to pose such problems. Thus, for example, two American commentators looking at the characteristics of services 'most frequently contracted by local government' in the United States claim that one of the defining features is that they have 'easily monitored outputs' (Chandler and Feuille 1991: 16).

However, while the problems are not as marked in the services that have been subject to CCT, the contrast can be exaggerated. In their argument for easily measured 'outputs', Chandler and Feuille refer to purely quantitative features, such as numbers of meals served; yet this says nothing about the standard of service provided (ibid.). These difficulties raise problems for claims of 'savings', and these can cut both ways.

Many critics of CCT have argued that the process is regularly accompanied by a decline in service standards. However, again there are difficulties in substantiating such claims. In Paton and Bach's case study of CT in a new District General Hospital a private contractor initially won the contract. However, following dissatisfaction with its performance, the contract was returned 'in-house'. Given that service management at District level in this case were sympathetic to CT, the return in-house is unlikely to be related to any anti-contractor bias. Paton and Bach claim that low staffing levels and training standards contributed not only to poor standards but also to a sharp increase in the spread of infection. They argued that the link to infection was the spread of a micro-organism, methicillin-resistant *Staphyloccus aureus* (MRSA), which can affect patients via infected dust (Paton and Bach 1990: 288). The private contractor was cleaning the hospital over the period February 1985–September 1986. In 1985 nine patients were identified as MRSA-positive, and sixty in 1986, with the peak of infection levels in August 1986. As part of the contract cleaning standards were monitored, and overall performance was expressed as 'satisfactory' inspections as a percentage of the total number of inspections (ibid.: 282). Paton and Bach go on to argue that the most virulent effects of MRSA were felt when the performance level was at its lowest. Furthermore, when the contract was returned in-house cleaning performance improved and the number of MRSA cases fell.

However, there are a number of difficulties in this account. It is not clear what criteria were applied to determine when cleaning was 'satisfactory'. Similarly, Paton and Bach admit that MRSA is not merely spread via infected dust, but also directly from person to person (ibid.: 288), and that 'the difficulties with MRSA cannot be solely attributed to standards of cleaning as screening processes and nursing practices have an impact on the spread of MRSA' (ibid.).

The subjectivity of standards of quality in services subject to CT can also be illustrated from a US study that comes to diametrically opposed conclusions to that of Paton and Bach. A study by Stevens concluded *both* that there were major cost differences between public and private sector after adjusting for levels of service and that 'without exception, differences in service quality were not found to explain differences in service cost' (Stevens 1984: 399 and 401). However, many of the measures of 'quality' used were either highly subjective or reduced quality to simple quantitative measures of activity, as Table 4.8 indicates.

The whole question of savings thus remains an ambiguous one. It is

Table 4.8. Measures of 'level of service' in public services

Service	Criteria for 'Level of Service'
Street sweeping	Sweepings/year
Refuse collection	Frequency and pick-up location
Payroll	% of cheques to salaried employees
Traffic signals	No. of preventive maintenance visits
maintenance	per intersection per year

Source: Stevens (1984).

common to find 'savings' when it is unclear whether the specification has been changed, and definitions of service 'quality' remain problematic.

The Impact on Labour

If the effects of CCT on service cost and quality have defined one of the areas of debate on competitive tendering, the effects on labour have raised issues of an even more directly political form. This issue turns on both an empirical question and an issue involving political values. The empirical question is: if CCT results in cost reductions (this term is chosen to bracket the question of whether such reductions constitute 'savings'), how far are these reductions at the expense of the labour force? The question of political values relates to how the sources of such cost reductions should be viewed. However, before that question can be posed, it is necessary to look at the question of the source of cost reductions.

Some accounts are quite unequivocal on this issue, arguing that cost reductions are derived from the effect of CCT on conditions of employment. Furthermore, such accounts do not exclusively derive from trade union sources, where there may be an interest in stressing the negative effects on workers. For example, the report of a multi-departmental review on competitive tendering in central government, cited earlier, which was favourable to CT, argued that 'Most of the savings from contracting out arise because contractors offer poorer conditions of employment . . . they eliminate costly bonus schemes and overtime working, provide little if any sick pay, and avoid national insurance payments by means of more part-time working' (Treasury 1986: 33). Equally, the report also stressed that contractor cost advantages were not an effect of technical superiority in methods used, but rather of the nature of the regime applied to direct labour: 'The evidence that contractors in the ancillary services are technically ahead of managers in the public sector is patchy. Where the contractors have the edge is in the toughness of their management' (Treasury 1986: 34).

Similar conclusions were reached by a survey of the effects of CT in the United States: 'a good deal of what taxpayers stand to gain from privatization comes at the expense of municipal employees' (Donahue 1989: 144–5).

In the British context there is evidence to support such contentions. Paton and Bach's case study provides valuable material on the cost structure and the sources of contractor cost reductions in hospital cleaning. In this particular service the role of direct labour in the total cost is striking. They found that, of the five bidders for the hospital cleaning contract (one in-house, four private contractors) labour costs accounted for over 90 per cent of the total cost in all cases (Paton and Bach 1990: 277). In this particular exercise the contract was one first by a private contractor. The study shows that the contract price quoted by the winning contractor (for a two-year contract) was nearly 30 per cent lower than the in-house bid. Examining the means by which the contractor could quote such a substantially lower bid Paton and Bach's findings are similar to the conclusions reached by the inter-departmental study of central government departments: the contractor's bid operated with staffing levels, in terms of Whole Time Equivalents, over 20 per cent below the level of the in-house bid (ibid.). This study also examined detailed costings, which showed the importance not just of total staffing levels, but also of the distribution of working hours. Thus, while there was little difference in basic pay rates between the in-house bid and the contractor, the latter reduced or eliminated bonus payments and substituted part-time for full-time labour. The effect of the latter was to bring a large percentage of staff below the national insurance threshold, thus eliminating the employer's national insurance contribution. A corollary of such a policy was that the employees concerned lost any cover from state contributory benefits.

A more recent study from the Equal Opportunities Commission (EOC) examined the impact of CCT on employment levels, pay and other conditions of service in building cleaning, catering in education, refuse collection and sports and leisure management. The employment data were based on seventy-one contracts in thirty-nine local authorities. The study compared pre- and post-contract levels in the services, and found that overall employment levels fell by 21 per cent in the services covered (Escott and Whitfield 1995: 147). In two services, building cleaning and education catering, the overwhelming majority of the workforce was part-time (ibid.: 150). The EOC study also found a pattern of hours reduction amongst part-time staff averaging 25 per cent in the case of cleaning and 16 per cent in the case of catering (ibid.: 153). It is, of course, important to enter the caveat that, given, for example, expenditure control pressures on local authorities, some deterioration in employment conditions might have been expected in any case: thus it is not possible to conclude that the fall was exclusively due to CCT. However, an interesting comparison emerges from the study (though it cannot count as a rigorous 'control') from the fact that the study also examined employment trends in community care services in the same authorities. In this area, which is not subject to such a prescriptive regime as CCT, there was a significant fall in employment (13 per cent), but this was also considerably lower than that for CCT (ibid.).

However, the idea that CCT has been damaging to employment conditions is certainly not a universal view. A British study of costs in refuse collection contrasted costs in local authorities that had put the service out to tender where an in-house win occurred, in cases of tenders won by private contractors, and in authorities that had not put the service out to tender. The data were drawn from 1984, and thus preceded the introduction of *compulsory* competitive tendering. The study attempted to measure differences in 'technical efficiency' between the local authorities concerned. The method seeks to identify a minimum volume of labour and vehicles that will be required to produce the output (for example, 1 tonne of refuse). Service providers operating at this minimum level are defined as 'technically efficient'. Conversely, authorities with inputs in excess of this minimum level diverge from 'technical efficiency'. A simple example can be used to illustrate what would count as an example of 'technical inefficiency'. Assume that two local authorities are providing a similar refuse collection service (e.g. number of collections in a given period, similar levels of spillage, etc.) and in a similar set of circumstances (e.g. proximity to the dump), and that both are using identical capital equipment; and suppose that authority A is operating at the frontier of technical efficiency with the minimum input of labour required, while in contrast, authority B is using more labour than A, and thus diverges from the norm of technical efficiency: it is now equally possible to quantify the gap between the authorities. Cubbin *el al.* use this methodology to examine the effects of CT, and the results are reported in Table 4.9.

Technical efficiency is represented here by a score of 1, and thus the nearer authorities were to 1 the more technically efficient they were. Equally, the technical efficiency gap would be defined by the ratio of mean scores. Thus in the table the 17 per cent efficiency difference is simply derived by expressing the mean technical efficiency score of the tendering and contracting out authorities with that for the not tendered authorities.

Table 4.9. 'Efficiency' comparisons: refuse collection, local authorities in England and Wales, 1984-5

	Mean	'Technical Efficiency' 'Efficiency' differences	Regression-based cost differences
1. All authorities (317)	0.8142	–	–
2. Tendered and contracted out (17)	0.9390	(2 and 3) 17%	22%
3. Not tendered (291)	0.8055	–	–
4. Tendered and retained in-house (9)	0.8608	(2 and 4) 7%	17%

Source: Cubbin *et al*. (1987).

It is important to bear in mind that the technical efficiency comparisons are contrasting variations in inputs in physical, not cost, terms. Thus in the example used above the efficiency standard is not defined by reference to the cost of labour (wages, non-wage benefits, etc.), but rather the volume of labour measured in labour hours. The next stage in the argument is to relate this 'physical efficiency' measure to an overall measure of cost differences between the sets of authorities covered. The cost difference figures are, in fact, drawn from a previous study. As can be seen from the Table, most of the cost difference between tendered and contracted out authorities and not tendered authorities (22 per cent) is 'explained' by the difference in 'technical efficiency'. Cubbin *et al*. draw the following conclusion from this study: 'Some commentators have asserted that the savings are largely the result of pecuniary losses of those in employment through lower wages and fringe benefits. Our results do not support that view. They indicate that for those authorities with private contractors the bulk of the savings can be attributed to improvements in technical efficiency – that is, physical productivity of both men and vehicles' (Cubbin *et al*. 1987: 53–4).

Some American commentators have also concluded that savings from tendering are derived from efficiency gains that are not achieved at the expense of labour. The Stevens study of eight activities supplied by municipal services and outside contractors cited average wage levels for contractors of $1,521 for private contractors and $1,442 for municipal providers.

Part of the reason for the difference in these conclusions relates to the aspects of the impact on the workforce considered. Thus, for example, Cubbin *et al*. are simply concerned with the issue of pay and fringe benefits, and thus have a narrow view of the interests of labour, ignoring such issues as hours of work and corresponding effort levels.

A further reason for discrepancies relates to the use of measures which are misleading. For example, the Stevens comparison of salary figures is an *unweighted* average figure. The significance of this fact can be seen from Table 4.10.

This shows that in only *one* service area, asphalt laying, were municipal wage levels lower than those paid by contractors. Equally, the gains to labour in this case are less significant because this is the most capital-intensive of the processes of the services studied (Donahue 1989: 143).

The significance of labour cost differences in the more labour-intensive activities are illustrated in Donahue's analysis of Stevens' figures on grass-cutting. Stevens found that municipal costs for mowing an acre of grass averaged $81, as against $58 for contractors. However, if contractors had been obliged to offer the same wage levels as municipal contractors their costs would have risen to $73 an acre (Donahue 1989: 144).

These differences are related in part to the range of issues examined and the measures deployed. However, there is also an important question of wider significance raised by studies such as that of Cubbin *et al*. In assessing the impact on at least those workers who remain in employment, this article concentrates simply on the pay ('pecuniary') aspect. Yet this is a peculiarly narrow approach, since it abstracts completely from the nature of the employment regime under which workers do their jobs.

In this respect it is instructive to return to this article and look at what Cubbin *et al*. argue concerning the nature of the efficiency improvements that they claim to have identified. In particular, two features are stressed: it is argued that 'task and finish' payment schemes, where employees are expected to finish a particular 'task' rather than work a given fixed number of hours, have become a 'major impediment to better productivity' (Cubbin

Table 4.10 Labour cost and privatisation in eight municipal services in the United States

Service	Average labour cost for the service as a share of city budget %	Municipal wages for the service relative to contractor wage %
Refuse collection	1.89	115
Turf maintenance	1.40	129
Tree maintenance	0.91	106
Traffic Signal maintenance	0.46	115
Street cleaning	0.41	103
Janitorial services	0.33	140
Asphalt laying	0.26	63

Source: Donahue (1989).

et al. 1987: 54). The basis for this argument is that such schemes can result in an increasing divergence between the original conditions assumed in the time set to complete a round and the conditions currently prevailing: 'The workload associated with a given "round" often diminishes with the passage of time following changes in routes and reductions in the number of units served. However, as payment levels remain the same, this has the effect of raising labour costs over and above the minimum required to collect a fixed volume of refuse' (Cubbin *et al.* 1987: 54).

The second factor that is claimed to be the source of 'efficiency' gains is the ability to vary crew size and rostering practices so that the deployment of crews and vehicles can be 'closely matched to the pattern of demand' (ibid.).

There are a number of points that should be noted in this argument. In themselves, the factors to which the study refers are speculative – they are not based on any attempt by the authors to investigate the actual working practices involved. However, what is striking is how far they refer to a deterioration in the conditions of employment. Thus, in the case of 'task and finish', what is assumed is that contractors will 'tighten up' and expect a given job to be completed in a shorter time. Note, incidentally, the ingenuous treatment of the bonus scheme here. The deliberations of work study engineers here take on a scientific and normative character. Thus a *de facto* loosening of conditions of labour here is treated as a move away from the norm. This fails to appreciate the contentious character of work study, and its inevitably subjective character.

The second feature emphasised also involves a deterioration in the conditions of labour: 'closely matching' labour requirements to levels of demand must involve a greater level of effort and less non-working time for the reduced labour force.

Thus, in their reductionist treatment of the impact on labour Cubbin *et al.* unconsciously reproduce the Hayekian assumption that the labour of the employee, once the contract has been struck, is and should be at the total discretion of the employer. Such a situation is not to be accounted a loss to labour. There is another crucial point here. The technical frontier concept used by Cubbin *et al.* suggests that such changes in the labour regime constitute an advance in 'technical efficiency'. Indeed, this is quite consistent with the concept itself, since a reduction in employment levels with a given level of output maintained represents such an 'efficiency' advance. Yet there is a paradoxical aspect to such a conceptual treatment. The claim that an efficiency advance has been achieved is derived from the idea that a given output has been achieved with fewer inputs. Yet these inputs are defined purely in terms of measures such as labour hours, abstracting from what happens in such hours. Yet, central to such an argument is, to use a term cited earlier, the role of 'tough' management in coercing labour to increase its input.

It is also worth noting that such abridgements to the freedoms of workers at the workplace are a characteristic of the contracting out and tendering process in the United States. Thus, Table 4.11 shows some systematic differences between municipal agencies and private contractors as employers.

It is important to bear in mind that the political issue of the effects of the policy on employment conditions is often not confronted directly. In many discussions of CT the whole issue is reduced to one of whether tendering is associated with lower costs at a given level of service. Indeed, this is the dominant standpoint adopted in contemporary *economic* analysis of CCT. In these analyses the producers of the service and their interests have virtually vanished from view.

A good illustration of this type of argument is provided by a debate on the sources of CT cost reductions between Ganley and Grahl (1988) on one side and Domberger *et al.* (1988) on the other.

Ganley and Grahl make a number of points similar to those made above with respects to the cost to labour involved in CCT: that changes in working practices under CT and CCT have been made under implicit or explicit threats of redundancy; that the costs to labour cannot be reflected simply in financial costs.

In response to these contentions Domberger *et al.* produce a rather confused argument. On the one hand, they seek to refute Ganley and Grahl's argument that CT cost reductions are not made at the expense of the labour force. The argument is somewhat puzzling, since they admit

Table 4.11. Differences between employment practices between municipal agencies and contractors in a sample of cities in the United States

	Cities using contractors	Cities using municipal agencies
Workforce unionised	20.0%	48.1%
Average age of workers	32.1 years	36.1 years
Vacation days per worker	10.1	14.0
Foremen with power to dismiss worker	53.7%	16.0%
Written reprimands used	33.8%	72.5%
Formal staff meetings held	53.8%	81.5%

Source: Stevens (1984).

that CCT will involve 'some redistribution of benefits from producers to consumers' (Domberger *et al.* 1988: 88).

This implicit view that labour *does* lose as a result of CCT is reinforced later when Domberger *et al.* attack Ganley and Grahl's argument on normative grounds: 'it seems likely that public sector monopoly provision enabled monopoly rents to be expropriated by the work force' and 'if it turns out that the best case that can be made for the retention of a public sector monopoly in refuse collection is that it provides the basis for expropriation of monopoly rents, then this seems to us to be compelling argument *in favour* of the introduction rather than the reverse (Domberger *et al.* 1988: 89; emphasis in the original).

However, this appears to lead to a rather extraordinary conclusion. The majority of the workforce that has been affected by CCT is either unskilled or semi-skilled, and often poorly paid. Surveys of groups like contract cleaners have generally found that they are all badly paid, but that unionised cleaners enjoy better rates (e.g. *Bargaining Report* 1990: 12). This is the kind of 'rent' that, according to this argument, ought to be removed. It is true that the protections accorded by the absence of con-testable markets will not help the group still subject to the effects of competition. Quite reasonably, it might then be argued that, if the aim is to protect all such low-paid employees, then this calls for regulation rather than public sector monopoly. However, this abstracts from the fact that the experience of labour market regulation is that legal rights do not tend to be effective in the absence of collective bargaining (Brown 1991: 219). It is, thus, difficult to reconcile at least cost-saving-oriented CCT with employment protection via a regulatory framework, since the CCT process tends to involve de-unionisation, as was demonstrated earlier.

There is also a more general political point with respect to the operation of CCT in local government. As was argued at the beginning of the chapter, the Audit Commission has argued that CT can be treated as a non-political tool. However, this assumes that it has no implications for broader cor-porate policies. Yet, for instance, the EOC study shows that not only has CCT been associated with job losses, but their effect is markedly uneven on a gender basis. Thus, comparing pre- and post-contract employment levels, women's employment fell 22 per cent in the services covered, but men's 12 per cent (Escott and Whitfield 1995: 152). The same study also found that, while employment levels had dropped sharply in refuse collection (22 per cent), with a predominantly male labour force half the DSOs studied had improved their bonus rates (ibid.: 159). By contrast, bonus payments to building cleaners, mainly women, had declined in all cases (ibid.). Such examples illustrate the questionable character of arguments like those of the Audit Commission. It means, as the EOC study points out, that local authorities can simultaneously be operating an equal opportunities policy which may be being undermined by the effects of CCT. To exclude CCT from the ambit of political debate is thus to have an impoverished and attenuated concept of the political.

–5–

Determining Public Sector Pay: Prescription and Practice

In this chapter we shall consider the approach taken by successive Conservative governments to the determination of pay in the public sector. With public sector pay representing roughly 60 per cent of current spending on goods and services (Bailey and Trinder 1989: 1), pay settlements in the sector have a major impact on total public spending. A concern with the latter became an issue of ideological significance for the Conservatives. With the shift to the right in the British Conservative Party in the 1970s, discussed in Chapter 1, the public sector became increasingly seen in negative terms. For example, criticising what he saw as the effects of public spending in the era of the 'middle way', Keith Joseph argued: 'The public sector, including central and local government, and more accurately named the state-sector or wealth-eating sector . . . spread like bindweed at the expense of the non-state sector, the wealth-creating sector, strangling and threatening to destroy what it grew upon' (cited in Eccleshall 1990: 236). This was in line with a view that had become increasingly fashionable among academics and journalists. A much-quoted work was that of Robert Bacon and Walter Eltis, *Britain's Economic Problem: Too Few Producers* (1978). These authors argued that the growth of the non-marketed sector of the economy drew resources (both financial and personnel) away from the marketed sector, that is the production of goods and services for sale. Yet it was the latter that was responsible for the creation of wealth. By the 1970s, a declining marketed sector was supporting a bloated non-marketed sector. It took only a small step to identify the latter as the cause of Britain's economic decline, a view clearly expressed in the Conservative Party's first White Paper on public spending when they came into office in 1979: 'Public expenditure is at the heart of Britain's economic difficulties. Over the years public spending has been increased on assumptions about economic growth which have not been achieved. If this continued our economy would be threatened with endemic inflation and economic decline' (Treasury 1979: 1).

Thus the *economic* desirability of shrinking the public sector in order to reduce inflation, encourage enterprise and efficiency and hence create the conditions for economic growth and employment was established as a central tenet of the philosophy of that and subsequent Conservative governments of the 1980s and 1990s (**5.1**). A policy of reducing public expenditure has implications for employment in the public sector: a really radical reduction in public spending would involve sharply cutting the number of public sector employees; and at first sight the figures on public sector employment seem to indicate that successive Conservative governments *did* pursue such a radical approach. The estimated workforce in employment in the UK in 1981 was 24.4 million, of whom 17.3 million (70 per cent) were in the private sector, and the remaining 7.1 million in the public sector. By 1995 the numbers employed by the public sector had fallen by 1.9 million (Hughes 1996: Table 4). This was due predominantly to the privatisation policies pursued in respect of nationalised industries and public corporations, the impact of CCT on local authorities, and reclassifications – for example, in respect of local authority education employment, where new universities, higher education institutions, further education colleges and grant-maintained schools are now classified as being in the private sector, not the public sector, although of course these institutions continue to remain publicly funded.

Even taking these changes into account, overall employment in the social welfare areas has remained virtually constant into the 1990s, with 20 per cent of the total workforce in employment continuing to work in the public sector.

Thus, if reluctantly, Conservative governments in the 1990s continued to remain substantial direct employers of labour and also responsible for funding a significant proportion of employment in the public sector as a whole. In line with other governments, they turned their attention to curbing the growth in the volume of public sector pay (OECD 1994). In this chapter we will examine how they discharged this role of paymaster to the public sector. The chapter is divided into three sections. The first will explore the Conservative philosophy on pay and employment, contrasting this with the pattern of pay determination that was *in situ* in 1979, and the challenges to this inheritance will be the focus of the second section; in both these sections it will be argued that the Conservatives operated with a norm that stressed the desirability of more individualised forms of pay determination. The third section will consider in detail one of the clearest manifestations of this approach, namely performance-related pay. The chapter ends with an a discussion of the overall effects of Conservative policy on public sector pay.

The Megaw Report (*Report of an Inquiry into Civil Service Pay* 1982), the Review Bodies on Doctors' and Dentists' Remuneration, the Review Bodies for Nursing Staff, Midwives and Health Visitors and the Interim Advisory Committee on School Teachers' Pay and Conditions (1988–91), which was succeeded by the School Teachers' Review Body (STRB) in 1992, provide forums where government could express its ideas on pay determination. The reports of these bodies have, therefore, been used as exemplary texts throughout the chapter.

Conservative Philosophy on Pay and Employment

In the argument developed so far it has been pointed out that pay determination in the public sector was relevant for the Conservatives in terms of the economic goal of controlling public expenditure. It was also significant for broader ideological reasons. As we saw in Chapter 1, concomitant with the rejection of Keynesian political economy was an alternative diagnosis of unemployment, where changes in the supply side and in particular the labour market were viewed as crucial if unemployment was to be reduced and inflation controlled. Such objectives were themselves congruent with the political philosophy that was embodied, in particular, in the Conservative legislation on labour law, which was virulently anti-collectivist.

The implications of these ideological concerns for employment policy can be seen in three White Papers, *Employment: Challenge for the Nation* (Department of Employment 1985) and *Employment for the 1990s* (Employment Department 1988), and *People, Jobs and Opportunities* (Employment Department 1992), which provide a clear statement of Conservative philosophy in the areas of pay and employment.

Eschewing the Keynesian approach to employment and unemployment, the 1985 White Paper states that the role of government in maintaining full employment is 'inescapably limited' to developing a framework of economic and industrial policy, removing obstacles to the creation of jobs and tackling the unemployment problems of groups with special needs (Department of Employment 1985: para. 4.2). For the Conservatives, 'the biggest single cause of high unemployment is the failure of our jobs market, the weak link in our economy'; 'the supply side is crucial, and that needs an efficient labour market' (ibid.: paras. 5.2 and 5.4). It is the responsibility of management, employees and the education system 'to ensure that the supply of labour meets demand in quality, quantity, cost and flexibility' (ibid.).

These themes are developed in the subsequent White Paper, where the barriers to employment are identified as industrial relations, pay and training. Trade union activity in the 1970s, it is argued, adversely affected labour costs, productivity and jobs; in short, such activity was synonymous with creating unemployment. For the future unions must accept that the job prospects of their members will be improved only 'by linking pay to the performance of the businesses for which they work and to local labour market conditions' (Employment Department 1988: para. 2.12).

Unlike the earlier White Paper, which says little on pay beyond reiterating familiar government themes of the 1980s, such as the view that government-imposed pay policies do not work and that hence pay bargaining is a matter solely for employers and employees, the institutions and the criteria by which pay is determined are a central concern of the 1988 White Paper. Following the by now expected genuflections to 'excessive pay increases' and 'pay settlements remaining too high' comes a key statement of the changes required in pay bargaining if future employment growth is to be secured. Thus the 'going rate', 'comparability' and 'cost of living increases' are attacked as 'outmoded concepts' (Employment Department 1988: para. 3.5). There were also criticisms of practice on both the timing of settlements and the level of bargaining; the assumption that pay should automatically rise annually was attacked; national pay bargaining was seen as engendering rigidities in the labour market (**5.2**).

Comparability was objectionable from two distinct points of view. It suggested that at least an element in pay determination should be a concern with equity. However, this raised the spectre of 'social justice' considerations entering into questions of pay determination. The rejection of such a position was an aspect of the Hayekian programme that had been embraced by the Conservatives, as instanced by the opposition to incomes policy minimum wage legislation and modification and subsequent abolition of the Wages Councils (**5.3**). In addition, comparability principles linked pay to the type of job performed, not to any measure of *performance* in the job. This was seen as inflationary, in that it encouraged a divorce between pay increases and productivity improvements. This was also the basis for opposition to the concept of a 'rate for the job'. 'Paying the rate for the job' assumes that all workers will be treated in a uniform way, and thus militates against rewarding individual performance and productivity. The extension of this form of argument also had implications for what was seen as the appropriate level at which bargaining should take place.

The White Paper put forward a particularly critical view of national pay bargaining. It argued that such agreements were a source of rigidity, in that they prevented employers from adjusting wages to take account of different circumstances. It was further assumed that national agreements tended to inflate wages by constraining employers from reducing pay in areas of high unemployment, and thus restricted the creation of job opportunities in such 'labour markets'. The preferred alternative would be decentralisation of pay bargaining (defined in geographical terms).

Underlying these arguments was a set of principles defining how pay determination should ideally operate. Of central importance here was the conception of an *individualised* employment relationship. This conception was most clearly set out in the 1992 White Paper. Thus, the centralised industry-wide collective bargaining and Government-imposed pay limits of the 1960s and 1970s are condemned because they 'resulted in a strong trend towards identical pay increases, regardless of individual employees' contributions to the organisations for which they worked' (Employment Department 1992: para. 4.3). The initiatives taken since 1979 to reverse this trend – the rejection of incomes policies, measures to check trade union power, steps to encourage profit-related pay and making pay more responsive to local needs – are noted (ibid.: para. 4.4). The result was claimed to be a move away from collective bargaining to decentralising pay to local levels and individually negotiated pay (ibid.: para. 4.5). 'Pay determination is increasingly responsive to individual effort' (ibid.: para. 4.6). A priority for the 1990s was to embed these changes in the public sector (**5.4**).

As was indicated in Chapter 1, the focus on an individualised employment relationship was central to Conservative legislation on individual and collective labour law: reducing the scope of individual employment rights and removing state protection from the employee and legislation on the trade unions narrowed the range of collective action via mechanisms such as 'enterprise confinement'. The attack on what were seen as prevailing patterns of wage determination was of a piece with such a stance. Thus linking pay with 'performance' meant that it was possible to move in the direction of distinct individual pay rates. The other arguments point in the same direction: decentralised bargaining is again a potential force for differentiation; the link to political anti-collectivism is clear.

The general approach to pay determination favoured by the Conservatives thus suggested a number of objectives: an attack on collectivist *institutions* of pay determination; an attack on *criteria* of pay determination that involved concerns of social justice or other impediments to 'flexible' and differentiated 'adjustments' of the labour market.

In the private sector Conservative attempts to advance such an approach were necessarily limited. After all, pay determination there was a matter of negotiation between employers and employees. Government could exhort private employers to follow the prescribed road, but that was as far as they could go. In contrast, in the public sector the government was either the direct employer or, where it was not, could exercise a crucial influence on pay determination. In the rest of this chapter the aim is to examine how the government used its power as paymaster. However, if one is to set this in context, it is necessary to look at the pattern of pay determination in the public sector when the Conservatives came into office in 1979.

Public Sector Pay Determination: 1979

Institutions

The 1979 Conservative government inherited a number of different arrangements for determining pay in the public sector: collective bargaining, review bodies, indexation and *ad hoc* pay inquiries. The majority of public sector employees had their pay determined by national collective bargaining, on either the Burnham or the Whitley systems. The former, for teachers, dated from 1945, and was a tripartite structure, with representatives of local authorities, central government and the unions. The role of the Minister of Education was to approve the settlements agreed by the employers and unions, which then had statutory force. The balance of power in this structure changed somewhat with the Remuneration of Teachers Act 1965. Under this Act central government secured a veto over the global sums available for teachers' pay and a weighted vote over the distribution of any award (Saran and Sheldrake 1988 : 13). The Act also introduced the principle of unilateral arbitration in the case of disputes.

The Whitley system originated in 1916 as a mechanism for improving employer–employee relationships in the engineering industry; it was extended to local authorities and the public utilities in 1918, and by 1979 covered civil servants, local authority employees, other than the police and teachers, and NHS employees, with the exception of doctors and dentists (Bailey and Trinder 1989: 16). Although the structure of Whitley Councils varies for the different groups, Bailey and Trinder have argued that Whitleyism itself is characterised by a number of principles: joint agreement between employers and employees on pay and conditions; negotiations between those two parties; collective bargaining within an agreed framework; and procedures for conciliation or arbitration (ibid.: 16–17).

Review bodies are appointed by the government, but are independent of it. They make recommendations on the size of the pay increase for particular occupational groups: the government is then free to accept or reject the recommendations or delay payment by staging the awards. The review bodies for the armed forces, doctors and dentists, and senior civil servants, senior officers of the armed forces and the judiciary were established in 1971 under the Heath government.

A pay formula was introduced for the police in 1978. This linked the rise in pay to the rate of increase in the average earnings index.

Finally, in the 1970s, governments resorted to *ad hoc* pay inquiries for specific groups of employees: for example, the Houghton Report on non-university teachers, 1974; the Halsbury Report on nurses, also in 1974; the Edmund Davies Report on the police, 1978; and the Clegg Commission on Pay Comparability, 1979–81. These inquiries usually followed pay freezes or incomes policies, and were attempts to circumvent industrial action.

Criteria

Until 1981, a key principle for determining pay in the public sector was that of 'fair comparison'. The seminal statement of this principle was that of the Priestley Inquiry into Civil Service Pay in 1955. Priestley was critical of its predecessor, the Tomlin Committee (1929–31), which had argued that the basis of remuneration for civil servants should be what was necessary to recruit and retain them without loss of keenness and efficiency (**5.5**), arguing that the State had an obligation to remunerate its employees fairly (**5.6**). Internal relativities could be used to supplement the primary principle of 'fair comparison'.

Priestley also outlined a methodology for determining civil service pay in the future: namely the establishment of a Pay Research Unit, which would have the task of comparing individual jobs inside and outside the civil service and reporting (to the government and civil service unions) on the actual rates of pay and all other relevant conditions of employment for the comparable jobs outside the civil service. This information would be the basis for the annual pay negotiations. (A fuller discussion of the pay research system can be found in Chapters 2 and 3 of the Megaw Report of 1982). Priestley's recommendations were put into effect by the government, and the pay research system, albeit with some modifications, continued until 1981.

Fair comparison became a significant influence in determining the pay of many other groups of public sector employees, not only civil servants, from the 1950s onwards. However, the concept experienced a number of challenges. For example, the National Board for Prices and Incomes (NBPI), created in 1965 with the objective of stimulating efficiency in

British industry, argued that comparability was incompatible with such an objective, which required pay to be linked with productivity (Thomson and Beaumont 1978: 55). The Board produced several reports in the late 1960s that identified different types of payment by results systems and merit bonuses schemes (e.g. NBPI 1968), and, in a general report of 1969 on the subject of salary structures, noted different mechanisms for linking pay progression to performance and the ways in which organisations could distinguish between the performance of different individuals (NBPI 1969). In addition, the incomes policies of the Labour Government in 1965 and the Social Contract of 1975 either downgraded or formally suspended all official comparability schemes. However, neither the NBPI nor incomes policies succeeded in eliminating the importance of fair comparison. Thus, by 1969, the Board accepted that there was little alternative to its use in setting the pay of many public servants (Brown and Rowthorn 1990: 9). Similarly the Labour government in its Social Contract of 1975 rejected comparability, but in 1978 accepted the result of an inquiry into police pay that recommended that it be indexed to average national earnings (Bailey and Trinder 1989: 31–2). Following the 'Winter of Discontent' of 1979, the then Labour Government 'expressed a readiness to see a greater role for measuring pay and conditions (in public services) by making comparisons with pay and effort in other occupations. Government has a responsibility both to be fair to public service employees and to avoid arrangements which could in themselves prove inflationary. Comparability studies must therefore be made in a systematic and thorough manner' (Hansard, vol. 963, col. 1252).

To undertake this work, a Standing Commission on Pay Comparability (Clegg) was established. Clegg produced ten reports in all, covering teachers, nurses and midwives, and NHS ancillary staff, among others. While not denying the relevance of labour supply and efficiency, Clegg was committed to the notion of 'fair comparison', as is demonstrated by its method of working, which attempted to use job-for-job comparisons. In all cases, Clegg recommended substantial increases in pay: e.g. 16.9 per cent for local authority and NHS ancillaries, and the equivalent of 18.2 per cent of the wage bill for teachers, in order to restore their wage levels to those of groups undertaking comparable work.

Thus public sector pay determination in 1979 was characterised by a mixture of collective bargaining, especially at national level, indexation, and the influence of recommendations by third parties, namely, review bodies, with comparability as a key principle. As already argued, such institutions and principles did not correspond with Conservative economic ideology in the 1980s.

Challenging the Inheritance

Changing the Philosophy

Comparability. The Conservative opposition had agreed to honour the findings of the Clegg Commission if there was a change of government following the 1979 election. The Conservative government did indeed honour the reports, which appeared after its return to office in 1979, but then abolished the Commission in 1981.

The events surrounding the 1981 civil service pay negotiations were the catalyst for a further attack on fair comparison. In August 1980, the Government informed the unions that economic circumstances required tight constraint on public expenditure, and this would influence the 1981 pay settlement. No agreed settlement was forthcoming over the following months. Thus, in October, the government withdrew from the pay agreements and pay research procedures for the 1981 settlement. Subsequent attempts to reach a settlement based on cash limits were unsuccessful, and the civil service unions took selective industrial action from March to July 1981, when a settlement was reached. This period of industrial activity was accompanied by the appointment of the Megaw Inquiry into Civil Service Pay in June 1981.

Megaw was critical of the 'fair comparison' principle espoused by Priestley. It argued that the pay research system introduced after Priestley was flawed in practice, pointing to such defects as the difficulties of finding comparator jobs in the private sector, the inflexibility and generosity of a formula that linked civil service pay to the median rate of pay of 'good employers' in the private sector, and the undervaluation of the index-linked pensions of civil servants and their relative job security. In addition, Megaw maintained that adherence to Priestley's primary principle of 'fair comparison' underestimated the importance of other factors such as internal relativities, recruitment and retention, financial and economic constraints, and management needs (**5.7**).

Taking account of both the adverse criticisms of the pay research system and the changed economic circumstances of the preceding years, namely, high levels of inflation and unemployment, Megaw recommended that in future, the governing principle for civil servants' pay should be what was necessary 'to recruit, retain and motivate them to perform efficiently the duties required of them at an appropriate level of competence' (ibid.: para. 91) – in fact a return to the Tomlin principles rejected by Priestley. In addition, internal relativities should play a more significant role than under the Priestley system (ibid.: Ch. 8).

The government pursued its attack on comparability by consistently urging the annual review bodies both for nursing staff and midwives (established in 1983, see below p. 127) and for doctors and dentists to reject it as a principle of pay determination (**5.8**).

The government also favoured market forces in setting teachers' pay in the period after the abolition of Burnham in 1987. Each of the remits provided by the Secretary of State for Education for Burnham's successor, the Interim Advisory Committee on School Teachers' Pay and Conditions, directed the Committee to have regard to 'The Government's view that school teachers' pay and conditions of service should be such as to enable the maintained school system to recruit, retain and motivate sufficient teachers of the required quality both nationally and at local level' (Interim Advisory Committee 1991: 7).

Decentralisation. The antagonism of Conservative governments to national pay bargaining has already been documented: their preferred alternative was for the decentralisation of pay, which in turn embodied two distinct ideas: (1) the delegation of decisions on pay to the unit of employment, e.g. school or hospital; and (2) the introduction of regional variations in pay. The former is usually linked to problems of recruitment and retention of staff in a competitive labour market, and encompasses the possibility of pay rates that are *higher* than those nationally agreed. The latter also viewed nationally agreed pay rates as a constraint, assuming that they were usually based on the 'going rate' in London and the South-East, and as such were assumed to contribute to high unemployment in areas of the country where the supply of labour exceeds the demand for it. Thus the objective of regional pay is to *reduce* overall pay levels.

In the Megaw Inquiry, the government (or rather individual departments) rehearsed their arguments on decentralisation and regional pay (**5.9** and **5.10**).

Support for decentralised pay can also be found in the Health Department's evidence to the Review Body for Nursing Staff, Midwives and Health Visitors from 1987 onwards (**5.11**). Although there have been changes of approach over the years, each proposed scheme has been justified by reference to one or more of the following reasons: local pay determination would enable Trusts to exercise control over how they rewarded their staff; permit services to react to the changing needs of patients; and enable Trusts to respond more flexibly to issues of recruitment and retention (Review Body for Nursing Staff, Midwives and Health Visitors 1996: para. 34).

The issue of local pay was of less concern for Health Departments in respect of doctors and dentists, and it was not until 1993 that the Departments announced their intentions to move away from centrally determined pay for NHS doctors and dentists, which would enable pay levels to reflect differences in labour markets; and that they were particularly keen to see greater scope for geographical pay (Review Body on Doctors' and Dentists' Remuneration 1994: paras. 19–20).

The Secretary of State for Education required each of the Interim Advisory Committees to consider what modifications should be made to the system of selective payments to increase flexibility, recruitment and retention, for example, changes to Incentive Allowances with respect to shortages of teachers in key subjects in particular geographical areas (see, for example, Interim Advisory Committee 1990: para. 1.4).

Paying for Performance.   Again, it is in the Megaw Inquiry that the government provided a statement of the government's philosophy on performance-related pay (PRP) as this applies to the public sector, in this instance the civil service (**5.12**).

PRP can be defined as a means of 'providing for periodic increases in pay which are incorporated into basic salary or wages and which result from assessments of individual performance and personal value to the organisation. Such increases may determine the rate of progression through pay scales or ranges. They are expressed either as percentages of basic pay, as pre-determined (variable) cash increments or as unconsolidated lump sums' (Incomes Data Services/Institute of Personnel Management, quoted in Murlis 1987: 29). Although the details of schemes vary, all have common elements: a system of performance appraisal and assessment and a means of translating performance assessment into financial rewards (or penalties).

Three major arguments are usually put forward for adopting PRP schemes: they are seen as operating to solve recruitment and retention problems in areas (both geographical and specialist) where there are severe shortages of staff; they offer an additional means of motivating staff, differentiating reward according to effort and thus producing a 'fairer', more equitable system of pay; and they are seen as a means of securing organisational change (Kessler 1994).

The fact that there has been continuity on this issue of policy is demonstrated by the commitment to PRP in the *Citizen's Charter*, which states the government's intention of linking pay in the public sector to a person's individual performance (**5.13**). The precise proportion of pay to be linked to performance is not specified. This commitment to linking pay and performance is reiterated in the remit given by the Government to various Review Bodies (e.g. STRB 1992).

Changing the Practice. Successive Conservative governments thus developed a distinctive ideology in respect of public sector pay determination, when seen in the context of the criteria and institutions that they inherited: as they have been in office from 1979 onwards, they have had ample opportunity to effect changes that corresponded with their ideological position, and it is these changes that will now be considered.

At first glance it does appear that public sector pay has undergone significant changes: performance-related pay schemes were introduced for civil servants, NHS employees and teachers. Local authority employers also use such schemes. Major groups of public sector employees were removed from collective bargaining. Burnham was disbanded in 1987 and replaced by the Interim Advisory Committee, which had similarities to a Review Board but was required to make its recommendations within a global figure given by the Secretary of State. In 1992, the Interim Advisory Committee was itself superseded by the School Teachers' Review Body. Nurses, Midwives, Health Visitors and Professions Allied to Medicine were removed from the arena of free collective bargaining in 1983, with the establishment of their Review Body. Several local authorities removed either single or several groups of employees from national agreements. The abolition of the Clegg Commission on Comparability in 1980 neatly indicates the government's view of comparability in public sector wage determination. Reforms of both the NHS and Education have introduced structural changes that either enable organisations to leave national pay bargaining (the establishment of NHS Trusts and grant-maintained schools) or at least introduce greater flexibility into pay units (with local management of schools (LMS)). NHS Trusts are allowed to negotiate their own pay rates and conditions of service for all staff, including junior doctors. Grant-maintained schools will be able to do the same if they choose to withdraw from the scope of the School Teachers' Review Body. With the introduction of LMS, local authorities must delegate a substantial and (increasing) proportion of the schools budget to Governing Bodies, who are responsible for appointing and paying staff.

Following the policy initiative announced in the 1988 Cabinet Office paper 'Next Steps', most civil service departments have been constituted as Executive Agencies. The Civil Service (Management Functions) Act 1992 delegated pay and grading to the departments and agencies, allowing them to design their own grading systems and award salary increases, thus linking pay to individual circumstances and labour markets (**5.14**).

By April 1996, there were in excess of 150 separate civil service bargaining units (*Pay and Benefits Bulletin* 1996: 5).

Thus the picture sketched above is one that would support the view that Conservative governments have transformed public sector pay determination in line with their ideology. However, a closer consideration of these changes does not necessarily sustain this picture.

Comparability Lives.   As has already been noted, Conservative governments eschewed comparability in the sense of social justice, preferring that rates of pay should be determined by market forces. Thus the Megaw Inquiry, and the annual Review Bodies on Doctors' and Dentists' Remuneration and for Nursing Staff, Midwives and Health Visitors, and later the Interim Advisory Committee for Teachers and its successor, the School Teachers' Review Body, were urged to link pay to what was necessary to recruit, retain and motivate staff. Each of these bodies, however, recognised that such objectives would oblige employers to use *external comparisons* in setting pay levels for civil servants, doctors, nurses and teachers. Thus, while Megaw agreed that the key principle for civil servants should be what was needed to recruit, retain and motivate them, the Inquiry also argued that this principle involved a form of comparability, in that recruitment and retention had to be underpinned by pay increases and levels of remuneration that 'broadly match those available in the private sector for staff undertaking jobs with *comparable job weight*' (*Report of an Inquiry into Civil Service Pay* 1982: para. 101; our emphasis). Not only did Megaw support the use of external comparisons, but the reference to assessment by reference to 'job weight' would appear to involve a commitment to job evaluation, the approach that underpinned the pay research method developed by Priestley.

The 1983 Review Body on Doctors' and Dentists' Remuneration argued that, while doctors' and dentists' position in the earnings hierarchy should not be fixed, 'we need to have proper regard to their relative position in the hierarchy' (Review Body on Doctors' and Dentists' Remuneration 1983: para. 12); and it added that one of the considerations of the review was that 'recommendations should not involve any significant change in the existing relationship between doctors' and dentists' earnings and those at comparable levels of skill, responsibility and workload in the economy' (ibid.). These views were reiterated the following year. While the Review Body did not subscribe to any concept of comparison that would entail more or less automatic indexation of pay, it maintained that 'Comparisons with remuneration outside the NHS must continue to have some part to play in our considerations' (Review Body on Doctors' and Dentists'

Remuneration 1984: para. 12). In 1987, the Review Body suggested that external comparisons were not irrelevant to the work of a Review Body that compensates to some extent for the absence of an independent labour market. Recruitment to and retention in the professions within their remit could be seriously affected if they were not properly rewarded (Review Body on Doctors' and Dentists' Remuneration 1987: para. 26).

The Review Body on Doctors' and Dentists' Remuneration continued to acknowledge the importance of comparability into the 1990s (**5.15**). Furthermore, the 1994, 1995 and 1996 Review Body reports found that the remuneration of groups covered by their remit were broadly in line with comparator groups, with the 1996 report outlining the methodology by which it reached this conclusion (**5.16**).

The Review Body for Nursing Staff, Midwives and Health Visitors, while accepting that it had to take account of the country's economic circumstances and financial constraints, argued that such concerns should not be allowed to override all other considerations (Review Body for Nursing Staff, Midwives and Health Visitors: 1984; 1987; 1989); identification of shortages in geographical areas and particular specialities exposed recruitment and retention principles as unsatisfactory (Review Body for Nursing Staff, Midwives and Health Visitors: 1987; 1988; 1991). On three occasions – 1985, 1987 and 1991 – the Review Body expressed disquiet about the idea that market forces could be used to determine pay in a situation where the NHS was a near-monopoly employer (**5.17**).

The Review Body frequently commissioned the Office of Manpower Economics to carry out surveys of relative pay levels, and such survey results were one of the factors that they considered in making their recommendations. Comparability studies led the Review Body to comment on at least two occasions that levels of remuneration for nurses were modest (Review Body for Nursing Staff, Midwives and Health Visitors 1987; 1988).

Comparability between the pay of nursing staff and similar occupations has continued to be a feature of the Review Body Reports on Nursing Staff. While they have accepted that recruitment and retention were key considerations in respect of comparability, they have also argued that if remuneration of nursing staff were to fall too far out of line with these similar occupations, this could effect morale and motivation, because of feelings of unfairness. In addition, this remuneration should be 'felt fair' not only by staff but by the community as a whole (**5.18**).

Similarly, the Interim Advisory Committee did not disregard comparability. While not advocating automatic rises in line with movements in pay levels outside teaching, its second report in 1989 commented that if increases were below the rate of those enjoyed by other groups, this would contribute to low morale within the profession, a view reiterated in its third report (Interim Advisory Committee 1990: para. 4.5). The fourth and final report of the Interim Advisory Committee pursued this theme: 'While teachers cannot expect automatic comparability with other groups, or periods, neither can they be considered in isolation from the rest of the economy' (Interim Advisory Committee 1991: para. 7.10). Each of the reports from the School Teachers' Review Body (with the exception of the first in 1992) compares teachers' earnings over time with those of non-manual employees in general (STRB 1993: para. 24; 1994: para. 30; 1995: para. 39; 1996: para. 35).

Neither has comparability been ignored by the government, whose evidence to the Review Bodies usually gives a detailed overview, from a variety of sources, on settlements in the private sector – 'a clear sign that the Government does not really believe that public sector pay bargaining can proceed without reference to what is happening in the private sector' (*Income Data Services Report* 1995: 25).

Conservative governments retained indexation for both the police and fire service, with pay rises for the former continuing to be linked to median pay increases for non-manual employees in the private sector, while for the latter the link is to the upper quartile of male manual earnings. In such cases comparability is explicit.

Decentralisation Rules? From the earlier discussion, it would appear that significant changes had been made by the government to the practices of public sector pay determination with respect to the decentralisation of pay. However, two dimensions of decentralisation were identified: delegation of decisions on pay to the unit of employment and the introduction of regional variations in pay. On the latter, the government has made no progress.

Megaw considered and rejected regional pay (**5.19**).

The first Interim Advisory Committee on Teachers' Pay was asked to consider regional/local pay and subject differentiation of pay. They rejected such proposals out of hand, pointing out that teaching was a collegiate activity, with teachers acting as a team: any variations in pay, beyond some informal differentiation to take account of recruitment and retention needs, would undermine such a concept. Other arguments were also advanced against the introduction of variations (**5.20**). The Interim Advisory Committee did not change its views in subsequent reports. The School Teachers' Review Body has not ever considered the issue.

The Review Body for Nursing Staff, Midwives and Health Visitors considered the proposals put forward by the Health Departments for decentralised pay, some of which contained a regional differentiation element, but was invariably critical of them (see for example Review Body for Nursing Staff, Midwives and Health Visitors 1994: 11–12).

However, it may be that government departments have not directly pursued regional/local variations in pay because they can introduce it via the other dimension of decentralisation, namely delegation of pay bargaining or determination to the unit of employment. Again, it should be noted that Megaw was critical of this dimension of decentralisation (**5.21**).

Under LMS, LEAs are required to delegate to the Governors of each secondary school and primary school the annual budget for running the school (see Chapter 3 for details). Thus the 'Governing Body will have freedom to deploy resources within the schools budget according to their own educational needs and priorities. They will determine the number of both teaching and non teaching staff at the school' (Department of Education and Science 1988, Circular 7/88: para. 21). However, once the Governing Body has decided on the number of teachers to appoint and at what grade, they must then abide by the national scales of pay. The discretion that LEAs had over certain elements of pay, for example to pay an additional allowance to an unqualified teacher, has, with LMS, been transferred to individual schools; but there is no evidence that in terms of the total teaching budget the sums involved are more than marginal. Although governors will have greater control over the pay of non-teaching staff, this constitutes, on average, only 9 per cent of a school's budget (Dixon 1991:60).

Grant-maintained schools will have the option of ignoring national pay settlements in favour of locally determined pay (Teachers Pay Act 1991). However, although Grant-Maintained schools are now a significant proportion of secondary schools, they are still marginal to the primary sector.

Both NHS Trusts and Executive Agencies have considerable autonomy in establishing conditions of service and pay. By April 1995, around 98 per cent of health care was provided by Trusts (Review Body for Nursing Staff, Midwives and Health Visitors 1996: para. 7) and by April 1996, Executive Agencies employed 71 per cent of all civil servants in Great Britain (Government Statistical Service 1996). Decentralisation would seem to be securely established in these two key areas. However, closer analysis of both the agencies and the Trusts would suggest that firm conclusions that decentralisation of pay determination has proceeded rapidly needs to be treated with some caution. In respect of the agencies, the Treasury requires each bargaining unit to supply it with a 'delegation' plan, which has to include a description of the employees in the unit, proposals for pay bill modelling and an outline of the pay strategy in place. Apparently departments are being required to send the Treasury a quarterly summary of key pay information (*Pay and Benefits Bulletin* 1996: 5). The development of local pay, which is in line with the logic of the organisational changes, has the potential to be frustrated by the Treasury's continuing concern to retain financial control (Kessler 1993: 333).

Indications that local pay determination has proceeded very slowly in the Trusts can be gleaned from the reports of the review bodies. Thus, in discussing developments in respect of doctors and dentists, the 1994 review body commented that 'we do not feel able to assume that many units will have a system of local bargaining in place by April 1994' (Review Body on Doctors' and Dentists' Remuneration 1994: para. 17). A similar comment was made in the following year: 'We have observed that the few Trusts which have reached the point where comprehensive local pay systems can be introduced have usually spent a long time in preparing the ground' (Review Body on Doctors' and Dentists' Remuneration 1995: para. 40). Although 17 per cent of consultants and almost 22 per cent of other career grades in NHS Trusts were on local contracts, they 'were said to "shadow" national terms and conditions' (Review Body on Doctors' and Dentists' Remuneration 1996: para. 2.8). Certainly in respect of hospital doctors, the Health Departments were prepared to accept this slow pace, as were the National Association of Health Authorities and Trusts and the NHS Trust Federation, which stated that 'the majority of Trusts had not yet found it necessary to address the issue of local pay for doctors . . . they should be allowed to approach local pay at a pace with which they feel comfortable' (ibid.: para. 2.11). Similar comments about the relative lack of progress towards local pay can be found in the reports of the Review Body for Nursing Staff, Midwives and Health Visitors (**5-22**). In 1995, 75 per cent of NHS staff remained on national conditions of pay: 20 per cent of the 25 per cent who were on Trust contracts had contracts that shadowed Whitley (Review Body for Nursing Staff, Midwives and Health Visitors 1996: para. 10). Further, the small survey undertaken by the Office of Manpower Economics for the 1996 report found that, although the majority of Trusts visited were committed to local pay, virtually all were at an early stage of implementation (ibid.: Appendix F).

However, by the time of its 1995 report, the Review Body was being proactive in respect of local pay negotiations. It explained the change of its position by saying that a Review Body always has 'to work within the broad framework for the NHS established by Government policies . . . In particular we felt that Trusts and staff representations should be able to use local pay bargaining to achieve greater flexibility and efficiency in delivering health services' (Review Body for Nursing Staff, Midwives and Health Visitors 1996: para. 16), and it recommended for 1995 a national rise of 1 per cent topped up by local negotiations. 'In 1995–96, for the first time the vast majority of nursing staff, midwives and health visitors employed in the NHS have received, as part of their annual pay settlement, an amount determined locally' (ibid.: para. 32).

However, the majority of Trusts reached pay settlements of around 3 per cent, with few attaching any conditions to the settlements (ibid.: para. 47). As the Review Body pointed out, the going rate of 3 per cent was not surprising given the continued refusal of 'the Staff Side to sanction any local pay negotiation [which] limited Trusts' freedom of action' (ibid.: para. 19).

In its 1996 report, the Review Body continued to support local pay negotiations, stating that the September 1995 agreement between the Health Departments and the Staff Side 'provides at least an interim framework in which local pay determination can be taken forward' (ibid.: para. 52). This agreement, which applies only to staff on national contracts, will work in the following way. Between April and August, the Nursing and Midwifery Staffs Negotiating Council (NMNC) will collect information on the levels of local settlements: the Council will then seek to reach agreement on the levels of increases to be consolidated in future national agreements. Thus 'national salary scales are to be raised annually to reflect the outcome of local negotiations in the preceding year' (ibid.: para. 21). In effect, as Income Data Services points out this process 'establishes national minimum pay rates' (Income Data Services 1996: 82). Indeed, the Review Body itself comments that the framework agreement will obviously affect the scope of local pay negotiations, with some Trusts content to work within it, while others regard it as an incentive to press ahead with developing local contracts (Review Body for Nursing Staff, Midwives and Health Visitors 1996: para. 32). In the 1997 report, the Review Body noted that Trusts were experiencing the framework agreement as a constraint (Review Body for Nursing Staff, Midwives and Health Visitors 1997: para. 59).

The limited progress on local pay determination in the Trusts was again noted in the Review Body's 1997 report (ibid.: paras. 24, 31, Appendix F), although the Health Departments argued that significant progress had been made (ibid.: para. 55). Several explanations can be suggested for the slow progress.

Firstly, there has been considerable opposition to the concept from many groups concerned that it would result in lower pay, could discriminate against women, would be expensive to implement and operate and had not worked well in other countries, at least in respect of nurses (**5.23**). Indeed, it could be added that it had proved unsatisfactory for nurses when used in Britain in the 1920s and 1930s (Thornley 1994).

Secondly, some Trusts have been critical of the role of the NHS Executive in relation to local pay determination, arguing 'that it is inconsistent with Trusts' freedom to manage . . . perceived about-turns have made Trusts' planning difficult and . . . central guidance has inhibited or undermined local progress' (Review Body for Nursing Staff, Midwives and Health Visitors 1996: para. 24). Trusts have also been critical of the Review Body itself, noting that its 1996–97 recommendations (a 2 per cent national increase for all nurses) inhibited local pay determination (Review Body for Nursing Staff, Midwives and Health Visitors 1997: para. 59).

Thirdly, there was an acknowledgement that there have been changes in the approach to, and meaning of, local pay. Taking the reports of the Review Body for Nursing Staff, Midwives and Health Visitors in 1987 and 1988, local pay was conventionally defined as linked to local labour market conditions: by the time of the Health Departments' evidence to the review body in 1991, local pay began to be linked both to local labour markets and individual performance-related pay. Indeed, in their 1992 report the review body pointed out that it was essential to distinguish the two, as they fulfilled different purposes. By the time of their evidence in 1994, the Health Departments were linking local pay to the performance of each employing unit (**5.24**).

Finally, the problem of differential systems of pay determinations should be noted. Thus if doctors remain on national salary scales, which Trusts have to meet, at a time of resource pressure, this would pre-empt additional locally determined increases for other groups, for example nurses.

Performance is All?

The Megaw Inquiry wholeheartedly supported the government's philosophy on performance-related pay (**5.25**), and schemes were introduced into most areas of the public sector in the mid-1980s; but they had limited coverage, and only a small proportion of the pay bill was allocated to them (cf. e.g. Foreman 1991: 9; *Pay and Benefits Bulletin* 1989; Income Data Services 1991: 41; Interim Advisory Committee 1991: para. 59). In the Citizen's Charter the government announced its intention to pursue PRP more vigorously. With the exception of the Civil Service, though

(Income Data Services 1996: 19–20), there is little to suggest that matters have changed in the 1990s. The most recent Public Sector Labour Market Survey by Income Data Services suggests that PRP in local government is confined to white-collar staff, and, in many cases, senior managers only (Income Data Services Report 1996b: 31); while in NHSTs there is limited use of PRP (Income Data Services Report 1996c: 28).

At the request of the relevant government departments, the Review Bodies on Doctors' and Dentists' Remuneration, for Nursing Staff, Midwives and Health Visitors and for School Teachers have all considered the case for introducing PRP for their respective professional groups. The School Teachers' Review Body (STRB) have been the most enthusiastic supporters of the principle; but even they have secured only modest change.

In its first report, in 1992, the STRB stated that 'we have no doubt that moves towards properly designed performance pay would be right in principle: providing better rewards for the best teachers and clearly offering worthwhile incentives to motivate all teachers to improve their performance' (STRB 1992: para. 62). While recognising that there were difficulties with the introduction of PRP, the review body considered that these were 'largely concerned with developing practicable and effective arrangements' . . . in particular the criteria on which teachers' performance should be judged and the means for making such judgements (ibid.: para. 62).

Over the years, though, the Review Body changed its position significantly. PRP for classroom teachers disappeared from the agenda (other than the award of excellence points), and the focus was on PRP for Heads and Deputy Heads. In a Consultative Document of July 1994 and its subsequent report in 1995, the Review Body proposed that a voluntary PRP scheme for this group should be introduced, and one-off pensionable bonuses (ranging from £600 to £1,500) should be paid when four essential performance indicators were met: namely, year-on-year improvement in a school's examination or test results; year-on-year improvement in pupil attendance; evidence of sound financial management; and, if there had been a recent Ofsted inspection, progress in meeting the requirements of the resulting action plan. Half the bonus would be paid where all these performance indicators were met, with the remainder linked to successful performance in other defined areas of management activity (STRB 1995: para. 70). These performance criteria have been incorporated into the annual salary review process for heads and deputy heads (**5.26**).

These performance indicators are, of course, not unproblematic (see Chapter 2 for a discussion of the general conceptual and methodological problems associated with performance indicators). Firstly, they might not be within the control of the headteacher. For example, unauthorised absences might be condoned by parents, or the reported rates of attendance so high that it would not be possible to improve them (Trade Union Research Unit 1992: 20). Test results could be distorted by having, in any one year, small numbers of either very bright children or children with severe problems (ibid.: 20). Secondly, linking pay to examination results could lead to manipulation – the refusal to enter pupils for examinations unless they were likely to pass or gain good grades; the use of rote learning to secure these passes (Mayston 1992: 24–6).

A more fundamental problem was that of linking pay to exam performance, which could lead to schools basing their selection of pupils on those likely to do well in examinations and, as there is a correlation between socio-economic class and success in examinations, increasing their intake of advantaged pupils. In turn, this would enable them to recruit and retain better teachers and further increase their powers of selection (ibid.: 21). Of course, such a process of selection, while advantaging some pupils/teachers, would disadvantage others (ibid.: 22–3). (See Chapter 3 for a fuller discussion of this issue.)

Returning to the deliberations of the STRB, a key question is: How is its repositioning to be explained? Two explanations suggest themselves. Firstly, there has been either universal opposition of the key groups of actors (teachers and headteachers' unions) or at the very least severe reservations by others (employers) over the principle and practice of PRP (cf. e.g. STRB 1995: paras. 73–80). Secondly, the focus on heads and deputy heads follows logically from a managerialism that states that it is the senior staff in an organisation that play the key leadership roles, who are responsible for overall performance or turning the organisation round. Thus, 'the role of heads, supported by deputies, is crucial to the success of schools' (STRB 1995: para. 61), and although teamwork in schools is important 'we also support the widely held view that heads and deputies are the main influence both in creating and sustaining such teamwork and on overall school performance' (STRB 1997: para. 104).

In discussing PRP for heads and deputy heads, or indeed any group of employees, there is research evidence of its negative impact, in that it frequently demotivates employees (Marsden and Richardson 1994; Thompson 1993), but there is little evidence of its beneficial consequences. No less a body than the Audit Commission had made this point: there is 'no clear evidence . . . that PRP improves staff motivation or performance' (Audit Commission 1995: 43). However, a scepticism as to whether PRP does or does not improve the performance of an organisation is to loose sight of its main rationales, namely, to individualise forms of remuneration, extend managerial discretion and control over employees, and change the culture of an organisation (Kessler and Purcell 1992: 21–3; Marsden 1993: 32–3; Kessler 1994). Thus the appeal of PRP is its consistency with the precepts of public sector managerialism of the 1980s and 1990s.

Conclusion

Successive Conservative governments in the 1980s and 1990s have sought to reduce both the size and the cost of the public sector. Such an intention would, inevitably, have implications for employment in the public sector. However, by the end of its fourth term of office, the government still remained a substantial employer of labour in the public services. Persistent attempts were made over the period to control pay in the public sector. A number of initiatives have been pursued here: a rejection of comparability; decentralised pay; individualised pay. These have been accompanied by robust attacks on incomes policies and national pay bargaining. Two themes have been dominant: that pay should be determined by market forces – that is, what is necessary to recruit, retain and motivate – and by individual performance. This approach has been underpinned by assumed models of pay determination in the private sector. The key question, then, is whether governments have succeeded in changing the agenda on pay in the ways that they have believed to be desirable. An evaluation of the policies on public sector pay suggests a rather complex story.

The Review Bodies for Doctors and Dentists, for Nursing Staff, Midwives and Health Visitors, and for School Teachers have been asked to disregard issues of comparability, basing their recommendations on what was necessary to recruit, retain and motivate staff. However, the Review Bodies recognised that such exhortations did not engender realistic pay prescriptions, and that pay for the groups covered by their remit must be seen in the context of the wider labour market. What was necessary to recruit, retain and motivate was related to comparability. Indeed, government did not eschew comparability in attempting to develop arguments on market forces: it invariably compared pay in the public sector to that in the private sector. The influential Audit Commission favoured 'market tracking' (Audit Commission 1995: para. 52). That the comparisons were usually undertaken to demonstrate that settlements in the private sector were running below those in the public sector is irrelevant to the point that comparability was/is heavily favoured by governments.

The evidence presented by government to the Review Bodies on the proposed pay increases for doctors, nurses and teachers, taking account of the settlements in the private sector, is one indication that governments have not withdrawn from this area of economic activity. Another is the acceptance of the Review body mechanism *per se*. Conservative govern- ments have not only tolerated third-party independent bodies, but indeed increased their number – creating additional bodies in 1983 for Nursing Staff, Midwives and Health Visitors and in 1992 for Teachers. Indeed, the rationale for their continued existence has been pondered upon by the Review Body for Nursing Staff, Midwives and Health Visitors, whose role and terms of reference have remained unchanged since 1983 despite the changes in the NHS. In their 1996 Report, the Review Body stated that the Minister of Health conceived their role as that of monitoring the implementation of local pay arrangements, while the Review Body itself maintained that their recommendations should provide the framework within which local Trusts negotiate pay and conditions (Review Body for Nursing Staff, Midwives and Health Visitors 1996: para. 12). Review Bodies also provide a forum for government to develop their policies on public sector pay.

Any notion that governments were pursuing a *laissez-faire* approach to pay came to an abrupt end in the Autumn Statement of 12 November 1992, by the then Chancellor of the Exchequer, Norman Lamont, announced that pay settlements for the following year (1993/4) throughout the public sector (even where employees were not subject to central arrangements, such as those on NHST contracts) would be restricted to between 0 and 1½ per cent (*Income Data Services Report* 1992: 6). Norman Lamont's successor as Chancellor, Kenneth Clarke, in his first budget speech stated that public sector running costs for 1994–5 would be frozen at 1993–4 levels, and pay increases for staff would have to be paid for by greater efficiency, or savings in the cost of running departments (*Income Data Services Report* 1993: 25). The government's commitment to freezing public sector running costs, and hence pay, at 1993–4 levels has been reaffirmed in subsequent years, and is due to continue until 1998 (*Income Data Services Report* 1995: 25; *Income Data Services Report* 1996a: 25).

Parallel with imposing limits on levels of pay settlement, governments have been anxious to increase local pay flexibility. In line with their economic theories there were attempts to link pay and local labour markets. However, jobs have different types of labour markets – local, regional and national; and, as the Audit Commission pointed out, for 'lower paid jobs the market is normally more local: the highest paid jobs often relate to a national market' (Audit Commission 1995: para. 52). Thus attempts to introduce regional/local pay for groups of professionals such as doctors, teachers, and nurses have met with little success. As Purcell and Ahlstrand (1994) have pointed out, the linking of pay to local labour markets has not been an influential aspect of decentralisation in the private sector.

Decentralising pay to the level of the unit – individual Trust, School, executive agency – has been another feature of the move towards local pay flexibility. However, providing the opportunity for a unit to introduce local pay does not necessarily mean that they will take advantage of this opportunity. Thus in respect of nurses, as was noted earlier in this chapter, most Trusts have similar pay settlements. There is also evidence that Trusts are sharing pay information (Gosling 1995: 28). During 1995, most government departments and agencies with delegated bargaining made salary awards worth between 2.5 per cent and 3 per cent of pay bills (*Pay and Benefits Bulletin* 1996: 2). Although the numbers of grant-maintained schools have increased, only two have used the powers under the Teachers Pay Act to set their own levels of pay. Here again, there is a misunderstanding of practice in the private sector: although there is evidence of decentralisation to unit or divisional level (Brown and Walsh 1991), this is more common in manufacturing than services (Purcell and Ahlstrand 1994: 126). This would suggest that in the public sector, which is predominantly service-based, with similar services being delivered by similarly qualified people across the whole country, decentralisation to the unit level is only likely to be feasible for a few groups of employees. As White also points out, even where such decentralised bargaining exists in the private sector, it is usually within a framework of strict pay guidelines from headquarters (White 1996: 111). Decentralised pay has been slow to advance for a variety of reasons; but of course a major one is the centralised control over public sector spending and pay, which is stronger and more explicit in the mid/late 1990s than in the earlier years since 1979.

Government policies on public sector pay determination throughout the 1980s and 1990s were marked by tensions and disjuncture between rhetoric and reality. However, in one area, successive governments did pursue a consistent policy, and that was in respect of the differential treatment meted out to different groups of public sector employees. A study by Elliott and Duffus using unpublished data from the New Earnings Survey points to the considerable diversity in real earnings growth between 1980 and 1992 – 40 per cent for doctors, female nurses, and primary and secondary teachers; and for the police, further education teachers and those in local authority clerical and secretarial grades growth was between 30 and 40 per cent; while for civil service clerical/executive grades, university academics and manual workers the growth was less than 20 per cent over these years (Elliott and Duffus 1996: 57).

However, despite certain groups' experiencing favourable treatment the authors conclude that the 'pay of almost all public sector workers (after 1980) has deteriorated relative to that of their private-sector counterparts' (ibid.: 76). Such deterioration is likely to be exacerbated by the changes in the patterns of employment in the public sector: 33 per cent of the total public sector workforce is now employed part-time, compared to 22 per cent in the mid-1980s (Hughes 1996: para 13); 42 per cent of all public sector staff taken on since 1992 are non-permanent (Elliott *The Guardian*, 10 February 1997). As women now represent 60 per cent of the public sector workforce (Hughes 1996: para. 12), such changes in both employment patterns and the structure of pay determination – moves to local pay determination that could lead to low pay, and PRP, with its increased discretion over employees (Rubery 1995) – will be particularly disadvantageous to them.

$-6-$

Conclusion: A Managerialist Future

In the first chapter it was argued that public sector managerialism in the UK needed to be located with respect to both the ideological changes in the Conservative Party and the politics of that party, and to a broad shift in political economy away from demand management towards supply-side economics. In this final chapter these issues are re-examined with respect to the current political situation in the UK and the immediate future of its politics. To do this the scope of the argument is extended to encompass both the Conservative and Labour parties. The aim is to examine the approaches of both parties to political economy and its connection with managerialism. The object of this analysis is to consider the question of the future of public sector managerialism whatever the outcome of the 1997 general election.

The chapter also addresses another key question: throughout this book a critical stance has been taken with respect to public sector managerialism. However, this is by no means the sole reading of this phenomenon, and a number of commentators have argued that positive claims can be made for public sector managerialism. This issue is discussed via a consideration of the concepts of Fordism and Post-Fordism on the one hand and 'New Wave' Management on the other.

The Conservative Legacy

In Chapter 1 the reasons for the shift in the approach of the Conservative Party to political economy were outlined. In the 1980s and 1990s they have become a party identified with the repudiation of demand management and the view that the control of inflation should be the primary economic objective. However, it is worth bearing in mind that the control of inflation was, itself, seen as a means of improving employment opportunities. For example, in Mrs Thatcher's first term Leon Brittain, then her Chief Secretary to the Treasury, argued that 'past inflation has been the cause of present unemployment' (cited in Bootle 1981: 25). Thus Conservative economic policy has been dominated by the notion that

Managing the Welfare State

government should establish a stable macro-economic environment, and
that labour market 'reforms', such as those discussed in Chapter 5, which
are designed to increase labour market 'flexibility', would provide the
basis for significant and sustainable employment growth.

At the macro-economic level there has, however, been a significant
disjuncture between what was promised by government and how policy
has operated. Thus, while the Thatcher governments of the 1980s repudiated Keynesianism, significant expansion of demand occurred in the early
to late 1980s as an effect of financial deregulation. As Godley (1996: 34)
demonstrates, this led to a sharp increase in the growth of money supply,
a marked boost in consumption over the period 1982–90, and a substantial
increase in consumer indebtedness. This last reached 100 per cent of
disposable income in 1991, three times the level of 1974 (ibid.).

While this did lead to a substantial fall in unemployment, ironically,
for a party that had emphasised supply-side economics, it also ran into a
supply-side constraint. The first eighteen months of Mrs Thatcher's first
administration saw a fall of 17 per cent in manufacturing output (ibid.:
29). Conservative monetary policy was strongly implicated in this huge
fall (Neale 1992), and the combination of this lack of industrial capacity
with the boost to demand flowing from financial deregulation led to severe
balance-of-trade problems. This, in turn, led to deflationary policies, which
were central to the recession of the early 1990s (Godley 1996: 38). Thus
the claims of the Conservatives to have created a stable macro-economic
environment sit uneasily with the experience of two substantial recessions
punctuated by an unsustainable boom.

The Record of 'Flexible' Labour Markets

This is perhaps contributory to an increasing Conservative emphasis on
the other key aspect of policy, the creation of a more 'flexible' labour
market. It is worth noting that this is, in some respects, a more modest
project. Thus, the aim is not so much to avoid economic 'shocks' as to
ensure that the economy respond to such shocks 'flexibly'. Manifestations
of such policy have already been discussed earlier in the book, and include
reductions in the scope of individual employment rights, removal of
minimum wage protection, reductions in the power of trade unions and in
the value of benefits paid to unemployed claimants relative to wage levels
(Morgan 1996: 530). Such changes are designed to make it more attractive
for employers to hire labour, because there are fewer obstacles to adjusting
employment levels to fluctuating demand levels and because wages may
fluctuate downwards in economic recessions. In turn, lower benefits levels

and tighter administrative controls are claimed to induce greater job search (Murray 1995).

Two types of claims can be made for these policies: first, that a more flexible labour market has been created and that, as a consequence, the 1990s recession has been significantly less damaging to employment than its early 1980s predecessor; and second, the stronger claim that the outcome of British flexible labour market policies has been significantly better for employment than the more 'rigid' labour markets of other European Union countries.

These claims have been subject to a critical review by Morgan (1996). He finds some evidence to support the first claim. Thus, comparing the first three years of the *recoveries* from the 1980s and 1990s recessions, he notes important differences. Generally, a pick-up in employment lags substantially behind an improvement in economic activity: thus unemployment continues rising even during periods of recovery. However, in the 1990s recession, by the beginning of the *second* year of the recovery employment began to level off and then rise. In contrast, in the 1980s increases in employment only began to appear in the *third* year of the recovery (ibid.: 533). However, while this might support a claim that British employers could have become increasingly willing to take on labour in the recovery, the stronger claim of superior *comparative* performance was not sustained.

In the 1990s recovery the British unemployment record was superior to those of France, Italy and Germany. However, it is important to bear in mind that unemployment is affected not just by patterns of employment, but also by trends in labour market participation. Morgan (1996: 531) breaks down the experience of the countries he studied into trends in employment, unemployment and non-participation. With respect to claims on flexibility, the experience with respect to employment is crucial. This is because the British government has argued that its measures have, *inter alia*, increased employment opportunities. Morgan's analysis shows, however, that, while Germany's employment record was inferior to Britain's in the 1990s recovery, those of France and Italy were superior. The better British unemployment record did not stem from more job creation, but came about because participation levels in the British economy were falling, while they were *rising* in France and Italy (ibid.). In part this reflected the substantial expansion of higher education in Britain, discussed in Chapter 3. It is also worth noting that it is not only the British government that claims that employment protection is tougher in these other European Union countries, but this is also the conclusion of the regularly quoted OECD 'Jobs Study', which included a ranking of employment protection in twenty-one countries. In the ranking the USA came out as the country with the 'least strict' form of protection (ranked 1), while the UK was ranked 7, France was ranked 14 and Italy (ranked 21) had, on the OECD arguments, the most rigorous employment protection regime of all the countries studied.

Morgan's conclusion was that the UK's move to a more flexible labour market engendered an employment performance that 'does not appear particularly impressive by international standards' (Morgan 1996: 531). However, such flexibility also has a price: deregulation of labour markets is associated with increasing inequalities of wages and evidence, at the bottom of the wage hierarchy, of static or falling real wages. Such inequalities are frequently measured by taking deciles at both ends of the wage distribution and looking at the relativities between them. Machin (1996), for example, looked at changes in relative earnings between 1980 and 1990 in eleven countries by comparing earnings at the top (90th) decile of the wage distribution to those at the bottom (10th) decile. In the UK case in 1980 men at the top decile earned 2.53 times what men at the bottom decile earned; by 1990 this differential had increased to 3.21; the same pattern was evident for women, with the respective figures being 2.40 (1980) and 3.02 (1990) (Machin 1996: 48). In contrast, France, Germany and Italy all experienced compression of these wage differentials over the same period (the Italian data cited were for 1987). Also, in the British case, data from the Family Expenditure Survey showed *no* growth in real earnings at the 10th decile over the 1980s (ibid.: 49).

As Morgan shows, the employment gain for such increased inequalities and static real wages for the poorest workers is hardly impressive. However, adherents of flexibility might want to argue that the relevant comparison is not between the British economy and the largest other European Union economies, but between the United States (the OECD's most deregulated labour market) and the European Union.

In Morgan's study US overall employment growth in the first three years of the 1990s recovery was superior to that of the four European Union countries surveyed (Morgan 1996: 531). Furthermore, another important claim is made for US labour market flexibility, and that is with respect to the *duration* of unemployment. Thus, in 1992, whereas 40 per cent of unemployed men in the European Union were out of work for over a year, the corresponding figure in the USA was 13 per cent (Freeman 1995: 70). This is significant, because it suggests that, while the US economy is characterised by much greater wage inequality than is the case in the European Union (Machin 1996: 48), this is consistent with a smaller proportion of the working population excluded from the labour market.

However, Freeman's analysis of US labour market data suggests that such positive claims must, at best, be highly qualified. Wage flexibility and a deregulated labour market are seen as being particularly helpful to less educated and qualified workers. However, Freeman shows (1995: 67–8) that the employment record of less-qualified men was worse than that of the better-educated, even though it is the former group that has experienced substantial falls in real wages.

He also throws doubt on the extent to which the US labour market minimises social exclusion. With respect to the latter, he argues, that it is important to take into account the size and rate of growth of the US prison population. This is a relevant consideration because there are some important demographic similarities between the US criminal population and the long-term unemployed in the European Union, with both groups composed disproportionately of less-qualified people. He points out (ibid.: 70) that, given the rate of growth of the US prison population (around 9 per cent per annum in the 1980s), if this is projected to the year 2000 then the United States will have a larger share of its male population in prison or long-term unemployed than the European Union will have long-term unemployed. This argument is put forward in the context of a European Union prison population around one-tenth the size of the American (ibid.).

Of course, to sustain such a claim it would be necessary to establish that the wage inequalities and very low (by international standards) levels of US real wages at the bottom of the wage hierarchy are a key cause of criminal activity and hence of this form of social exclusion. On this latter point Freeman (ibid.: 71) argues that there are similarities between the prison population and groups who have suffered 'huge losses in real earnings' (ibid.): viz US criminals are mainly drawn from less-qualified men; survey evidence suggests that real pay increases would reduce criminal participation; and studies of criminal participation show a connection between such activity and the relative rates of return from criminal activity and legitimate work. While all these arguments can be disputed, they are important for raising relevant doubts concerning the extent to which such positive claims for the US labour market can be sustained.

These considerations are also important to the framework within which public sector managerialism operates. As was indicated in Chapter 1, a key contextual feature was the combination of government continuing to dominate the finance and provision of welfare services, but operating in a context of parsimony with respect to public expenditure. It is likely that, if the Conservative Party were to win a fifth successive term in office, this framework will remain substantially unchanged. As was indicated above, the government claims that flexibility has led to a substantially better employment performance than in other large European Union countries. These claims are indicative that the Conservatives would continue down this road. This is likely to lead to the further encouragement of low-wage employment and, as a correlate, harsher administration of benefits paid to the unemployed, via measures like the Job Seeker's Allowance. However, arguments like those of Freeman suggest that going down the American road will not necessarily lead to reductions in public expenditure, but rather a reorientation of such expenditure to repressive and containment objectives. In such circumstances the current pressures for 'more for less' in services like health and education will continue, and hence the political space in which public sector managerialism operates will remain substantially unchanged. This raises the question of whether Labour offers a political alternative, and the possible role of public sector managerialism should Labour be in a position to implement its policies after the 1997 general election.

Does Labour Offer an Alternative?

Old Labour

Labour fought and lost the General Elections of 1979, 1983 and 1987 on social and economic policy programmes that were clearly distinct from those of their Conservative opponents. However, the defeat of 1987 was the prelude to the party's reassessing such programmes.

In its 1987 Manifesto the Labour Party approach to social policy could be seen to exhibit a continuity with traditional Labour commitments to the welfare state – the reduction in NHS waiting lists, cuts in prescription charges, the need to reward nurses and other public sector staff fairly, the use of the voluntary sector to supplement statutory services and a commitment to expand nursery and post-school education. Thus, the main concern throughout was with the identification of welfare needs and the development of policies to meet them, 'collective provision for private use' (Labour Party 1987: 8).

Labour economic policy in the early to mid-1980s was also distinct from that of the Conservatives, and was identified with what came to be known as the Alternative Economic Strategy (AES). While the AES appeared in a number of variants, a common feature was a commitment to reflationary policies and a willingness to contemplate measures, such as import controls, to underpin such an employment-creation policy. The

AES thus involved a commitment, in contrast to the Conservatives, to demand-side employment policies, even to the extent of risking (over import controls) a confrontation with the European Commission as the guardian of intra-community free trade (Williams *et al*. 1992: 12).

Labour: the Conversion to a Conservative Agenda?

However, by the late 1980s the economic policy of the Party was under-going major changes: reduction of inflation, rather than the return to full employment, became the key objective of macro-economic policy. For example, Labour supported British membership of the Exchange Rate Mechanism (ERM) as a means of securing low inflation. Thus, in an interview, published in the *Financial Times* (27 September 1991) John Smith, then Shadow Chancellor, committed Labour to maintaining the parity of the pound against the Deutschmark at 2.95 DM, a rate that was regarded by many commentators as too high, and proved to be unsustainable. The fact that this posed a potential threat to British com-petitiveness and hence to employment might have been expected to have concerned Labour, given its traditional emphasis on maximising employment. However, the fact that it did not is demonstrated by the commitment, expressed in the 1992 Manifesto: 'to curb inflation Labour will maintain the value of the pound within the European Exchange Rate Mechanism' (Labour Party 1992: 12). In addition, Labour was cautious on employment policy, claiming that it was determined to make a 'swift reduction in unemployment' (ibid.); but there was no hint of the term 'full employment', and no target for such reductions. Parallel with the change in priorities at the level of macro-economic policy was the emphasis on the efficiency and competitiveness of the economy. While this was in no sense novel for Labour, it now involved a virtually exclusive emphasis on supply-side policies. Thus the 1992 Manifesto stated 'Britain [is] in a race for economic survival and success. Faced with intense competition, companies and countries can succeed only by constantly improving their performance' and that meant more 'cost-effective pro-duction, continuous product and process innovation, the flexibility of a highly skilled workforce' (ibid.). Thus supply-side economics has come to dominate Labour thinking in this policy area, where it has mirrored that of the Conservatives (Thompson 1996: Ch. 18). This shift has also led to attempts to reconcile traditional socialist values of equity and social justice with the emphasis on the virtues of efficiency and competition. For example, the Shadow Chancellor, Gordon Brown, has argued that investment in education and training will enhance the competitiveness of the British economy at the same time as expanding opportunity and promoting greater equality of incomes (Brown 1994). This view is reflected in the title of his Fabian pamphlet 'Fair is Efficient'.

Labour and Public Sector Managerialism

As the Labour Party has accepted central aspects of the political economy of the Conservatives, so it also accepted their public sector managerialism. The 1992 Manifesto shows some continuity on social policy issues with its predecessors: for example, it included a commitment to end what was seen as the privatisation of the NHS, and included policies to expand the provision of nursery-school places and the expansion of higher education. There was also a commitment to increase spending on both the NHS and education, £1 billion and £600 million respectively over a period of 22 months. There were also policies that were consistent with traditional Labour approaches to social policy, like the return of opted-out schools and hospitals to local authority and health authority control. However, the Manifesto moved on to a different terrain by adopting the language and ideas of its opponent – targets, monitoring, performance.

A Health Quality Commission would 'monitor the quality of care and raise standards' (Labour Party 1992: 16). To achieve the higher priority accorded to care of the elderly and sick Performance Agreements would be negotiated with each Health Authority, and an Incentive Fund would reward authorities that performed well. Hospital managers would be accountable for meeting their targets, but otherwise given maximum freedom of decision-making (ibid.) – a clear commitment to devolved management.

In education, standards were to be raised by a Reading Standards programme and national tests. They were to be guaranteed by an Education Standards Commission, which would 'monitor the performance of every school' (ibid.: 18). It would have powers to bring under-performing schools up to standard, and parents dissatisfied with a Local Education Authority or school could complain to the Commission and 'get action taken' (ibid.). While Local Management of Schools would be reformed, it would continue, and schools would be 'free to manage their day to day budgets, with local education authorities given a new strategic role' (ibid.). Equally, the role of voluntary organisations would now change from one of supplementing statutory services to 'playing a key role in developing services' (ibid.: 20).

New Labour

Under the leadership of Tony Blair the move to the terrain of the Conservatives has continued with respect to both economic and social policy. Shortly after his election as leader, Blair gave an interview to the *Daily Telegraph* (26 July 1994), pledging that, if Labour were elected, it would shed its image as a tax and spending party, and orientate the Welfare State to getting people off dependency rather than keeping them on it. In an interview in the *Financial Times* (16 January 1997) he stated that 'New Labour is pro-business and pro-enterprise', and that the government's role in relation to business is to 'set a framework within which business has the stability to plan and invest in the future'. To reinforce this view of the limited role of government, he added that he had no wish to raise the share of income taken by public expenditure.

This stance has also been reinforced by Gordon Brown. In a speech in January 1997 he stated that 'there would be no new commitments in our manifesto' that would require additional spending, and he committed himself to spending plans that would rise by only a ¼ per cent per annum in the first three years of a Labour government. This contrasts with an annual growth rate of nearly 2 per cent per annum over the period 1985–95 (*Financial Times*, 21 January 1997). Brown has also stated that he would retain the departmental allocations for 1997–9 already agreed by government (Glennester 1997). On tax he aims to reduce the basic rate of tax for the low-paid (ibid.), while pledging not to introduce a new higher rate of tax or to increase the basic rate of tax (*Financial Times*, 21 January 1997; for a concise statement of New Labour economic policy and policy on public expenditure and taxation see Mandelson and Liddle 1996: Ch. 4 and 103–9).

Labour has also taken up key elements of the Conservative social welfare agenda. In a speech to the Institute for Public Policy Research in May 1996, Chris Smith, Shadow Secretary of State for Social Security, said: 'Surely it is time to get away from the sterile battle lines of public and private and, instead, to look at how the two can best work together in the interests of the citizen – and in the interests of all citizens' (*The Guardian*, 8 May 1996).

The conception of a partnership between public and private sectors in the provision of welfare would, of course, lead to a redefined role for the state: 'The principle must surely be that the state acts as the guarantor of all provision, the regulator of all provision – and the administrator of some' (*The Guardian*, 8 May 1996). Mandelson and Liddle support universal welfare, but argue that it should not be uniform, and that welfare services should permit greater freedom of choice and seek to marry public and private finance and provision (Mandelson and Liddle 1996: 143).

Where services do remain provided by government, then public sector managerialism will be applied. In *Renewing the NHS* (Labour Party 1995a) it is stated that the 'aim is to ensure the maximum number of people are treated to the highest possible standards within a budget acceptable to the taxpayer' (ibid.: 18). To achieve this, a number of managerialist techniques, some inherited from the Conservatives, some introduced by New Labour, would be used. Health Authorities will be expected 'to meet new national standards on quality, access to services and information' (ibid.: 19); hospitals will continue to have 'complete managerial responsibility' (ibid.: 21), and a range of levers would be used to improve quality and cost-effectiveness. These include audit and the use of comparative data on hospitals, which 'will be powerful tools in levering up standards' (ibid.: 22). Financial incentives will be used to ensure that hospitals deliver the range and quality of services required (ibid.: 23), and monitoring and feedback procedures will be used to improve the quality of patient care (ibid.). Finally there will be 'a strengthened role for the Audit Commission' (ibid.: 25).

There are similar commitments to key features of public sector managerialism in Labour education policy. *Excellence for Everyone: Labour's Crusade to Raise Standards* (Labour Party 1995b) argues that crucial to the raising of standards is the role of the headteacher and the local education authority (LEA). To ensure that the former can make a significant contribution, 'Labour will improve headteacher training to boost leadership and management skills with a new national qualification' (ibid.: para. 2.7). While, in respect of the latter, 'Labour will expect [them] to set strategic Education Development Plans on a three year rolling basis detailing how standards will be raised in schools in their area' (ibid.: para. 3.13). The plans will set clear targets to raise standards. In turn, the performance of LEAs will be monitored by the Office for Standards in Education (OFSTED) and the Audit Commission (ibid.: para. 3.12). Each school will be required to set clear targets for improvement in pupil attainment (ibid.: para. 4.4). Finally, 'Labour will develop better information for parents and teachers, using value-added measures and comparisons with a school's previous performance to help raise standards' (ibid.: para. 4.13), although this information should not be used to develop a competitive market in education.

Thus, by the late 1990s Labour policy has moved to conform closely with Conservative policy both in the sphere of the economy and on the role of public sector managerialism. As was argued in the first chapter, the two aspects are interrelated, in that public sector managerialism is likely to thrive in conditions of weak economic growth and a political commitment to restraint of public expenditure. However, we now turn to consider whether the phenomenon of public sector managerialism can be considered in an alternative way.

Fordism and Post-Fordism

Throughout this book the analysis of public sector managerialism offered has been critical of the phenomenon. However, it is necessary in this conclusion to address two different ways of conceptualising these changes, which suggest, at least in part, that they might be viewed more positively. These alternative conceptualisations relate to, on one hand, the distinction between 'Fordism' and 'Post-Fordism'; and, on the other, the concept of 'new wave management'. The argument will proceed by examining these alternative conceptualisations and outlining their implications for the analysis of public sector managerialism. Having delineated these approaches, we shall develop a critical evaluation of their worth.

Definitions

The concepts of 'Fordism' and 'Post-Fordism' raise definitional problems for two main reasons: because they refer to distinct 'levels' of the social; and because, with respect to social policy, they involve a transfer of concepts, originally developed to explain manufacturing production processes, to areas that are, arguably, of a quite distinct character to that of this original sphere of application.

The operation of Fordism and Post-Fordism at different levels relates to the different theoretical traditions that have been involved in the development of these concepts. One crucial form of definition relates to conceptualisations of production processes in manufacturing industry, and a central work has been Piore and Sabel's *The Second Industrial Divide* (1984). In this work a distinction is made between 'mass production' (ibid.: 4) and 'flexible specialisation' (ibid.: 17) as production processes. In turn, this distinction has been used to distinguish 'Fordist' and 'Post-Fordist' forms of production process. Thus, for example, Jessop (1991: 1) defines 'Fordism' at this level as 'a particular configuration of the technical and social division of labour involved in making long runs of standardized goods'. Such long production runs go along with the idea that Fordism is conceived as an 'inflexible' production process. In contrast, Post-Fordism at this level is seen as 'flexible production process based on flexible machines and systems and an appropriately flexible workforce' (Jessop 1991: 12).

However, while one form of definition relates to the characterisation of Fordism and Post-Fordism production processes, another derives from the body of 'regulation' theory. In this approach capitalist economies operate with modes of 'regulation' that can be seen as means of averting or coping with crises. In this respect Fordism and Post-Fordism can be seen as alternative 'modes of regulation'. With respect to Fordism, a key feature of regulation is the 'Keynesian Welfare State' (KWS), which Jessop (1994: 17) argues 'tries to adjust demand to the supply-driven needs of Fordist mass production, with its dependence on economies of scale and full utilisation of relatively inflexible means of production'. Thus, the KWS is a means of seeking to generate sufficient demand to ensure that there is an adequate market for 'standardised' produced goods.

In contrast, in this respect, Post-Fordism involved the displacement of the KWS by the Schumpeterian Workfare State (SWS), whose 'distinctive objectives . . . are to promote product, process organisational and market innovation . . . in order to strengthen structural competitiveness of the national economy by intervening on the supply side' (Jessop 1994: 24). The point here is that the contrast in modes of regulation involves, as Carter and Rayner (1996: 354) argue, a distinction in forms of relationship between 'welfare, capital and the state'. Thus, under the KWS, expansive features of welfare such as 'indexed welfare benefits financed from progressive taxation' operate to generalise 'mass consumption norms to the economically inactive' (Jessop 1991: 3), and mean that the welfare state is seen as providing a mechanism to sustain demand. In contrast, the SWS means that state welfare provision is more likely to have a 'supply-side' role.

Fordism and Post-Fordism as Production Processes

The object of this section will be to evaluate the use of the concepts of Fordism and Post-Fordism as a means of analysing production processes. It is divided into three sections: in the first a more developed version of the concept is presented; in the second, examples are given of attempts to transfer these production-process-based concepts to social policy – such examples present, in some respects, a more positive role of public sector managerialism than the view developed earlier in this book; and finally, a critical analysis of these concepts will be given.

As was indicated above, the distinction between Fordism and Post-

Fordism related to an opposition between processes producing standard-ised products and those producing differentiated products. However, a more developed version of the concepts requires that we distinguish four features. Firstly, there is the idea of a shift in methods, from Fordist standardised products produced on inflexible or dedicated equipment to a Post-Fordist 'flexible production process based on flexible machines or systems and an appropriately flexible labour force' (Jessop 1994: 19). A central role in flexible production is the increased use of information technology (IT): thus 'its crucial hardware is micro-electronics-based information and communication technologies' (ibid.; see also Piore and Sabel 1984: 260–1).

The second key element is that flexible production processes are seen as opening up the possibility of producing a wide diversity of products. In turn, this shift is related to a postulated third element, consumer resist-ance to standardised mass-produced products. Thus, Jessop (ibid.) argues that part of the crisis of Fordism was 'the relative saturation of markets for standardised mass-produced goods and/or . . . the growing demand for more differentiated products'. It is also important to note that there is another implicit feature here. If consumers, in general, are going to have access to more differentiated products, then this suggests that such differentiation does not lead to a significant cost penalty. There has always been a market for customised and quality products: but this has gone along with high prices, which restrict them to particular market segments. What is claimed with respect to Post-Fordism is that now the run-of-the-mill consumer will also have access to such variegated products.

The final element concerns the implications for relations between employers and workers. Fordism is characterised as linked to 'Taylorism', i.e. a distinction between the conception of a task and its execution. Thus, under 'Taylorism', it is the role of management and professional staff to design the way in which a job should be done, and the role of the employee is to execute these tasks. This also meant that labour was predominantly conceived of as 'semi-skilled' and able to perform only a highly circum-scribed set of tasks (though, for a more qualified account, see Piore and Sabel 1984: 116 and 173).

Under Post-Fordism such forms of employment relations are seen as incompatible with flexible production. Thus Jessop (1991: 14) argues that Post-Fordism is linked to industrial relations strategies that 'focus on integrating core workers into the enterprise and mobilising the production intelligence of workers by dissolving the Taylorist distinction between conception and execution'. Similarly, Sabel claims that under 'flexible specialisation' 'firms know that they do not know precisely what they will have to produce, and further that they must count on the collaboration of workers and subcontractors in meeting the market's eventual demand' (Sabel 1994: 139).

Fordism and Post-Fordism in the Public Sector

One of the central ways in which concepts like Post-Fordism have entered social policy debates is by attempts to transfer these concepts into discussions of public sector services. Thus, Hoggett has argued that such a parallel can be found in what he calls decentralisation. Decentralisation is said 'to lead to new organisational and managerial forms . . . leaner and flatter managerial structures, decentralised cost and innovation centres' (Hoggett 1987: 225). As with Post-Fordism in the manufacturing sector, there is a postulated connection with IT, which generates 'technical advances . . . in the control of production processes' (ibid.: 221). There is also the link to what is seen as consumer resistance. Thus there is the emergence of 'the legitimate demand for a more differentiated state product' (ibid.: 224). This demand 'comes directly from a new actor whose appearance over the last decade corresponds to an important change in the environment of most welfare state organisations – the "differentiated consumer"' (ibid.). Finally, such shifts are claimed to involve increases in worker autonomy. Thus the 'flatter' structures are seen as going along with 'enlarged and more generic roles, teamworking, flexibility and informality' (ibid.: 225).

What is interesting about this characterisation is how, from a radically different political standpoint, Hoggett identifies his position as 'socialist' (ibid.: 227). A Post-Fordist account of the transformation of the public sector mirrors the claims of supporters of Conservative-inspired managerialisation of the welfare state. Thus the 'classic' welfare state is portrayed as a failure: Hoggett talks of the 'massivity and remoteness, inflexibility, inefficiency and unresponsiveness of the welfare state' (ibid.: 224). He also goes on to argue that 'it would seem that the technical conditions are beginning to emerge for a welfare state form which is more consumer oriented, more efficient, less hierarchical and managerially more participative' (ibid.: 225).

In evaluating arguments like those of Hoggett it is important to explore two dimensions: the first is to pose the question as to how far, if at all, the public sector managerial changes, introduced under the Thatcher and Major governments, can be understood in terms of a shift to Post-Fordist production processes; the second, reflecting the fact that commentators like Hoggett do not identify with Thatcher's or Major's politics, is to ask how far a Post-Fordist welfare production process might be seen as having the potential for the gains that Hoggett identifies, even though they may not be realised under anti-collectivist regimes.

In both Post-Fordist arguments and arguments put forward by the government it is claimed that public sector consumers require a more differentiated product. Arguably, the clearest instance of reforms ostensibly designed to achieve this objective has been in secondary education, where, according to Mrs Thatcher 'we had gone as far as we could towards a "public sector voucher"' (Thatcher 1993: 591).

However, as was argued in Chapter 3, there are a whole series of reasons why these changes sit uneasily with a production-process concept of Post-Fordism. 'Product' choice was circumscribed because of the National Curriculum, and choice was also prescriptively guided both by the emphasis given to measured scores of academic attainment and by Conservative hostility at national and local level to comprehensive education. Unit autonomy and decentralisation were compromised by the fact that the state imposed obligations on schools to publish test and examination results. Finally, it is implausible in such a regime to argue that there was necessarily an overall increase in responsiveness, given the implicit privilege accorded to academic success in judging school performance. This was likely to lead schools to respond to the parents of students likely to be academically successful, but to be less interested in parents of students who might expect a lower level of attainment.

Of course, it is possible to argue that what is problematic here is not the Post-Fordist process *per se*, but rather the 'neo-liberal' version offered by Thatcher and Major. However, Chapter 3 also revealed a more fundamental problem. As was argued above, the production-process version of Post-Fordism claims that the transformation of production methods allows for a combination of greater choice of product with an absence of cost penalties. However, the discussion of secondary education showed quite the opposite to this supposed pattern. Thus, to maintain 'choice' required the toleration of surplus places, and hence production 'inefficiencies'. Equally, as the examples from the Scottish experience showed, even with surplus places choice was heavily circumscribed in rural areas. In other words, while Post-Fordism in manufacturing promised (see below for critical discussion of this) the combination of low cost and product differentiation, public sector education would appear to require a trade-off between the extent of choice and cost.

A second claimed manifestation of Post-Fordism in the public sector is the shift from bureaucratic structures to decentralised or devolved structures, a process which, it is argued, has been driven, at least in part, by the diffusion of IT. However, again there are problems with reconciling this account with the experience of public sector managerialism. Thus, while Post-Fordist arguments link devolved management and performance measurement to unit freedoms, it can also be argued that they are means of increasing centralisation. Thus in Chapter 2 it was argued that the Audit Commission takes a highly prescriptive view of how public services should be managed, and value for money reports are often designed to encourage emulation of 'best practice'. Equally, the importance of top-down measures means that those subject to them have little or no influence on what is measured.

Again, it can be argued that this reflects a politics that fails to realise the potential of devolved management. Yet, as Chapter 2 showed, there are fundamental conceptual and methodological problems with respect to performance measurement. Thus, for example, the difficulties and contentiousness of outcome measures means that they often lead to procedural or 'bureaucratic' means being reinvented. For example, Teaching Quality Assessment runs into the problem of defining what constitutes 'quality'. To avoid this can of worms, such assessments often operate with a set of rule-based guidelines. An example would be to expect front sheets on student essays, that require the tutor to comment on issues like presentation, structure of argument and referencing. No doubt such practices can be criticised on the grounds that they encourage mere conformity with procedure, which is not necessarily of any substantive value: but, arguably, they reflect an attempt to avoid the political divisions that arise with outcome measures.

The same difficulties arise with the notion of Post-Fordism going along with employee 'empowerment'. In contrast, there are numerous examples of more authoritarian forms of management operating. The 1990 GP contract, for example, included a range of precise contractual requirements of GPs that involved replacing discretion with imperative controls of, arguably, doubtful value to individual patients or public health (Morrell 1991). Similarly, research on Local Management of Schools has demonstrated how the gap between senior teachers in a management role and front-line teachers has increased (Gewirtz *et al.* 1995); this, in turn, is reflected in the fact outlined in Chapter 5, that performance-related pay is restricted to such senior teachers.

Furthermore, Post-Fordist arguments fail to grasp the ambivalent character of empowerment: thus, increasing the range of tasks expected can be accompanied by work intensification. Furthermore, in a restrictive budgetary context 'soft' human resource approaches focusing on training and employee development can be effectively negated (see below p. 165).

While the argument developed so far has sought to illustrate attempts to develop parallels between a claimed shift to Post-Fordism in the private sector and a supposed analogous process in the public sector, there is one noticeable difference. In the private sector version the deployment of IT is usually seen as contributing to a transformation of the production process that yields increased product diversity without cost penalty. Thus Piore and Sabel (1984: 260) argue that flexibility without cost penalties is possible because changing a product in a 'mass production' system involves 'physical adjustments', while 'with computer technology, the equipment . . . is adapted to the operation of the computer program . . . therefore the equipment can be put to new uses . . . simply by pro-gramming'.

In the argument developed below, the validity of such claims will be discussed; but it is important to note that public sector welfare versions of this argument tend to point not to the role of IT in changing *production methods*, but rather to its operation at the level of *management control*. This omission is symptomatic, since it suggests that, broadly speaking, the way in which services are provided has not been significantly altered. Thus, it is hard to see how it is possible to resolve cost–choice tensions like those in schools or in community care discussed in Chapter 3.

Finally, to complete the critical discussion it is worth going back to the concepts themselves in their original sphere of application. This is important because much of the literature on the transfer of these concepts to public sector services assumes both that the basic conceptual distinctions are sound and that they give a realistic account of the changes in private sector manufacturing. However, this ignores the fact that there are sub-stantial problems in this original sphere, some of which echo the issues discussed in relation to public sector applications.

The first problem relates to the simplistic character of the basic concepts used. Thus, for example, Williams *et al.* (1987: 415–16) point out that, in what are characterised as mass-production or Fordist car plants, particular important parts of the production process cannot be seen as 'inflexible'. They point out that hydraulic presses, used to shape car bodies, usually have a working life of around thirty years, and are used to produce a variety of car bodies in any one period. They are thus quintessentially 'flexible', accommodating both to changes of model over time and to a variety of models in any given time-period.

They also point out (ibid.: 416) that situations where mass producers concentrate on a single model, like the Ford Model-T or the Volkswagen Beetle, are the exception rather than the rule. Usually 'mass production' means a variety of models. Theorists like Piore and Sabel (1984: 51) regard such differences as superficial; but they provide no basis for distinguishing 'real' as against 'presentational' product differences (Williams *et al.* 1987: 416).

The potential for this conceptual distinction to degenerate into stereotype is also criticised by Warde (1994) with respect to patterns of consumption. Thus, he points out (ibid.: 235) 'from the way . . . the term "mass consumption" is used, one might be forgiven for thinking that for a period of modern history everybody has owned the same goods . . . that needs and desires were universal'. This potential for stereotype is strengthened by the absence of empirical support for claims of a transformation from universal to differentiated consumption. Thus, for example, research on food consumption (Tomlinson and Warde 1993) showed stability in differences in patterns of food purchasing on class lines between 1968 (usually regarded as part of the Fordist period) and 1988 (periodised as Post-Fordist) – i.e. there was no apparent shift to a random individualised pattern of consumption.

Treatment of pattern of consumption issues also reveals further conceptual difficulties. Thus Williams *et al.* (1987: 427) point out that arguments like those of Piore and Sabel conflate the concepts of market fragmentation and product differentiation. Thus, market fragmentation can occur where a large choice of brands is available, and this could reflect, for example, the entry to a sector of producers from newly industrialised countries, such as those in East Asia. This, in turn can raise problems for established producers, since fragmentation could reduce their market share. However, this is quite distinct from product differentiation, since the brands concerned (as in the case of, for example, washing machines) could well be broadly of the same type and might reflect a lack of demand for a more differentiated product.

Finally, the point was made earlier that applications of the concept of Post-Fordism to the public sector may have involved an exaggerated view of the productive significance of IT. This is also reflected in the literature on applications in manufacturing industry. Thus, Williams *et al.* (1987: 430) point out that, while robots can be used to weld a greater variety of car body parts than jig multiwelders, this does not mean that reprogramming is costless. Thus, the introduction of a new generation of models will require an expensive recommissioning process. Furthermore, discussions of the relationship between IT and flexibility often assume that the whole of the production process is transformed. Yet, for example, while in car body welding more 'flexible' equipment is used, engines are still produced on dedicated equipment with very long production runs (Williams *et al.* 1987: 430–1).

Conclusion: A Managerialist Future

Fordism and Post-Fordism as Modes of Regulation

The argument so far has sought to demonstrate the weaknesses in the use of the concept of Post-Fordism in its 'production-process' version. However, there is also the use of the concept as a mode of regulation, particularly in the form of the idea of a shift from the Keynesian Welfare State (KWS) to the Schumpeterian Workfare State (SWS). A difficulty with evaluating this argument is that it is not entirely clear what it involves with respect to social policy. In one sense it could mean a reorientation of state expenditure away from social welfare to industrial policy objectives. However, it might also be argued to refer to a redistribution of resources *within* social policy in a supply-side direction.

As was argued earlier in this chapter, both Conservative and Labour parties are now committed to a supply-side economics that, while having different emphases, stresses the importance of labour's responding 'flexibly' to changes in product markets. In both parties there is also an emphasis on the potential role of education and training in facilitating such adjustments. Thus, in the case of the Conservatives, what are claimed to be improvements in 'learning and skills', in part stemming from changes introduced into primary and secondary education, are seen as contributing to competitiveness (Department of Trade and Industry 1996: Ch. 4). Similarly, as was argued in Chapter 3, the rapid expansion of higher education under the Conservatives has been presented as improving the supply side of the economy.

In the case of New Labour, Gordon Brown's emphasis on the expansion of education and training as a means of reconciling the supply-side goals of greater efficiency with the socialist objectives of greater equality of incomes has already been cited. Furthermore, it is also possible to find evidence of a business lobby with similar views – for example the Confederation of British Industry (CBI) has supported an even greater expansion of higher education to reach a 40 per cent age participation ratio (Keep and Mayhew 1996). The CBI rationale for this expansion is that increased participation rates in higher education have fuelled the economic success of faster-growing economies. These features would thus appear to support the SWS variant of Post-Fordism. Thus, it could be argued that here is a major shift in the key political parties and in business to adopt a form of social welfare that subordinates public provision to the demands of the supply side.

However, it is important to note an equivocation in arguments on the SWS. In some respects this shift is seen as *resolving* a crisis of the KWS by creating a more flexible economic structure. However, such shifts could also be seen as operating more at the level of rhetoric. This equivocation is, for example, present in Jessop's characterisation of the SWS, which, he says, 'could . . . be seen as having a post-Fordist nature to the extent that its emerging functions resolve (*or are held to do so*) the crisis tendencies in the KWS' (Jessop 1994: 27, our emphasis).

This equivocation is crucial in assessing the phenomenon of an increased emphasis on education and training. Thus the SWS can be treated as either an effective set of supply-side measures or as a gestural political response. While this is a big question, there are considerable doubts that can be expressed regarding the effectiveness of education and training policy. For example, the emphasis on the importance of training is often underpinned by reference to research undertaken by the National Institute for Economic and Social Research (NIESR) (for a critical review see Cutler 1992b). NIESR work assumes that training is an economic input analogous with investment in physical capital, and that a central problem of the British economy is the under-supply of trained labour and thus of this relevant input. This argument has been developed in the context of international comparisons, where the British training record has been compared unfavourably with European Union competitors, particularly Germany.

However, it is important to realise the difficulties stemming from treating training as an isolated 'input'. This makes the implicit assumption that it can be taken out of the economic and industrial relations context of the nation-state concerned. For example, as Heyes and Stuart (1994: 43) point out, Germany remains an industrial relations system with formidable trade union strength. This, in turn, means that German labour may be able to block low-wage deregulated routes to business profitability. If this is so, then simply expanding the supply of skilled labour in the UK will not have the same effect, because of the contextual difference. This is, of course, relevant to Conservative policy, and raises the tension between both embracing deregulationist approaches and expanding the supply of skilled labour. However, it also has potential implications for Labour, since the move to the right has been accompanied by an attempt to distance the party from the trade unions. Thus Labour is unlikely to be a vehicle for radically improving the bargaining or political power of trade unions.

Analogous problems arise with respect to the expansion of higher education. Thus the rapid expansion of higher education has raised questions as to whether such labour is 'under utilised'. While there are measurement problems here, such situations can be argued to occur when graduates go into jobs that have been traditionally non-graduate and have not been redesigned to utilise the skills that graduates might bring to the job (Mason 1995). Mason's research in financial services (banks and building societies) found clear evidence of such under-utilisation.

In this case, in the ten enterprises for which data were available, 45 per cent of graduates entering employment in the twelve-month period studied had entered (unchanged) 'clerical, cashier and similar jobs' (ibid.: 22). Such jobs were paid only 60 per cent of median graduate salary levels, and, while it was possible that these jobs could be a basis for advancement within the enterprise, Mason did not regard their prospects as promising (ibid.). It would, of course, be dangerous to generalise these findings to the manufacturing or service sectors as a whole; but it is worth stressing, since, as most graduates enter the service sector, how they are deployed there is particularly significant. Thus, whereas in 1983 23 per cent of first-degree graduates entered manufacturing and 39 per cent services, by 1993 the respective figures were 15 per cent and 50 per cent; the banking, insurance and finance sector alone accounted for 5 per cent of graduates, one-third of the intake of manufacturing (ibid.: 33).

Thus, while the concept of a shift to a SWS might be seductive, the evidence presented here suggests that policy moves that give greater weight to education and training are not equivalent to a supply-side policy that resolves contemporary economic problems.

New Wave Management

The second alternative means of conceptualising public sector service management that, again, has a more positive view of the phenomenon has been characterised as *new wave management* (Wood 1989). This position derives from the 'excellence' approach, in particular work stemming from Peters and Waterman's (1982) book *In Search of Excellence*. There are various respects in which this approach has similarities with the discussion of Post-Fordism. For example, again the conception has been applied to the public sector, but originates in a framework applied to the private sector. However, there is also an important difference in the nature of the literature from which the 'excellence' approach to management stems and that on Fordism and Post-Fordism. In the case of the latter the argument stemmed from theoretical work in the social sciences seeking to explain what were seen as important social changes either at the level of production processes or in the relationship of different social 'levels'. In contrast, the 'excellence' literature derives from management and Peters and Waterman's own backgrounds were as management consultants at the firm of McKinsey.

Stemming as it does from this source, the excellence approach is prescriptive rather than theoretical. For example, the subtitle of the book stresses that what is offered is 'lessons from America's best-run companies'. *In Search of Excellence* was written in a context when American corporate performance was being unfavourably compared with, in particular, Japanese industry. However, Peters and Waterman claim that, if the appropriate 'lessons' were learnt from American corporate experience, then importations of foreign practice were not required; thus they state, 'it dawned on us that we did not have to look all the way to Japan for models with which to attack the corporate malaise which has us in its vicelike grip. We have a host of big American companies that are doing it right from the standpoint of all their constituents – customers, employees, shareholders and the public at large' (Peters and Waterman 1982: xxii). An important feature in this quotation is the suggestion that well-run private sector practice delivers benefits for all the 'stakeholders', 'all constituents'. This, in large part, accounts for the appeal of New Wave Management. Thus, if such a claim can be taken at face value and if such 'lessons' can be transferred to the public sector bodies, then it might be possible to reconcile the potentially conflicting interests of these groups. Naturally, if this is the case, then an 'excellence'-based public sector management could be seen as offering a substantial advance on the 'classic welfare state'. In evaluating such arguments the analysis will follow a different order to that used in the discussion of Fordism and Post-Fordism. In that discussion the problems of applying the concepts in the public sector were discussed before the weaknesses in the original area of application (the private sector). In the case of New Wave Management the approach will be outlined and discussion will focus on the private sector application via a critical discussion of *In Search of Excellence*. It will then be possible to link this critical discussion to arguments on the weakness of the 'excellence' approach in the public sector.

The 'Excellence' Approach

Peters and Waterman argue that 'excellent' business enterprises can be characterised by eight organisational features. They have a 'bias for action', i.e. there are few or no obstacles to experimentation, including the introduction of new products. Secondly, they are 'close to the customer', with an emphasis on discovering customer needs and satisfying them. Thirdly, they foster autonomy and entrepreneurship: individuals who are 'product champions' are encouraged to pursue new ideas and mistakes are tolerated. Fourthly, such companies operate 'productivity through people': 'excellent companies treat their rank and file as the root source of quality and productivity gain' (Peters and Waterman 1982: 14). Fifthly, they are 'hands on and value-driven': thus it is seen as important to have a clear set of corporate values and that managers be in touch with production. Sixthly, companies should 'stick to the knitting', i.e. be involved in a limited range of related businesses rather than attempting to run a wide range of diversified businesses. Seventhly, there should be a simple organisational form that is not overstaffed. Finally, there should be a 'tight–loose' combination, 'tight' in the sense that employees should be expected to adhere to corporate values, but 'loose' in the sense that controls should not stifle autonomy.

The argument suggests, therefore, that companies exhibiting these characteristics will also have superior performance. However, in so far as this is an empirical proposition, it would require means by which such characteristics could be measured. Yet, a feature of the text, which has been much discussed by critics, is the very impressionistic approach that the authors have to the identification of such characteristics. For example, a paradoxical feature, given the emphasis on empowerment of staff in the position taken, is that the text is littered with statements by senior corporate managers that are taken as evidence of the organisational characteristics of the firms concerned. Thus, as Carroll (1983) has argued in a review of *In Search of Excellence*, 'The lessons are conveyed via anecdotes and quotations from the leaders of excellent companies. There is in this use of leader quotations an important but unstated implication that the leader knows and understands in an unimpeachable way what has happened in the excellent company and is capable of expressing that happening without any loss of potency and accuracy.' He also points to further use of impressionistic material. For example, one of the features that stems from the 'bias for action' is the idea that product experimentation is highly desirable. It is also assumed not to involve prohibitive costs in 'excellent' companies, although, presumably, it could in the non-excellent. However, as Carroll argued 'since the authors give no evidence of having catalogued and priced those research endeavours one has to wonder whether and how Peters and Waterman are qualified to rank Digital, HP (Hewlett Packard) and Wang (all 'excellent') and their many electronic competitors' (ibid.: 84).

The vagueness of the evidence is also illustrated in the treatment of training. Given that productivity through people is an excellent characteristic, it might be expected that such companies put a high priority on training. Peters and Waterman (1982: 264, emphasis in the original) comment 'We haven't the systematic data, so we can't conclude with finality that our excellent companies are far above the norm in the amount of time they spend on training activities. On the other hand, there are enough signs of *training intensity* to suggest that this might be the case.'

However, even if a serious attempt were made to tackle the issue of identifying 'excellent' characteristics, two other conditions would need to be addressed to support the argument. Firstly, 'non-excellent' companies would have to be shown not have the organisational features that characterise 'excellence'. And secondly, 'excellent' companies would need to be shown to have superior performance.

In the text neither of these conditions are met. The initial project was defined when the authors were working at McKinsey, and excellence was then defined as 'continuously innovative big companies' (Peters and Waterman 1982: 13). They focused on 'seventy-five highly regarded companies' (ibid.). It is not clear how these companies were chosen or what 'highly regarded' meant. Then 'intense structured interviews' were conducted 'in about half of these organisations' (ibid.). No details were given regarding who was interviewed or what they were asked. The other companies 'we initially studied through secondary channels, principally press coverage and annual reports for the last twenty-five years' (ibid.). It is on this basis that the 'eight attributes emerged to characterise most nearly the distinction of the excellent . . . companies' (ibid.).

While the term 'distinction' is used here, it would appear to be a misnomer, since no comparisons with 'non-excellent' companies were made at this stage. Peters and Waterman do raise the question of a comparison with such companies, but they comment: 'We also studied some underachieving companies for purposes of comparison, but we didn't concentrate much on this, as we felt we had plenty of insight into underachievement through our combined twenty-four years in the management consulting business' (Peters and Waterman 1982: 13). In other words no attempt is made to *demonstrate* any systematic differences between excellent and non-excellent companies.

Though this is damaging to the overall argument, its weakness is further emphasised if we consider the performance measures and their relationship to excellent companies. At first sight this might appear to be harder evidence. Thus, Peters and Waterman argue (ibid.: 22) 'we reasoned that no matter what prestige these companies had in the eyes of the rest of the business world, the companies were not truly excellent unless their financial performance supported their halo of esteem'. There is another irony here, for, despite all the reference to 'constituents', the only measures of performance used relate to shareholder interests. These were embodied in six financial performance criteria relating to rates of return and growth in corporate asset values over the period 1961–80 (ibid.: 22–3). 'Excellent' financial performance meant that the company 'must have been in the top half of the industry in at least four out of six of these criteria over the twenty-year period' (ibid.: 23). In the final analysis in the book the original seventy-five companies were reduced to sixty-two. However, of this sixty-two only thirty-six (58 per cent) met the financial performance criteria. This again weakens the argument, in that over 40 per cent of 'excellent' companies were not so in terms of financial performance, the only quantified performance criterion. Furthermore, the hurdles might be considered not particularly stringent. To meet them, the company only had to be in the top half of its industry, and, given that the book was written in a context of 'corporate malaise', at least for the later years this suggests that this would have meant the top half of a poor group.

Some commentators (e.g. Hoggett 1987) have seen devolved management in the public sector as embodying principles of new wave management. However, it is important to stress that there is a key difference. As was indicated earlier in the book, devolved management crucially involves performance measurement. Yet Peters and Waterman are highly critical of 'managing by numbers'. Thus, they argue, 'the companies that seemed the most focused – those with most quantified statements of mission, with the most precise financial targets – had done *less* well financially than those with broader, less precise, more qualitative statements of corporate purpose' (ibid.: 281, emphasis in the original). This observation supports arguments that the recent shifts in public sector management are inconsistent with new wave management. Thus, Walby and Greenwell (1994) point to features such as attempts to exert greater control over consultant contracts and the use of health care assistants in nursing as inconsistent with the notion of staff empowerment. Similarly, Cunningham and Hyman's (1996) research in NHS trusts in Scotland found that, while line managers did feel empowered, non-managerial staff, subject to work intensification and a tighter disciplinary regime, felt that their organisational commitment was reduced.

In this study, problems with empowerment were seen as stemming from short-term budgetary constraints on managers, which militated against investment in employee development. These analyses arguably connect back to the weaknesses of the claims of 'excellence' management. Thus, as was indicated above, the approach was seen as one that claimed to reconcile stakeholder interests. However, not only did *In Search of Excellence* not demonstrate this, because it contained no measures of performance other than those relating to shareholder interests, but even on these narrow criteria over 40 per cent of the selected companies were unable to meet these (relatively modest) financial targets. This is not, of course, to say that employee or user empowerment is not desirable; but the idea that it is a panacea that reconciles conflicting interests is, at best, unproven.

Managerialism and the Politics of Distribution

Both the production-process variant of Post-Fordism and New Wave Management are distinguished by the claim that they can reconcile variant stakeholder interests. This has parallels with the claims of public sector managerialism to deliver not just efficiency but also effectiveness. However, the experience of public sector managerialism does not support such claims. Thus a feature of changes in the public sector is that, while they have radically altered organisational structures and forms of management control, they have, to a large extent, left production methods unchanged. There are, in our view, two fundamental consequences of what has been changed and what has been left unchanged, and both have important political implications. The first is that the plethora of information on public sector 'performance' is effectively part of a presentational politics where, often, increases in activity and claims regarding quality are tendentious. This point has been made in the book with respect to a number of issues relating to performance measurement and the role of evaluative bodies in the public sector in Chapter 2, and with regard to government claims on quality in higher education in Chapter 3. Such developments reflect the need to appear to be doing more and at a higher quality level, and sit uneasily with claims for greater 'accountability'.

The second key feature is the distributional implications of public sector managerialism. This is effectively suppressed by managerialist discourse, which is dominated by the claim of 'more for less' and general stakeholder benefits. However, the effect of public sector managerialism is not so much to produce more as to redistribute existing resources. Thus many claims for increased unit efficiency and throughput involve displacing costs on to other providers (Department of Health 1997) and/or informal carers. There has also been a strong trend to increasing work intensity in the public sector, uneven treatment of different groups on a class and gender basis, and casualisation of employment relationships. Such a distributional politics is even more marked in the case of education, where the attempt has been made to remodel the service to serve individualist goals (Cutler and Waine 1997). Thus, while New Labour has promised reconciliation of equity and efficiency via education and training, there is, arguably, more compelling evidence that what is happening is a competitive credentialisation process to distribute existing limited employment opportunities. The emergence of an effective political consensus on public sector managerialism is likely, however, to continue to marginalise the necessary political debate on these central distributional issues.

Documents

1.1

The problem most relevant to the complaints that have been made to us is how to provide safeguards against inefficiency when an authority is acting within its legal powers. This matter is not simple. What is the most efficient and economical way of doing something is very often a question of judgement. Councillors are elected to local authorities to exercise such judgement and any procedures that are instituted to allow the government or any other body to investigate their decisions represent an intrusion into the responsibilities of the council.

We believe that the best way of promoting efficiency and securing value for money by external means is through the dissemination of comprehensive but intelligible information on the methods employed by local authorities and the results they achieve.

One of the suggestions made to us was that the government should set up a special monitoring unit for local government which would be concerned solely with issues of efficiency, value for money and prevention of extravagance and would be charged with carrying out regular comparability exercises in financial efficiency based on common yardsticks. It would publish reports on its findings from which individual local authorities and the public would be able to measure the relative efficiency of local administration.

We believe that, of all the external bodies at present concerned with efficiency or of the possible new bodies suggested to us in evidence, only the auditors are in a position to base studies in comparative efficiency on information sufficient to achieve savings sufficiently greater than the costs of procuring the information in the first place. But because of the present limitation on efficiency auditing . . . we believe that there is a need to review the structure and procedures of the audit service in order to equip it to fulfil a wider role.

The head of audit should make regular reports on issues of general interest or public concern relating to more than one authority. These reports should be available to the public.They should be concerned particularly with comparisons between the methods employed by local authorities and the results achieved.

Documents

Committee of Inquiry into Local Government Finance (Layfield Committee), *Report*, CMND. 6453, London: HMSO, Ch. 6, paras. 19, 20, 27, 29 and 32

1.2

We recommend that 'agencies' should be established to carry out the executive functions of government within a policy and resources framework set by a department. An 'agency' of this kind may be part of government and the public service, or it may be more effective outside government. We use the term 'agency' not in its technical sense but to describe any executive unit that delivers a service for government. The choice and definition of suitable agencies is primarily for Ministers and senior management in departments to decide. In some instances very large blocks of work comprising virtually a whole department will be suitable to be managed in this way. In other instances, where the scale of activity is too small for an entirely separate organisation, it may be better to have one or several smaller agencies within departments.

These units, large or small, need to be given a well defined framework in which to operate, which sets out the policy, the budget, specific targets and the results to be achieved. It must also specify how politically sensitive issues are to be dealt with and the extent of the delegated authority of management. The management of the agency must be held rigorously to account by their department for the results they achieve.

The framework will need to be set and updated as part of a formal annual review with the responsible Minister, based on a long-term plan and an annual report. The main strategic control must lie with the Minister and Permanent Secretary. But once the policy objectives and budgets within the framework are set, the management of the agency should then have as much independence as possible in deciding how those objectives are met. A crucial element in the relationship would be a formal understanding with Ministers about the handling of sensitive issues and the lines of accountability in a crisis. The presumption must be that, provided management is operating within the strategic direction set by Ministers, it must be left as free as possible to manage within that framework. To strengthen operational effectiveness, there must be freedom to recruit, pay, grade and structure in the most effective way as the framework becomes sufficiently robust and there is confidence in the capacity of management to handle the task.

Jenkins, K. (1988) *Improving Management in Government*, London: HMSO, paras. 19–21

1.3

Outputs are neglected

While the introduction of management systems has helped make civil servants cost conscious, there is less consciousness about results. Departments regard the major central influence on them as the PES process. However, many people told us that the PES system gave the wrong signals. They felt that the emphasis was on inputs, not outputs or value for money.

This is not surprising. The Treasury has two goals with the PES round: to ensure that public spending does not exceed a specified total and to press departments to achieve maximum output from the resources they are allocated. The two are not mutually exclusive, but as the PES round progresses, attention inevitably focuses on the absolute levels of spending. Furthermore, at the later stages, the debate is about spending at the margin of the total bid. The combination of these two factors — emphasis on inputs and 'marginality' — leads departments to feel that although increased stress is being put on results and outputs, it is inputs which still really matter.

There are, however, encouraging signs of change. The 1986 Public Expenditure White Paper included 1,200 output measures; the 1987 White Paper cites some 1,800 measures of output. The April 1987 guidelines for PES asked departments to provide the Treasury with a full statement of output and performance measures to support their baseline expenditure. These will be discussed between the Treasury and departments. Any proposals for additional resources must be supported by information on what indicators and targets for outputs will be used to evaluate their use.

There are also some signs in particular areas of government of an increasing awareness of the importance of outputs. For example, in 1986 the Foreign and Commonwealth Office undertook a scrutiny of existing output measures to see to what extent they could be improved and applied systematically to the full range of work of the FCO at home and overseas.

It is apparent that the closer staff are to the sharp end, the more conscious they are of outputs. In many areas staff are strongly motivated by a wish to serve the public. A common source of frustration in many local offices is the inadequacy of the service staff feel they are giving. Our evidence suggests that very few departments set themselves formal targets for improving the quality of service to the public.

ibid.: paras. 32–6

1.4

Mr. Nicholas Winterton: Did my right hon. Friend watch the interesting Panorama programme last night in which Friedrich Hayek indicated that a constructive and meaningful reform of industrial relations was vital if the economic policies of this Government were to succeed? Will she assure the House that she will have discussions in the near future with her right hon. Friend the Secretary of State for Employment in order to outlaw the closed shop, which I believe is an evil and an infringement of personal freedom, to which my right hon. Friend has referred so often?

The Prime Minister: I did not see the broadcast, as I was in my constituency, but I am a great admirer of Professor Hayek. Some of his books are absolutely supreme – "The Constitution of Liberty" and three volumes on "Law, Legislation and Liberty" – and would be well read by almost every hon. Member.

Hansard (Column 756) 10 March 1981 (Oral Answers)

1.5

Mr. Prior: As we look back over 20 years . . . none of us can take great comfort in our achievements. Productivity and performance have deteriorated. Our record has been worse than that of almost any other country.

There is no doubt that bad industrial relations have greatly contributed to our bad performance . . . There is no doubt that the public generally, including trade unionists and trade union activists, were shocked and alarmed by the events of last winter and that they believe, with the rest of the country, that some reform is necessary.

What are the reforms that are required? First of all there is the right to work free from intimidation and obstruction. Secondly, there is the provision of protection for those not concerned with the dispute but who find their jobs threatened. Thirdly, we must encourage the voice of the majority to prevail over the actions of the minority. Fourthly, we must give proper protection to the individual against loss of employment in a closed shop situation.

Having said that, let me place firmly on the record our view on both the changes that have to be made and the part that the law can play. The law should always give full recognition to the inherent weakness of the individual worker *vis-à-vis* his employer, to the need for him to be organised in a union and to the need for his union to have such exceptional liberties as may be necessary to redress the balance. That is fundamental, but, having accepted that, the very nature of privilege is that it must always be restricted to what is necessary and never go beyond that.

Hansard (Columns 823–4) 21 May 1979

1.6

Since 1979, the Government has acted to improve labour market performance

In the UK, as in many European countries, structural unemployment rose steadily from the 1960s to the 1980s. By 1979, there was clear evidence from the economy's low level of productivity, rapid wage inflation and poor industrial relations that the labour market suffered from deep-rooted problems.

During the last 17 years, the Government has implemented many labour market reforms. It has:

• implemented a step-by-step approach to the reform of industrial relations and trade union law
• reformed employment protection legislation – preserving necessary employee rights while ensuring that legislation does not act as a disincentive to recruitment
• removed or reduced regulations which impede job creation
• introduced a series of education and training reforms to help provide the skills and knowledge needed for the flexible labour market
• developed active labour market policies to help and encourage unemployed people to compete more effectively in the labour market and succeed in getting jobs
• introduced a series of reforms in the system of unemployment benefits to encourage unemployed people to make efforts to find work
• improved incentives to work
• encouraged the development of new, decentralised and more flexible pay determination arrangements.

Flexibility will bring more jobs and allow a diversity of employment patterns. More people can find a way of working that suits them. It is no coincidence that the UK, which has the most deregulated labour market in the EU, has more of its people in work than almost any other EU country.

Europe has seen the consequences of inflexible labour markets over the last 20 years. In the UK, there are clear signs that performance has improved. The best way to help unemployed people is to improve their chance of getting a job. UK unemployment now stands at 8.6 per cent. The more flexible labour market has helped ensure that unemployment is below that in Germany (9.1 per cent), France (11.6 per cent), Italy (12.4 per cent) and Spain (22.5 per cent).

Department of Trade and Industry (1996) *Competitiveness: Creating the Enterprise Centre of Europe*, CM. 3300, paras. 5.2, 5.3, 5.6 and 5.7

1.7

The Government concentrates on customers while continuously improving performance . . .

The Citizen's Charter improves the standard of public services and makes them more responsive to users. Forty main charters and over 8,000 local charters set out the standards that the public expects.

Charter Mark is the Government's award for excellent public service. To win, services must satisfy a number of criteria, including user satisfaction and value for money. The 417 holders include local authorities, hospitals, schools and GPs. The public plays an important part in the scheme — more than 4,000 people nominated over 2,000 separate organisations in 1995. The 1996 campaign was launched in February.

Government is too big and diverse to be effectively managed as one unit whilst concentrating on the customer. The solution in most cases is to set up free-standing Agencies with well-defined responsibilities, clear aims and objectives and targets or key performance indicators. By the end of 1997, three-quarters of civil servants will work in Agencies.

Employment Service performance

- 93 per cent of employers who were Jobcentre users said they were dealt with quickly.
- 89 per cent said that they were dealt with efficiently.
- 86 per cent said they were dealt with professionally.
- 72 per cent of users agreed that Jobcentres produced candidates quickly.
- 67 per cent of employer users considered that Jobcentre staff had a good knowledge of the local labour market.
  Source: CBI and Employment Service.

. . . which means published targets . . .

The 1995 Competitiveness White Paper announced that the 1995 Next Steps Review[1] would include three years of trend data on Agencies' success in meeting their targets. In fact the Review went further by including details of running costs, savings achieved and, in many cases, unit costs. The results show that there has been incremental improvement but that there is scope for more challenging targets. Too often agencies set targets at a level lower than they have already shown they can deliver. Agencies are expected to deliver annual improvements to match those achieved on average by the private sector and targets will be set accordingly.

. . . effective monitoring . . .

The 1996 Next Steps Review will provide more information, enabling Agencies to compare trends in business results, levels of customer service, commitment to training and other aspects of performance, so that they can identify and adopt best practice.

In addition, the Government is working to develop models of organisational performance that will enable Agencies to benchmark against each other and with the best private sector business. In due course, comparisons will also be made with other international leaders in delivering public services.

The Government is also committed to improving further the efficiency, standards and responsiveness of non-departmental public bodies (NDPBs). On 1 April 1996, there were 1,227 NDPBs, 188 fewer than in 1994 and 940 fewer than in 1979. The Government is currently carrying out a study into objective setting and monitoring in executive NDPBs and will report in Summer 1996. The 1996 Public Expenditure Survey will look closely at NDPBs' administration costs.

Performance information for schools, hospitals and local authority services allows people to find out how their local services compare with others and to demand that their services match the best.

ibid.: paras. 13.14–21

2.1

In considering whether the best use is made of the available beds, the length of time each bed is in use for one patient is of importance. An index of this can be found by means of a bed use factor: the higher the

1. *Next Steps, Agencies in Government Review* (1995) (Cm 3164) [HMSO]

factor the more patients are passing through one bed. The number of patients discharged and died divided by the number of beds yields this index. It has been worked out for a number of large hospitals in relation to the two main categories of patients suffering from general medical and general surgical conditions. The same method is of course applicable to other categories of patients. It has been found that there is considerable variation in these factors in hospitals which appear prima facie comparable as illustrated below in relation to the Teaching General Hospitals.

			London Undergraduate Teaching Hospitals	*Provincial Undergraduate Teaching Hospitals*
General	Highest	–	17.35	31.2
Medicine	Lowest	–	10.1	12.45
	Overall	–	12.3	19.1
General	Highest	–	30.45	33.5
Surgery	Lowest	–	14.55	18.8
	Overall	–	19.4	25.0

In some instances, of course, there is an obvious reason for the differences, e.g. certain hospitals have separate pre-convalescent units to which they transfer their patients for the final portion of their stay, but in many instances the reasons for the differences are not apparent. Local thought might profitably be directed to those reasons.

Ministry of Health (1953) *On the State of Public Health* (Annual Report of the Chief Medical Office 1952) CMD. 9009, London: HMSO

2.2

Hospital and community health services – performance

Activity trends

Table 15 gives details of hospital activity levels for each of the main sectors based on information collected directly from NHS hospitals and other health care providers.

- Between 1984 and 1994–95, the number of general and acute ordinary admissions and day cases grew by an average of 3.4 per cent a year.
- Within this increase there is a continuing shift towards treating patients on a day case basis. Since 1984, the number of day cases has grown to 2.4 million in 1994–95, 28 per cent of all general and acute episodes.

Table 15. Health service activity

'000s, days and percentages

	1984	1989–90	1990–91	1991–92	1992–93	1993–94	1994–95 (thousands)	Annual average % change 1984 to 1994–95	% change 1993–94 to 1994–95
Ordinary admissions									
General and acute	5,246	5,677	5,685	5,913	5,987	6,127	6,210	1.7	1.4
Geriatric	344	447	468	508	527	554	548	4.6	-1.1
Maternity	869	968	990	1,010	1,015	1,056	1,059	1.9	0.3
All specialties	6,867	7,477	7,524	7,755	7,828	7,988	8,065	1.6	1.0
Day cases									
General and acute	872	1,152	1,251	1,535	1,785	2,080	2,439	10.5	17.2
All specialties	903	1,163	1,261	1,547	1,808	2,106	2,474	10.3	17.5
All finished consultant episodes									
General and acute	6,118	6,829	6,936	7,448	7,772	8,207	8,649	3.4	5.4
All specialties	7,770	8,639	8,785	9,302	9,635	10,094	10,539	3.0	4.4
New outpatients (referral attendances)									
New outpatients	8,508	8,519	8,502	8,942	9,342	9,683	10,363	1.9	7.0
General and acute	7,577	7,621	7,593	8,036	8,488	8,832	9,513	2.2	7.7
Geriatric	51	60	72	70	77	83	94	6.2	12.3
Maternity	731	689	695	684	612	600	588	-2.1	-2.1
Mental health	198	207	211	218	238	245	257	2.6	4.8
Learning disabilities	3	3	3	3	4	5	5	6.1	-10.9

Table 15. Health service activity (*continued*)

'000s, days and percentages

	1984	1989–90	1990–91	1991–92	1992–93	1993–94	1994–95 (thousands)	Annual average % change 1984 to 1994–95	% change 1993–94 to 1994–95
New A & E (first attenders)	10,213	11,207	11,204	11,035	10,993	11,365	11,943	1.5	5.1
Ward attenders	n/a	900	981	1,008	1,029	985	980	–	–0.6
Occupied bed days								1984 to 1993–94	1992–93 to 1993–94
Mental health	24,700	20,800	19,300	17,100	15,400	13,900	–	–6.0	–9.7
Learning disabilities	14,300	9,100	8,600	7,600	6,500	5,500	–	–9.8	–15.4
Average length of episode (ordinary admissions) days									
General and acute	10.6	8.3	8.0	7.4	7.0	6.7	–	–4.4	–4.3
Geriatrics	53.3	35.9	32.1	26.4	23.3	20.8	–	–8.8	–10.8

(1) The figures for 1984 are estimates of finished consultant episodes based on 1984 discharges and deaths adjusted using 1988–89 data where information was collected using both methods.
(2) Excluding well babies.
(3) Obstetrics and GP maternity.
(4) From April 1992 patients seen by medical staff on a ward are recorded as outpatients rather than ward attenders.
(5) Figures from 1988–89 onwards are estimated based on data obtained directly from Regions.

Managing the Welfare State

Statistics on activity in the community health and paramedical services over the period 1988–89 to 1993–94 collected from health care providers are reported in **Table 16**.

- Following a decline in the early part of the period, activity has remained broadly constant in some areas, whilst increasing in others.
- Since 1984 the number of practice nurses has increased by 370 per cent.

Performance on Patient's Charter Standards

Patient's Charter
The Patient's Charter came into force on 1 April 1992 to improve the quality of health service delivery to patients as part of the Government's Citizen's Charter programme. The Patient's Charter sets out the rights of

Table 16. Community health and paramedical services activity statistics[1]

'000s of episodes

	1988–89	1989–90	1990–91	1991–92	1992–93	1993–94
Health visiting	4,100	3,900	3,600	3,700	3,700	3,700
Community nursing services (total)	2,800	2,800	2,600	2,700	2,800	2,800
District nursing	2,400	2,300	2,100	2,200	2,200	2,200
Community psychiatric nursing	230	240	250	270	300	340
Community learning disability nursing	20	20	20	20	20	20
Specialist nursing	195	200	190	220	270	270
Chiropody services	880	920	910	940	970	1,010
Clinical psychology	150	150	140	150	160	170
Dietetics	650	630	620	640	640	670
Occupational therapy	770	750	740	840	880	940
Physiotherapy	3,100	3,200	3,200	3,300	3,400	3,500
Speech therapy	240	230	240	250	270	290
Community dental services	n/a	n/a	1,160	1,190	1,210	1,160

(1) Owing to changes in definitions which occurred in 1988–89, it is not possible to provide comparative statistics to 1988–89.
(2) Number of new episodes commenced in the year except health visiting (number of different persons seen at least once in a year) and community dental services (number of episodes of care completed in the year.)
(3) Estimated national totals based on those districts supplying data.
(4) Data for 1988–89 to 1992–93 revised to take account of late and missing returns and correction of major errors.
(5) Includes a small number of discontinued episodes of care.
(6) Not collected on a comparable basis.

patients, and the standards of service they can expect to receive from the National Health Service. To ensure that the Patient's Charter is being delivered, the Department of Health regularly collects information on a number of key Charter standards. This shows that NHS performance on the majority of these standards has improved markedly over the year.

HCHS standards Performance against the immediate assessment in accident and emergency departments, and thirty minute wait in outpatients standards continued to improve. By the end of 1994–95, 93 per cent of patients were assessed within five minutes of arrival at accident and emergency and 88 per cent of patients were seen within thirty minutes of their appointment time in outpatients clinics.

Waiting times

Half of all admissions to hospital are immediate. The other half are elective, with a waiting time before the admission takes place. The median waiting time for elective admissions is six weeks with nearly three-quarters admitted within three months.

The NHS has been working to end the longest waits for treatment whilst ensuring that urgent cases continue to receive priority. Waits of two years or more for admission have now been ended and the Patient's Charter guarantee is that no one should now wait longer than eighteen months for admission. Progress is also being made on outpatient waits with a standard set that no one should wait longer than 26 weeks for an initial outpatient appointment, with 90 per cent of patients seen within 13 weeks.

Inpatients and day cases In March 1991 patients on the waiting list had waited an average of seven and a half months for treatment; by March 1995 the average waiting time had been reduced to four months. During 1994–95 the total waiting list fell by 2 per cent, a reduction of around 21,000. This trend has proved difficult to maintain however with a 1 per cent increase during the first three quarters of 1995–96. The number of people waiting less than 12 months rose slightly during 1994–95 and this trend has continued into 1995–96. Progress continues to be made on reducing the numbers waiting long times for treatment. The number of people waiting over 12 months has been reduced sharply since the beginning of 1994–95 from 64,508 to 20,892 at 31 December 1995. The number of very long waiters has also been driven down. At the beginning of 1994–95 428 patients were waiting more than 2 years. Over the course of that year and the first three quarters of 1995–96 waits of more than 2 years have been eliminated and at 31 December 1995 only 3 patients were waiting more than 18 months.

Outpatients Information on the time patients wait between referral by their GP and being seen in an outpatient clinic was first published in 1994–95. Figures for the quarter ended March 1995 show 95 per cent of first appointments seen within 26 weeks of referral and 82 per cent seen within 13 weeks. By the quarter ended September 1995 performance had improved and 97 per cent were seen within 26 weeks and 83 per cent seen within 13 weeks.

Acute, geriatric and maternity sectors unit costs

- Between 1983–84 and 1990–91 the average cost of treating an acute patient declined by almost 13 per cent.
- The number of patients treated on a day case basis has increased by on average 10 per cent per year since 1983–84, while the length of stay for patients occupying a bed overnight has been cut by over a third to an estimated 4.3 days in 1993–94.
- The average cost of each geriatric case has declined by 37 per cent between 1983–84 and 1990–91, with length of stay falling by almost a half.
- The average cost of a maternity case declined by 20 per cent over the same period.
- Average cost for all these sectors have gone down between 1991–92 and 1993–94.

Mental health and learning disability sectors

- Average costs per day for mental health and learning disability inpatients rose by 31 per cent and 58 per cent respectively between 1983–84 and 1990–91 and by 13 per cent and 30 per cent respectively between 1991–92 and 1993–94.

Target payments GPs make a substantial contribution to the health of the population by achieving high targets for vaccination against childhood illnesses and for cervical cytology to detect cancer. At April 1994 over 91 per cent of GPs were reaching the higher 90 per cent target for childhood immunisation, and 96 per cent reaching the 70 per cent target. On cervical cytology 89 per cent were reaching the higher 80 per cent target and 99 per cent the 50 per cent target. There are, however, fairly substantial variations in performance across the country. The Department is encouraging health authorities to support GPs in improving coverage in poorer performing areas.

Department of Health (1996) *The Government's Expenditure Plans 1996–97 to 1998–99* Departmental Report CM. 3212, London: HMSO, paras. 4.61–4.70: 4.98

2.3

As part of the monitoring process of institutions, the Funding Council use a range of indicators. The three main indicators used to monitor the financial health of the sector as a whole are:

- Strength ratio which is calculated by dividing general reserves by total recurrent expenditure and multiplying by 365. The strength ratio indicates that 37 days recurrent expenditure could be met from general reserves in 1990–91. This rose to 44 days in 1992–93 and is projected to rise to 56 days in 1997–98. General reserves represented about 10 per cent of recurrent expenditure in 1990–91 and 12 per cent in 1992–93. They are projected to increase to around 15 per cent for 1997–98;
- Current asset: current liability ratio which is a measure of short term liquidity, calculated by dividing total current assets by current liabilities. Current assets for the sector were sufficient to cover current liabilities about 1.5 times in 1990–91 and over 1.7 times in 1992–93. Projections show current liabilities being covered 1.8 times in 1993–94 dropping to 1.6 times by 1997–98; and
- Gearing ratio which indicates the extent to which the sector is using long term finance (borrowings) to fund development. It is calculated by dividing long term liabilities by general reserves. The gearing ratio has increased from 1.2 in 1990–91 to 1.5 in 1992–93 and is projected to increase to 1.7 in 1997–98 reflecting mainly a move to greater borrowing. This is consistent with the Government's support for increased private financing of higher education.

National Audit Office (1994) *The Financial Health of Higher Education Institutions in England*, London: HMSO, para. 2.14

2.4

Shorter waiting times

The first *Patient's Charter* was published in England in 1991. It set out, for the first time, patients' rights and the standard of service they could expect from the NHS. The themes on which it focused were reducing patient waiting times, improving communications with and information to the public, and preserving patient privacy and dignity. In March 1991, over 50,000 patients had been waiting two years or more to go into hospital. Now nobody waits this long.

A new *Patient's Charter* was published in January 1995. The new charter guarantees that from April 1995 patients will be admitted to hospital within 18 months of being put on a waiting list, and this has been largely achieved. Patients can expect to wait no longer than 12 months for in-patient treatment for coronary artery bypass grafts and some associated procedures. In fact, patients will normally be seen much sooner than these times. Of those admitted from waiting lists, half are admitted within six weeks, and nearly three-quarters within three months.

Procedures have changed in out-patient clinics, too. All patients are now given a specific appointment time, and should be seen within 30 minutes of that time. In 1994–95, the NHS met this standard for nearly nine out of every ten patients, a six per cent improvement over the previous year.

For the first time, a national standard has been set for the maximum time patients should wait to receive their first out-patient appointment after referral by their GP or dentist. Nine out of 10 people can expect to be seen within 13 weeks, and everyone should be seen within 26 weeks.

In England, in March 1995, around 32,000 patients had been waiting over a year for hospital admission, compared with over 200,000 in March 1990.

In March 1995, 93 per cent of patients in England were assessed immediately on arrival in an accident and emergency department, compared with 75 per cent in June 1993.

Documents

The 1991 *Patient's Charter* also set national standards for patients attending accident and emergency departments. Patients can now expect to have their need for treatment assessed as soon as they arrive in the accident and emergency department. More than nine out of 10 patients receive this standard.

Performance against three key patient's charter standards in England

	Quarter Ending 31 Dec. 1993	Quarter Ending 31 Dec. 1994	Quarter Ending 31 Mar. 1995
Patients assessed immediately in Accident & Emergency Departments (%)	83	91	93
Out-patients seen within 30 minutes of appointment time (%)	80	86	88
Number of patients not admitted within a month of first cancelled operation*		1,343	2,005

* This standard came into effect in April 1994

Prime Minister's Office (1995) *The Citizen's Charter: The Facts and Figures* CM. 2970, London: HMSO, paras. 2.16–2.20

Managing the Welfare State

National performance:	Outpatient appointments % of patients seen within 30 minutes of appointment time 90%	Accident and emergency % of patients assessed within 5 minutes of arrival 94%	Operations cancelled Number of patients not admitted within a month of cancellation of their operation 8
Addenbrooke's NHS Trust	84% ★★▲	95% ★★★★★▲	39
Allington NHS Trust	100% ★★★★★	–	0 ★★★★★
Anglian Harbours NHS Trust	99% ★★★★★	98% ★★★★★	–
Aylesbury Vale Community Healthcare NHS Trust	100% ★★★★★	98% ★★★★★	–
Bedford & Shires Health & Care NHS Trust	97% ★★★★★	–	–
Bedford Hospital NHS Trust	91% ★★★★★	99% ★★★★★	17 ★
East Berkshire Community Health NHS Trust	98% ★★★★▲	100% ★★★★★	0 ★
East Berkshire NHS Trust	100% ★★★★★	–	★★★★★
East Suffolk Local Health Services NHS Trust	100% ★★★★★	100% ★★★★★	–

HOSPITAL/TRUST NAMES	Column 1	Column 2	Column 3
Heatherwood & Wexham Park Hospital NHS Trust	94% ★★★★▲	96% ★★★★★	0 ★★★★
Hinchingbrooke Healthcare NHS Trust	90% ★★★★▲	94% ★★★★	60 ★
Horton General Hospital NHS Trust	85% ★★★	81% ★★★	0 ★★★★★
Ipswich Hospital NHS Trust	94% ★★	99% ★★	27 ★
James Paget Hospital NHS Trust	96% ★★★★★▲	93% ★★★★	4 ★★★

HOSPITAL/TRUST NAMES

Most hospitals are now part of an NHS Trust. If you can't see the hospital you are looking for, use the index beginning on page 231 to find out which NHS Trust it comes under. Then look up the Trust for the combined figures of all the hospitals within it.

THE PERFORMANCE MEASURES

Column 1: Outpatient appointments – The figures show percentages of patients seen within 30 minutes of their appointment time. *Column 2: Accident and emergency*

The figures show percentages of patients assessed immediately. Figures for major accident and emergency units are shown in **bold**. *Column 3: Operations cancelled* – The figures show actual numbers (not percentages) of patients who had an operation cancelled at the last minute, and then had to wait more than a month after that.

STAR RATINGS

Stars (★) are given depending upon performance: the better the performance against the standard, the more stars. Star ratings have been given where we know that the Audit Commission's auditors were satisfied with the data collection systems. In other cases we have published the data, but without stars.

CHANGE IN PERFORMANCE

An upward arrow (▲) indicates that this year's performance is significantly better than last year's. A downward arrow (▼) indicates a significantly worse performance. Arrows have only been given where the hospital has not been affected by a merger since last year and the Audit Commission's auditors were satisfied with the data collection systems in both years. Note: Arrows are not applicable in Column 3.

BLANK ENTRIES

A blank entry (–) means that the NHS Trust or hospital concerned does not provide the service in question. A dot (●) indicates that the NHS Trust or hospital concerned failed to provide data.

PERIOD

1 January 1996 to 31 March 1996

Table 4b. Waiting times: % of patients admitted within 12 months (continued)

	All Specialties	General surgery	Urology	Trauma and orthopaedics	Ear nose and throat	Ophthalmology
National performance:	**97%**	**97%**	**97%**	**93%**	**96%**	**95%**
Forest Healthcare NHS Trust	83% ★	88% ★★▼	86% ★★	54% ★▼	80% ★	63% ★▼
Great Ormond Street Hospital NHS Trust	98% ★★★★	–	96% ★★★★	92% ★★★▲	99% ★★★★★	100% ★★★★★
Hammersmith Hospitals NHS Trust	98% ★★★★	98% ★★★★	98% ★★★★	90% ★★★	99% ★★★★★	88% ★★
Harefield Hospital NHS Trust	99% ★★★★★	–	–	–	–	–
Haringey Healthcare NHS Trust	–	–	–	–	–	–
Harrow & Hillingdon Healthcare NHS Trust	–	–	–	–	–	–
Havering Hospitals NHS Trust	95% ★★★★	96% ★★★★	93% ★★★▲	93% ★★★	95% ★★★★▲	78% ★▲
Hillingdon Hospital NHS Trust	100% ★★★★★	100% ★★★★★	100% ★★★★★▲	100% ★★★★★▲	–	100% ★★★★★▲
Homerton Hospital NHS Trust	98% ★★★★	98% ★★★★★▲	100% ★★★★★	95% ★★★★▲	–	–
Hounslow & Spelthorne Comm. & Ment. Health NHS Trust	–	–	–	–	–	–
Mid-Essex Community & Mental Health NHS Trust	100% ★★★★★	–	–	–	–	–
Mid-Essex Hospital Services NHS Trust	87% ★★	84% ★	81% ★	77% ★	90% ★★★	72% ★▼
Moorfields Eye Hospital NHS Trust	99% ★★★★★	–	–	–	–	99% ★★★★★
Mount Vernon & Watford Hospitals NHS Trust	90% ★★★	94% ★★★	98% ★★★★	90% ★★★	–	100% ★★★★★

HOSPITAL/TRUST NAME Most hospitals are now part of an NHS Trust. If you can't see the hospital you are looking for, use the index beginning on page 231 to find out which NHS Trust it comes under. Then look up the Trust for the combined figures of all the hospitals within it.
THE PERFORMANCE MEASURE There are 14 types of medical procedure listed. The Table shows percentages of patients who had their operations within 12 months.
Note: The 'All specialties' column shows percentages of *all* patients who had their operations within that time period, including those specialties not listed in this Table.
STAR RATINGS Stars (★) are given depending upon performance. The better the performance against the standard, the more stars. Star ratings have been given where we know that the Audit Commission's auditors were satisfied with the data collection system. In other cases we have published the data, but without stars.

Oral surgery	Plastic surgery	Gynaecology	Cardiothoracic surgery	Cardiology	Paediatric surgery	Paediatrics	General medicine	Gastroenterology
95%	93%	99%	96%	99%	98%	100%	100%	100%
75% ★▲	–	94% ★★★	–	+	–	+	100% ★★★★★	100% ★★★★★
–	93% ★★★▲	–	100% ★★★★★	–	100% ★★★★★	99% ★★★★★	–	100% ★★★★★
100% ★★★★	95% ★★★★	93% ★★★	90% ★★★	100% ★★★★★	100% ★★★★★	100% ★★★★★	98% ★★★★	100% ★★★★★
–	–	–	97% ★★★★	100% ★★★★★	100% ★★★★★	98% ★★★★	–	–
–	–	–	–	–	–	–	–	–
–	–	–	–	–	–	–	–	–
85% ★★	–	98% ★★★★	–	+	–	+	100% ★★★★★	–
100% ★★★★	–	100% ★★★★★	–	–	–	–	–	–
99% ★★★★	–	98% ★★★★	–	–	–	–	100% ★★★★★	100% ★★★★★
–	–	–	–	–	–	–	–	–
–	–	–	–	–	–	–	–	–
93% ★★★▲	80% ★	91% ★★★▼	–	–	–	–	100% ★★★★★	99% ★★★★★
–	–	–	–	–	–	–	–	–
84% ★▲	78% ★▼	99% ★★★★★	–	–	–	–	97% ★★★★	99% ★★★★★

CHANGE IN PERFORMANCE An upward arrow (▲) indicates that this year's performance is significantly better than last year's. A downward arrow (▼) indicates a significantly worse performance. Arrows have only been given where the hospital has not been affected by a merger since last year and the Audit Commission's auditors were satisfied with the data collection systems in both years. Note: there are no arrows in the 'All specialties' column or the six columns furthest to the right as this is the first year that these indicators have formed part of the Table.

BLANK ENTRIES A blank entry (–) means that the NHS Trust or hospital concerned does not provide the service in question. A (+) indicates that the NHS Trust or hospital provided the service to only a few people. A (●) indicates that the NHS Trust or hospital concerned failed to provide data.

PERIOD 1 April 1995 to 31 March 1996.

NHS Executive (1996b) *The NHS Performance Guide 1995–96* (*selected* NHS Trust entries), London: HMSO

2.6

11. (1) For the purposes of this Part of this Act there shall be a body to be known as the Audit Commission for Local Authorities in England and Wales.

    (2) The Commission shall consist of not less than thirteen nor more than seventeen members appointed by the Secretary of State after consultation with —

    (a) such associations of local authorities as appear to him to be concerned; and

    (b) such bodies of accountants, such bodies representing local authority employees, and such other organisations or persons as appear to him to be appropriate.

    (3) The Secretary of State shall, after the like consultation, appoint one of the members to be chairman and another to be deputy chairman.

    Establishment of Audit Commission.

14. (1) The Commission shall prepare, and keep under review, a code of audit practice prescribing the way in which auditors are to carry out their functions under this Part of this Act.

15. (1) In auditing any accounts required to be audited in accordance with this Part of this Act, an auditor shall by examination of the accounts and otherwise satisfy himself —

    (a) that proper practices have been observed in the compilation of the accounts; and

    (b) that the body whose accounts are being audited has made proper arrangements for securing economy, efficiency and effectiveness in its use of resources.

    (2) The auditor shall comply with the code of audit practice as for the time being in force.

    (3) The auditor shall consider whether, in the public interest, he should make a report on

    General duties of auditors.

– 188 –

any matter coming to his notice in the
course of the audit in order that it may be
considered by the body concerned or
brought to the attention of the public, and
shall consider whether the public interest
requires any such matter to be made the
subject of an immediate report rather than
of a report to be made at the conclusion of
the audit.

Local Government Finance Act 1982, section 11: 14–15

2.7

26. (1) The Commission shall undertake or
promote comparative and other studies
designed to enable it to make recommendations for improving economy, efficiency
and effectiveness in the provision of local
authority services and of other services
provided by bodies whose accounts are
required to be audited in accordance with
this Part of this Act, and for improving the
financial or other management of such
bodies.

Studies for
improving
economy etc
in services.

ibid.: section 26

2.8

Councillors are, of course, politically accountable, but interest in local
elections is often quite low. Many electors do not pay rates – or at least
not directly – so that the connection between policies and their cost is not
made. Even those electors who are ratepayers do not pay the full cost of
local services. Substantial contributions to local authority funds are made
by government in the form of grants which vary from year to year, and
these diminish rather than improve local accountability.

In recent years there has been a demand for the 'sharpening up' of
accountability in local government. This is reflected, for example, in the
requirement for local authorities to publish an annual report. However,

accountability means more than that the accounts should be presented fairly and that councillors should present themselves periodically for election. There is a need for local authorities to check and to demonstrate that they are effective, efficient and economic. Auditors have a new responsibility to satisfy themselves that the authorities they audit can do this.

Audit Commission (1983) *Performance Review in Local Government: A Handbook for Auditors and Local Authorities*, London: HMSO, p. 3

2.9

Value-added evaluation of A-level work is used by a number of groups and individuals as a tool to inform institutions' internal management. The longest-established and most widely applied value-added evaluation system forms part of the A-level Information System (ALIS) operated by the School of Education of the University of Newcastle upon Tyne. ALIS is a collaborative research and development project to which more than 170 member schools and colleges subscribe. A range of data and inform-ation are gathered from the institutions and from the A-level students. Analysis of data from all members yields comparative information which is fed back without identifying any member's results to the other members.

One school which is a member of ALIS recently identified that its students' biology results were below expectations, even after taking account of their overall prior GCSE results. The students who had done least well were found to be those who were not simultaneously studying chemistry A-level and those who had only achieved grade C in GCSE mathematics. The chemistry and mathematics teaching within the biology A-level course has since been amplified and biology A-level results have improved. Another school found that ALIS data were critical to gaining the acceptance by teaching staff of a need to examine mathematics teaching methodology. The school reports that by following up the ALIS data with investigation of the reasons for under-achievement in mathematics A-level, it has now partially solved the problem of under-achievement in mathematics.

Audit Commission (1993b) *Unfinished Business: Full-Time Education Courses for 16–19 Year Olds*, London: HMSO, paras. 83–4

2.10

Performance in local government has two key aspects: service efficiency and service effectiveness.

Effectiveness means providing the right services to enable the local authority to implement its policies and objectives. *Efficiency* means providing a specified volume and quality of service with the lowest level of resources capable of meeting that specification.

These ideas may be expressed visually as follows:

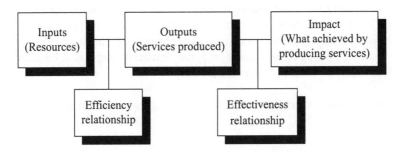

To these concepts may be added the third of the Audit Commission's three Es

– *economy*. This means ensuring that the assets of the authority, and services purchased, are procured and maintained at the lowest possible cost consistent with a specified quality and quantity.

Audit Commission (1983) *Performance Review in Local Government: A Handbook for Auditors and Local Authorities*, London: HMSO, p. 8

2.11

Reletting empty homes

When a property which the council manages becomes empty, the council will generally check its condition and make any minor repairs that may be necessary before a new tenant can view the property, sign up for the tenancy, and move in. If the quality of a council's housing is poor, it may delay the time it takes to relet a property. It may also mean the council has more empty properties than other authorities. Less desirable properties are usually harder to let. The high rise housing found in inner city and urban areas is generally considered less desirable than traditional housing in rural and suburban areas. Many authorities with this 'hard to let' housing have found ways to let it quickly and successfully – for example, by letting to young single people. Where the condition of council housing is poor, more properties could be empty because they are having repairs or improvements made to them, or are awaiting these repairs. A high 'capital spend' for each property should suggest that major improvement programmes are taking place.

In areas where there is a greater demand for housing, new tenants are less likely to turn down offers of a home and properties are less likely to stay empty. But some councils offer new tenants more than one property. This means the time taken to relet a property could be longer because a property may be offered to several different tenants before it is let. So the council's policy on how many properties it offers a tenant will lengthen or lessen the time a property stays empty.

Audit Commission (1994) *Watching their Figures*, London: HMSO

2.12

As Ministers have repeatedly made clear, the government's overall priority in setting up the new capital expenditure control system has been to contain the total of local authority net capital expenditure and related net borrowing within the overall cash limit provided in the relevant public expenditure plan.

Because the government's financial planning is on an annual basis government is seeking conformity with annual cash limits. So a respectable performance over four years is not good enough, from the standpoint of the government's economic strategy.

The present system for controlling local authorities' capital expenditure on a year-to-year basis is resulting in the following unnecessary inefficiencies.

(i) Projects are often delayed by the need to discuss the details with officials.
(ii) There is a risk that project appraisals will be hurried (or even non-existent) when authorities need to commit capital expenditure before the year end.

(iii) Costs are increased by abrupt reductions in capital programmes
(iv) Assets remain under-utilised, because many authorities consider that the incentive to sell off assets that they do not need in the short-term is not worth the longer term risks.

Audit Commission (1985) *Capital Expenditure Controls in Local Government in England*, London: HMSO, paras. 15 and 29

2.13

Set and Pursue Consistent, Achievable Objectives

Local authorities determine their own objectives, and there would be little purpose in local democracy if these did not differ from one authority to another. This is the most important contribution of members and the central focus of politics.

Setting clear objectives has always been a central characteristic of good management. In future it will be even more important that these objectives are **consistent** with each other and **achievable**:

– limitations on resources also make it much more important to be realistic. Plans for expanded service in one area will not be realised unless the funds can be found by economies of improved value for money elsewhere. Objectives for one without the other are inconsistent, unachievable, and quite simply pointless;
– the competition legislation will require councils to specify what the contractor **will actually do**, not what the council would ideally like to be done. If a perfect standard is required, then the cost has to be faced at the outset. If the cost has to be lower, then the consequent shortfalls in service have to be made explicit and accepted.

Audit Commission (1988) *The Competitive Council*, London: HMSO

2.14

Summary

Although London is the richest city in the United Kingdom, large parts of it face desperate social and economic problems. In some boroughs, unemployment among young men exceeds 45%; in some places, among young blacks, it exceeds 60%. More than one child in three is born into a single parent family. Half the school leavers have no 'O' levels or their CSE equivalents. Homelessness, housing conditions, crime, are worsening year by year, as the cycle of urban deprivation becomes more established. In such circumstances, although extra capital spending will be needed, money alone is not the answer; the need is for outstanding management of each of these problems. This is not evident in many London authorities.

Management problems can be clearly identified and include: reductions in grant, housing in poor conditions, failure to act promptly on opportunities to reduce waste, difficulty recruiting and keeping staff, and generally poor industrial relations. And the consequences are serious: expenditure around double that in similarly deprived areas *after* allowing for the extra costs associated with employing people in London, poor services, a cash gap in prospect next year of over £400 million – as much as 40% of current revenue expenditure in some places – and over £700 million of deferred purchase arrangements which will load extra costs onto tomorrow's ratepayers.

The size of the looming cash gap and the scale of the problems has led the Commission to publish this paper now.

Once the cycle of decay becomes established it will be immensely difficult to reverse. Prevention is the only viable strategy; and this will undoubtedly cost money. There is therefore no time to lose if effective action is to be taken to prevent the emergence in London of the urban dereliction that now affects some large North American cities.

Since it was established in early 1983, the Audit Commission for Local Authorities in England and Wales (The Commission) has become increasingly concerned about the cost and quality of the services delivered by Inner London authorities. This *Occasional Paper* summarises in turn the Commission's views on:

(i) The nature of the problems facing Inner London authorities. Unless their magnitude and causes are understood and the serious consequences of neglect more generally appreciated, the Commission will have failed in its duty as an independent watchdog over local government management and finance.

(ii) The evidence that improved local management could make a significant difference to the quality of local services.

(iii) The immediate financial prospects. There is a gap between current levels of revenue expenditure and the funds likely to be available next year in the most deprived London boroughs, of over £400 million.

(iv) The steps that will be needed in the near term by central government as well as local authorities to reverse the present decline. If local authorities in Inner London cannot be persuaded to adopt the steps necessary to improve their management performance, it will invite the imposition of new organisational arrangements.

Problems facing Inner London

Inner London comprises a dozen boroughs and the City of London. These authorities, with the Inner London Education Authority (ILEA), provide local government services to a population of some 2.3 million people and around 1.3 million commercial and domestic ratepayers. Members and officers in the boroughs in question face a desperately difficult situation: Inner London and four Outer London Boroughs – Brent, Haringey, Newham and Waltham Forest which have many of the same characteristics – include some of the most deprived in England and Wales on almost any indicator of social and economic deprivation.

There are very disturbing parallels between the situation in parts of London and that in parts of New York and Chicago. The South Bronx and the Southside of Chicago represent a future to be avoided at almost all costs. There, a combination of poor housing and education, high crime rates much of it drug-related, large scale immigration and associated racial tensions, an exodus of jobs and the more well off to the suburbs, high youth unemployment and welfare dependency and the break-up of traditional family structures (with a very high proportion of single parent families), have served to create what some commentators in the United States have described as an urban 'underclass'.

Local authorities often lack the powers and resources to tackle these problems. But it is not for the Commission to propose policies for the solution to the 'Inner City' problems, nor to comment on government policy towards Inner Cities generally or London in particular. But it is clear that faced with such challenges, the management of local services in London cannot afford to be less than outstanding. And this *is* the Commission's legitimate concern. Poor management was an important contributory factor to New York's problems in the early 1970s: incompetent appointments to key management positions, workforce opposition to any changes in working practices, tension between the police and the local black community and heavy use of so-called creative accounting to mask the reality that the City was borrowing heavily to finance current expenditure all played their part. The situation in New York is described, graphically, by Charles Morris in *The Cost of Good Intentions*. Good management of Inner London boroughs is a necessary, if not sufficient, condition of preventing similar problems here.

Some London authorities have argued that higher spending reflects greater needs, and that these can only be tackled with more resources and that increased government grant and extra borrowing alone were required. However, increased investment only makes sense if it can be managed effectively: one of the lessons of the past is that 'throwing money at the problem' all too often simply means more waste. So the Commission has undertaken a further review of the available information on the cost and quality of services in Inner London. It has reviewed the reports of its auditors both on the local arrangements for securing economy, efficiency and effectiveness and on individual services: housing management and maintenance, social services for children in care and the elderly, refuse collection, vehicle maintenance, cash flow management and internal audit. And evidence has been obtained from some North American cities facing the problems described earlier: New York, Boston, Chicago, Washington DC, Philadelphia and Atlanta.

This further work has confirmed the Commission's concerns. Even though there has recently been a welcome change in the atmosphere in which auditors have been working and some useful progress has been made, a very serious situation is in prospect. Not to put too fine a point upon it, large parts of London appear set on precisely a course which will lead to financial and management breakdown. In the Commission's view, the problems now facing some London boroughs are not due solely to social and economic factors over which they have no control. Of course these constitute a daunting management challenge. But management makes a vital difference – for good or ill: there is a marked contrast between the performance in terms of economy, efficiency and effectiveness of similarly deprived authorities in London and the provinces. This conclusion emerges from analysis of three groups of authorities shown below.

Group A Eight deprived London boroughs: Brent, Camden, Hackney, Haringey, Islington, Lambeth, Lewisham and Southwark.

Group B Eight other London boroughs facing similar problems of housing deprivation: Hammersmith and Fulham, Greenwich, Kensington and Chelsea, Newham, Tower Hamlets, Waltham Forest, Wandsworth and Westminster.

Group C The eight most deprived Metropolitan boroughs (excluding Liverpool for which information was not available): Birmingham, Bradford, Coventry, Kirklees, Knowsley, Manchester, Sandwell and Wolverhampton.

In terms of economy, there is a clear difference between Group A on the one hand and Groups B and C on the other in the level of staffing and expenditure ranking for Block Grant (excluding police, fire and education services) per capita in 1985–6:

Group	£ per resident	Whole-time employees per '000 residents
A	£470	19
B	317	14
C	152	10

The inclusion of Kensington and Chelsea and Westminster in Group B has the effect of very slightly *increasing* expenditure per resident.

If Group A authorities had been spending at the same rate per capita as Group B, their total annual expenditure would have been some £260 million a year less, worth well over £350 million to the local ratepayers because of lower grant 'penalties'.

Some of the difference between expenditure levels in London and the provinces is due to the higher cost of employing people in Inner London. This is reflected both in the London weighting allowance and the higher gradings often necessary to recruit people to posts in London. Some experts have calculated that this adds as much as 30% to the staffing costs of London authorities. Even assuming that it costs 40% more to operate in London than in the provinces for reasons outside the control of London authorities, there is still a gap of well over 100% between expenditure per head in Inner London in Group A and the most deprived authorities outside the capital; and expenditure in Group A is nearly 50% above that in Group B for the same range of services. Moreover, as Exhibit 3 shows, there is an evident contrast between the three samples of authorities in the expenditure trends over the past six years.

Council house management

The task of managing more than 400,000 Council owned dwellings in Inner London is arguably the most important service that the Inner London boroughs provide – over a million people are directly affected, and the cost (of general management, excluding caretaking, cleaning, wardens etc.) exceeds £80 million a year. The Commission's recent report, *Managing the Crisis in Council Housing* contrasts the recent performance of the three groups of authorities referred to above:

REAL CHANGE IN RATE AND GRANT-BORNE EXPENDITURE FY 1980–1986

Exhibit 3

```
160                                    GLC
150
140                                    Index:
130                                    FY 1980=100
120                                    Group A
110                                    Group B
100                                    Group C
    1980  81    82    83    84    85    86
            Financial Year ending 31 March
```

Source: Analysis of CIPFA Finance and General Statistics, adjusted for changes in the retail price index and financial reserves. GLC excludes London Transport.

		Group	
	A	**B**	**C**
Arrears (% of annual rent)	19.9	7.0	6.7
Relet period (weeks)	20	13	9
Management cost per dwelling	£201	£206	£101
Average rent for 3-bed house*	£18.55	£21.55	£17.83

* April 1986, not weighted; excludes Lambeth (no data), Kensington and Westminster (not representative)

Audit Commission (1987b) *The Management of London's Authorities: Preventing the Breakdown of Services*, London: HMSO, paras.1–3: 7: 9–12: 18

2.15

There are two influences outside the control of local authorities which are the main causes of many of the problems faced by local authorities. Firstly, there is in Inner London an unprecedented concentration of poverty and unemployment. There are for example more unemployed people in London than in the whole of Scotland. There is an appalling housing shortage especially for those unable to buy their own property. There are over 30,000 homeless families. There is deep rooted racial prejudice which has led to discrimination in employment, housing and elsewhere amongst the most ethnically diverse population in the country.

Many of the problems faced by Inner London authorities are intrinsically different from problems faced by other London boroughs and Metropolitan Districts. For example, 70% of Inner London housing stock consists of high rise blocks of flats compared to 35% as the next highest figure (in Manchester). Furthermore only in Inner London is there a high concentration of very large estates. The cost and difficulty of maintaining a housing stock of this nature leads to geometrically higher costs rather than simply arithmetically higher. This has been accepted by the Government's own Priority Estates Project.

These problems have been exacerbated by the perverse local economy, providing jobs mainly for people living outside Inner London. London as a centre of commerce and banking and the seat of Government has a unique dynamic of its own. However, the consequence is mainly to drive up property prices and wage levels which raises local authorities' costs and makes it harder to raise people out of poverty. It also has the effect of attracting the young unemployed from other depressed parts of the country – usually only intensifying their own misery as they are forced into homelessness and even greater reliance on state and local institutional support.

Much has been made in press reports of the Commission's work of their use of the three groups of authorities and the comparisons between them. These groups have been the "target" group of eight allegedly inefficient and badly managed Inner London authorities; a second group of eight London authorities and a group of eight Metropolitan districts with high needs both of which are meant by contrast to be well run authorities. It is the contrast which is important if the conclusion is to be drawn that the "target" eight are indeed inefficient. Therefore two things have to be established:

(a) That the social problems, financial difficulties and special factors are the same in all three groups;
(b) That despite similar problems the second groups are in fact better managed.

. . . The problems facing the "target" group are much more severe than in the other two groups. The Government's own measure of relative need (Grant Related Expenditure or GRE) shows this for the two largest services for Inner London authorities. Social Services need is 9% higher compared to the other London authorities and 76% higher than the authorities outside London. The differences are even greater when Housing is considered –

over 100% greater than other London authorities . . . a massive 645% greater than those out of London authorities. This in itself is not conclusive, because GRE's themselves are flawed and reflect Government policy decisions as well as need, but the Government could not be accused of bias in favour of the "target" group of authorities.

The Metropolitan Police force is the only Police force in England and Wales which is directly and solely responsible to the Home Secretary. Police costs in London are substantially higher than those in the rest of England including other Inner City areas.

. . . Even when costs are presented on a per officer basis the Metropolitan Police is significantly more expensive than police forces elsewhere in the country. Overall costs per officer are 38% higher but non-employee costs are 49% higher.

A significant performance indicator for the Police, from the point of the general public at least, is their ability to solve and clear up serious crime. Outside London Police forces on average spend £1969 for each crime cleared up. That figure rises by 269% to £7269 in London.

This analysis might seem a little unfair on the Metropolitan Police by failing to take account of outside factors which must have influenced police costs. However it is a reasonable summary of the way in which many Audit Commission reports have been presented to local authorities.

One of the main thrusts of Audit Commission criticisms of housing authorities . . . has been the problems of rent and rate arrears.

There are, however, a number of factors which affect levels of rent arrears which are beyond the control of the local authority

(i)   . . . It is not possible for a local authority to declare "intentionally homeless" any person in "temporary" accommodation. Thus, the local authority is obliged to provide such accommodation to many families each year and a substantial number fall into serious arrears whilst in temporary accommodation.

(ii) The amount of individual arrears . . . is aggravated by constraints imposed by legislation, the protracted procedure for serving notice of seeking possession, to obtaining a court order, right up to the final repossession.

(iii) Unlike a private landlord a local authority has a statutory duty to provide housing accommodation and therefore cannot be selective in accepting individual tenants.

(iv) Authorities report communication difficulties with individual DHSS offices which result in significant arrears accruing due to back-dated adjustments to benefits or failure to notify the Authority of changes. The Greater London Citizens Advice Bureaux Service conducted a survey on DHSS local offices in London; the conclusion was that the system for administering benefit has virtually collapsed in many local offices.

Association of London Authorities (1987) *London's Financial Problems – A Response to the Audit Commission*, London, Association of London Authorities, mimeo, paras. 1.24: 1.27: 2.13: 2.16–2.18: 2.20: and 3.13

2.16

The cost of libraries

Longer opening hours and a large number of small libraries are more convenient, but add to the cost of the service. The geography of the authority will also influence the costs and the kind of libraries the council runs. In rural communities, it may be harder for people to visit a library because they have to travel further. It will cost councils more in these areas to run libraries which are as easy to get to as they are in urban areas. Councils have to strike a balance between making it easy for people to visit libraries and the costs of running the service. One way of solving these problems is to run mobile libraries or 'book buses'. These are also used in inner city areas where fears about safety mean people, especially children, are reluctant to travel even short distances to libraries.

Audit Commission (1994) *Watching Their Figures*, London: HMSO

3.1

The Government is proposing seven key measures to achieve these objectives:

First: **to make the Health Service more responsive to the needs of patients, as much power and responsibility as possible will be delegated to local level**. This includes the delegation of functions from Regions to Districts, and from Districts to hospitals. The detailed proposals are set out in the next chapter. They include greater flexibility in setting the pay and conditions of staff, and financial incentives to make the best use of a hospital's assets.

Second: **to stimulate a better service to the patient, hospitals will be able to apply for a new self-governing status as NHS Hospital Trusts**. This means that, while remaining within the NHS, they will take fuller responsibility for their own affairs, harnessing the skills and dedication of their staff. NHS Hospital Trusts will earn revenue from the services they provide. They will therefore have an incentive to attract patients, so they will make sure that the service they offer is what their patients want. And in turn they will stimulate other NHS hospitals to respond to what people want locally. NHS Hospital Trusts will also be able to set the rates of pay of their own staff and, within annual financing limits, to borrow money to help them respond to patient demand.

Third: **to enable hospitals which best meet the needs and wishes of patients to get the money to do so, the money required to treat patients will be able to cross administrative boundaries**. All NHS hospitals, whether run by authorities or self-governing, will be free to offer their services to different health authorities and to the private sector. Consequently, a health authority will be better able to discharge its duty to use its available funds to secure a comprehensive service, including emergency services, by obtaining the best service it can whether from its own hospitals, from another authority's hospitals, from NHS Hospital Trusts or from the private sector.

Fourth: **to reduce waiting times and improve the quality of service, to help give individual patients appointment times they can rely on, and to help cut the long hours worked by some junior doctors, 100 new consultant posts will be created over the next three years**. This is in line with the number of fully trained doctors ready for consultant appointments in the relevant specialties. The new posts will be additional to the two per cent annual expansion of consultant numbers already planned.

Department of Health (1989a) *Working for Patients*, CM. 555, London: HMSO, para. 1.9

3.2

The powers, responsibilities and assets of each self-governing hospital will be vested formally in its NHS Hospital Trust. Each Trust will be run by a board of directors and will have a range of powers not available to existing NHS health authorities and hospitals. This section describes some of these powers in more detail.

All NHS hospitals will be given a greater devolution of management responsibility under the White Paper provision. Self-governing hospitals, having demonstrated the capacity for effective self-management, will be given further freedoms as of right. These freedoms will operate in the following important areas:

- acquisition, ownership and disposal of assets to ensure the most effective use of them;
- borrowing, subject to an annual financing limit;
- retention of operating surpluses in normal circumstances, after meeting interest obligations including those to the Government, and building up of reserves;
- determination of their own management structures without control from districts, regions or the NHS Management Executive;
- determination of their own staffing structures and of the terms and conditions of service for staff;
- advertisement of their services, subject to professional codes of practice on advertising.

Department of Health (1989b) *Self Governing Hospitals: Working Paper*, London: HMSO, paras. 2.2–2.3

3.3

Figure 6: Allocation of main functions to the new structure

Wider Department of Health

- Advising Ministers
- Formulating health policy
- Public health
- Family Health Services (exc. General Medical Services)
- Personal social services (including children)
- Managing relationship with rest of Government
- International relations
- Managing relationship with other agencies and statutory bodies

NHSME (Headquarters)

- Setting NHS Strategic Framework;
  - *Assessing health needs*

 — *Research and development*
 — *Formulating operational policy*
- Securing and allocating resources
- Human resources management
- Working with clinical staff
- Performance management
- Developing and regulating the internal market
- Managing General Medical Services
- Supporting Ministers

NHSME (Regional offices)

- Ensuring compliance with the regulatory framework for the internal market
- Managing performance of purchasers and providers
- Disputes arbitration
- Approving GPFH applications and budgets
- Purchaser development
- Targeted contribution to central work on policy and resources

Purchasers (DHA/FHSA)

- Setting purchasing strategy – targeted to meet local needs
- Purchasing services in accordance with local strategy
- Ensuring delivery to quality and cost targets in contracts
- Primary Care Development
- Administration of GPs' (& dentists', opticians' and pharmacists') terms of service
- Patient Registration

Providers

- Providing services to purchasers' specifications
- Managing delivery to quality and cost targets in contracts
- Meeting the terms of the 'established order' and mandatory financial duties
- Meeting purchaser and NHSME VFM targets
- Contributing views and information to local strategy

Department of Health (1993b) *Managing the New NHS: A Background Document*, London: Department of Health, 12

3.4

Different approaches would be required for fund-holders and non-fund-holders. For fund-holding GPs, the practice agreement could be set annually as an extension of the annual fund-setting process. **Such an extended process should continue to include fund-setting, monitoring of financial management and quality of care, and use of savings.** But it could also be extended somewhat to allow commissioning authorities to take a wide view of practice performance, raising the level of accountability of fund-holders; and it would in return allow fund-holders to discuss authority policies and strategies for secondary care and other issues. In this way commissioning and local action by practices would be brought into a closer relationship. The delegation of responsibility for setting GP fund-holding budgets to commissioning authorities would be a natural extension of this relationship, but would require legislative change. As authorities become increasingly involved with fund-holders, some strengthening of expertise and skills would be necessary.

Audit Commission (1993a) *Practice Makes Perfect: The Role of the Family Health Services Authority*, London: HMSO, para. 164

3.5

Summary of key requirements Annex A

Management accountability

- preparation of an annual practice plan
- signalling major shifts in purchasing intentions
- preparation of an annual performance report
- review performance with the health authority within the national framework

Accountability to patients and the wider public

- publishing information (e.g. annual practice plan and performance report)
- involving patients in service planning
- ensuring an effective complaints system

Financial accountability

- preparation of annual accounts for independent audit
- providing monthly information for monitoring by the health authority
- securing agreement to proposed use of savings for material or equipment purchases (including those relating to health education), improvement of premises, clinical audit, research and training
- stating planned contribution to the local efficiency targets set by the NHS Executive

Clinical and professional accountability

- participating in clinical audit of GMS activities
- ensuring that agreed audit programmes are completed by hospital and community health care service providers

NHS Executive (1995b) *An Accountability Framework for GP Fund-holding: Towards a Primary Care-led NHS*, London: Department of Health: 11

3.6

Although more money could always be spent to advantage, the current levels of expenditure from public funds could provide a community-based service for elderly, mentally ill and handicapped people. But some underlying problems must be tackled first:

- While the Government's policies require a shift from hospital-based (health) services to locally-based (local authority and health) services, the mechanisms for achieving a parallel shift in funds are inadequate. In fact, expenditure on NHS mental illness and mental handicap in-patient services has actually increased, by almost £100 million a year (in 1984–5 prices) since 1976
- Meanwhile, local authorities are often penalised through the grant system for building the very community services which government policy favours and which are necessary if the NHS is to be in a position to close its large long-stay psychiatric hospitals and release the capital assets – conservatively valued at over £500 million

- The funds being made available to bridge the transition phase are limited. For example, NHS revenue expenditure on joint finance and 'dowries' for patients transferred to local authorities is currently about £100 million a year (out of a total NHS expenditure on services for these clients of some £3 billion a year)
- Supplementary Benefit policies fund private residential care more readily than community-based care of which there is still relatively little in the private sector. Partly as a result, private and voluntary homes are expanding very rapidly, particularly on the South Coast – there are now nearly ten times as many places **per 1,000 people aged 75 or over** in private and voluntary residential homes for elderly people in Devon and East Sussex than there are in Cleveland, for example
- While central government attempts to achieve equitable distribution of public funds across the country, through the use of complex formulae both within the NHS and local government, the effects can be largely offset by Supplementary Benefit payments for board and lodgings. If all residents now in local authority care or NHS geriatric and mental health hospitals were to be transferred to private residential care (an unlikely eventuality – but a useful illustration of the forces at work) Supplementary Benefit payments for board and lodgings would increase up to a theoretical upper limit of more than £2 billion a year
- Responsibility for introducing and operating community-based services is fragmented between a number of different agencies with different priorities, styles, structures and budgets who must 'request' co-operation from each other. For community care to operate these agencies must work together. But there are many reasons why they do not, including the lack of positive incentives, bureaucratic barriers, perceived threats to jobs and professional standing, and the time required for interminable meetings (joint planning alone could easily be occupying the equivalent of 30 professional staff full-time in a large county)
- Staffing arrangements are inadequate. A new impetus in training and a different approach to manpower planning are required. The future of staff in institutions which have a limited life is not clear in many cases; as a result, staff anxiety is high. At the same time, inadequate provision is being made to train staff for community care.

Audit Commission (1986) *Making a Reality of Community Care*, London: HMSO, 2–3

3.7

Exhibit 1

Spectrum of Care Settings

Own Home Alone	Group Home (Unstaffed)	Sheltered Lodgings	Residential Home	Hospital
£133	119	133	210	255

£ per Week

⇦

Increasing
Independence

The policy of successive governments has been to promote community-based services allowing the reduction of long-stay hospital provision. This is generally considered better in most situations. It is also more economical in many cases: a frail elderly person living in their own home with day and domiciliary support would typically cost public funds some £135 per week; the same person would cost about £295 per week in a NHS geriatric ward.

The change-over to community care is, therefore, a fundamental shift, not only in the location of services, but also in the type and range of services provided and in organisational attitudes and skills of staff involved. It thus presents a considerable challenge to management. Any failure to meet the challenge of community care will result in a lower quality service and reduced value for money. While the total cost of community care may be comparable with the cost of institutional care, different individual placements have markedly different cost implications as Table 4 shows.

Table 4: COSTS OF CARE IN DIFFERENT SETTINGS £ per week, 1986 prices

Care Setting	Example A	Example B
Own Home		
– domiciliary service	£97.35 per week	
– as above, plus day care	135.35	132.50
Local Authority		
– sheltered housing	151.55	
– residential (Part III) home	133.25	190.25
Private and Voluntary		
– residential home	138.55	
– nursing home	183.55	
NHS Hospital	294.75	254.75

The table provides two examples to illustrate the order-of-magnitude differences in the costs incurred by the public sector as a whole for care in different settings:

— Example A shows the costs for a frail elderly single person on a state pension, without substantial savings. The client qualifies for Attendance Allowance at the lower rate, for a disability incurred after retirement age.
— Example B is a mentally handicapped adult with no savings or other income. The client qualifies for Severe Disablement Allowances, but not for Attendance Allowance.

ibid.: 1: 11–12

3.8

Hence, while there are a number of possible strategic options for organising and funding community care, the Commission considers the following to be promising enough to warrant serious examination by an independent review:

(i) Local authorities should be made responsible for the long term care where required of **mentally and physically handicapped people in the community**; except for the most severely disabled who require medical supervision, and the resources necessary to do this should be identified and, where appropriate, transferred from the NHS.

(ii) For **care of elderly people in the community** a single budget in an area should be established by contributions from the NHS and local authorities the amount to be determined in each case by a formula agreed centrally. This budget should be under the control of a single manager who will purchase from whichever public or private agency he sees fit the appropriate services for elderly people in the community in the areas for which he is responsible. The manager's activities should be overseen by a small joint board of NHS and local authority representatives.

(iii) For **mentally ill people in the community**, the NHS will inevitably remain the prime authority responsible for care but nevertheless there remains an important role for social services. Two alternatives should be evaluated:
   — Assigning to the NHS responsibility for all services; but that when

it requires services from local authorities it should purchase these, with the local authority acting as the contractor.
- An arrangement similar to that proposed above for services for elderly people.

In addition, for all client groups, care funded by Supplementary Benefits in the private or voluntary sector should be co-ordinated with care provided by the relevant local social services department or NHS authority.

ibid.: 75–6

3.9

Local authority social services authorities should be responsible for identifying people with community care needs in their area.

Where a social services authority has identified someone with community care needs, and that person has other needs e.g. for health care or housing, the authority should be responsible for ensuring that the other relevant public authorities consider whether, and if so what, they should do to contribute to the person's care and support.

Social services authorities should themselves be responsible for arranging for the needs of an individual for social, domestic and personal care and support to be assessed (and regularly re-assessed) in full consultation with the person concerned and any informal carers, so that these assessments take account of the individual's wider circumstances.

The social services authority must decide then what action to take itself. At the lowest level, support for informal care may be all that is needed. At the other extreme, multiple services may have to be arranged. It is recommended that social services authorities should develop and manage packages of care tailored to meet most effectively, within their budget and priorities, the needs of individuals.

In cases where a significant level of resources are involved a "care manager" should be nominated from within the social services authority's staff to oversee the assessment and re-assessment function and manage the resulting action. Where care is already being effectively managed, this proposal will amount to little more than making existing roles explicit.

Even when the situation is fairly stable, it is important that the individual and everyone else involved, including any informal carer, knows to whom to turn for immediate support. This might sensibly be the person with whom the individual has the most day-to-day contact. That person, regardless of their parent organisation, could be given responsibility for providing information to the social services authority about changes in the individual's circumstances that may affect the need for care and support.

Social services authorities should have sufficiently wide powers to enable them to provide goods and services to maintain or establish people, who might otherwise need to have institutional care, in their own homes. To that end, I propose that the community care element of the Social Fund should be withdrawn from the social security system and the funds ear-marked for that purpose transferred to social services authorities. I do not recommend any extension of social services authorities' limited powers to make cash payments to individuals.

Social services authorities should:

(i)   ensure that information is readily available about community care and where and how to seek services that will contribute to that care. This should cover services provided by public authorities, the voluntary sector, and private businesses;
(ii) develop and sustain informal and voluntary community care resources by supporting informal carers, volunteers, and voluntary organisations;
(iii) maximise choice and competition by encouraging the further development of private services.

Griffiths, R. (1988) *Community Care: Agenda for Action*, London: HMSO, 14–15 paras. 6.2–6.9

3.10

First, local authorities are to become responsible, in collaboration with medical, nursing and other interests, for assessing individual need, designing care arrangements and securing their delivery within available resources;

second, local authorities will be expected to produce and publish clear plans for the development of community care services, consistent with the plans of health authorities and other interested agencies. The Government will take new powers to ensure that plans are open to inspection, and to call for reports from social services authorities;

third, local authorities will be expected to make maximum use of the independent sector. The Government will ensure that they have acceptable plans for achieving this;

fourth, there will be a new funding structure for those seeking public support for residential and nursing home care from April 1991. After that date local authorities will take responsibility for financial support of people in private and voluntary homes, over and above any general social security entitlements. The new arrangements will not, however, apply to people already resident in homes before April 1991;

fifth, applicants with few or no resources of their own will be eligible for the same levels of Income Support and Housing Benefit, irrespective of whether they are living in their own homes or in independent residential or nursing homes;

sixth, local authorities will be required to establish inspection and registration units at arm's length from the management of their own services which will be responsible for checking on standards in both their own homes and in independent sector residential care homes;

seventh, there will be a new specific grant to promote the development of social care for seriously mentally ill people.

Department of Health (1989c) *Caring for People: Community Care in the Next Decade and Beyond*, CM. 849, London: HMSO, para. 1.12

3.11

The Government's proposals have six key objectives for service delivery:

- *to promote the development of domiciliary, day and respite services to enable people to live in their own homes wherever feasible and sensible.* Existing funding structures have worked against the development of such services. In future, the Government will encourage the targeting of home-based services on those people whose need for them is greatest;
- *to ensure that service providers make practical support for carers a high priority.* Assessment of care needs should always take account of the needs of caring family, friends and neighbours;
- *to make proper assessment of need and good case management the*

cornerstone of high quality care. Packages of care should then be designed in line with individual needs and preferences;

- *to promote the development of a flourishing independent sector alongside good quality public services.* The Government has endorsed Sir Roy Griffiths' recommendation that social services authorities should be "enabling" agencies. It will be their responsibility to make maximum possible use of private and voluntary providers, and so increase the available range of options and widen consumer choice;
- *to clarify the responsibilities of agencies and so make it easier to hold them to account for their performance.* The Government recognises that the present confusion has contributed to poor overall performance;
- *to secure better value for taxpayers' money by introducing a new funding structure for social care.* The Government's aim is that social security provisions should not, as they do now, provide any incentive in favour of residential and nursing home care.

ibid.: para. 1.11

3.12

5.6 Local authorities will need to have clear plans for the development of their community care provision against which their performance can be monitored and assessed. The purpose of such plans will be to enable social services authorities to:

- set out strategic objectives and priorities and, over realistic planning periods, set specific targets, in collaboration with relevant agencies;
- take account of the needs of people who have been in hospital a long time, and need help to re-establish themselves away from large institutional settings;
- assess other local needs, taking account of the results of assessments in individual cases;
- organise their move away from the role of exclusive service provider to that of service arranger and procurer;
- ensure that service arrangements respect and preserve individual independence, include adequate quality control systems, offer freedom of choice, and provide services in a sensitive and responsive way;
- monitor performance; and inform the public.

ibid.: para. 5.6

3.13

The Government will bring proposals before Parliament to:

- require local authorities to draw up and publish plans for community care services, in consultation with health authorities and other interested agencies;
- enable the Secretary of State for Health to call for reports and information from local authorities where he has reason to think these may be needed, and to specify the form in which they are to be provided;
- enable the Secretary of State for Health to issue directions and give guidance over the full range of personal social services activities by local authorities.

These powers will provide the basis of new planning and monitoring arrangements for community care. The Government has no intention of establishing an over-bureaucratic or heavily centralised system. Its aim will be to satisfy itself that authorities are developing and implementing plans in line with national objectives and priorities, at a reasonable pace. For that purpose the Social Services Inspectorate will play an active part in inspecting plans, monitoring performance and offering advice and guidance to authorities and the Secretary of State. Where necessary, the Government will not hesitate to intervene in order to stimulate improvements.

ibid.: paras. 5.3–5.4

3.14

Statutory Direction on Choice of Residential Accommodation

Purpose

This direction (text attached) is intended to ensure that people who are assessed as needing residential care are able to exercise a genuine choice over the place where they receive that care. It is intended to formalise the best practice which most authorities would in any case have adopted.

Summary

If an authority assesses someone as needing residential care which is not otherwise available to them it has a duty provide or arrange for the provision of that care.

If the individual concerned expresses a preference for particular accommodation, or other accommodation ("preferred accommodation") within the UK the authority must arrange for care in that home, provided

- the accommodation is suitable in relation to the individual's assessed needs
- to do so would not cost the authority more than it would usually expect to pay for someone with the individual's assessed needs
- the accommodation is available
- the person in charge of the accommodation is willing to provide accommodation subject to the authority's usual terms and conditions for such accommodation.

The authority must also arrange for care in accommodation more expensive than it would normally fund provided there is a third party willing to pay the difference between the cost the authority would usually expect to pay and the actual cost of the accommodation.

Department of Health (1992a) *Memorandum on the Financing of Community Care Arrangements After April 1993 and on Individual Choice of Residential Accommodation*, Annex D, London: HMSO paras. D1–D4

3.15

There appear to be three main reasons for the Government's rejection of Sir Roy Griffiths' proposal. These are:

(i) the disruptive consequences of introducing a new basis for social security funding so soon after the new arrangements for local government funding as a whole;
(ii) the incompatibility between the existence of a substantial specific grant for one service and the Government's presentation of (a) the community charge as a mechanism for enhancing local discretion and accountability and (b) the allocation to local government of additional responsibilities for community care as a reflection of the requirement for local flexibility/accountability; and

(iii) (possibly) the requirement it would place on central government explicitly to specify or endorse the levels of need and activity which it regards as legitimate for social services authorities to meet and sustain.

The Social Services Committee (1990) *Community Care Funding for Local Authorities Session 1989–90*, HC 277, London: HMSO, para. 30

3.16

The Government considered Sir Roy Griffiths' proposal that health authority spending on community care should be ring-fenced. It concluded, however, that attempting to do so would carry too great a risk of distorting future spending in this area. The growth of community care will depend crucially on the availability and growth of community-based alternatives to care in long-stay institutions. Setting aside a fixed sum for this purpose will not provide the flexibility which will be needed to respond to this diversity of opportunity. Community health services will play an important part in enabling people to live in the community, although it is not possible to say what proportion of in-patients may, in future, be supported outside hospital, nor what proportion of, for example, district nursing or health visiting comes within community care for these groups.

Department of Health (1989c) *Caring for People: Community Care in the Next Decade and Beyond*, CM. 849, London: HMSO, para. 8.29

3.17

It is recognised by all involved that close and effective collaboration between local authorities and the NHS will be central to the effective implementation of new community care arrangements. The Government's own monitoring and that of the Audit Commission has shown that this aspect of implementation needs to be strengthened significantly.

The letter sent by the Chief Social Services Inspector and Deputy Chief Executive of the NHS Management Executive to all Directors of Social Services and Health Authority General Managers on 25 September 1992 (the "Foster-Laming" letter) which was discussed with health and local authority interests set out the need for all authorities to have in place before the end of the year,

• agreed strategies governing health and local authority responsibilities for placing people in nursing homes, and the numbers likely to be involved during 1993–4

- agreement as to how hospital discharge arrangements will be integrated with assessment arrangements.

The Government considers that these are minimum requirements which all authorities must achieve if arrangements for providing care are to be secure and agreed between health and local authorities. **For that reason, the Government proposes to make the payment of the grant to authorities in 1993/4 conditional on them having provided evidence that such agreements have been reached with the relevant DHA(s).**

Department of Health (1992a) *Memorandum on the Financing of Community Care Arrangements After April 1993 and on Individual Choice of Residential Accommodation*, paras. 22–4

3.18

General Principle to be Observed by Minister and Local Education Authorities

76. In the exercise and performance of all powers and duties conferred and imposed on them by this Act the [Secretary of State] and local education authorities shall have regard to the general principle that, so far as is compatible with the provision of efficient instruction and training and the avoidance of unreasonable public expenditure, pupils are to be educated in accordance with the wishes of their parents.

Education Act 1944: section 76

3.19

6. (1) Every local education authority shall make arrangements for enabling the parent of a child in the area of the authority to express a preference as to the school at which he wishes education to be provided for his child in the exercise of the authority's functions and to give reasons for his preference.
   (2) Subject to subsection (3) below, it shall be the duty of a local education authority and of the governors of a county or voluntary school to comply with any preference expressed in accordance with the arrangements.

  (3) The duty imposed by subsection (2) does not apply

      (a) if compliance with the preference would prejudice provision of efficient education or the efficient use of resources.

Education Act 1980: section 6

3.20

26. For the purposes of section 6(3)(a) of the 1980 Act (which excludes the duty to comply with a parent's preference as to the school at which education is to be provided for his child if compliance with the preference would prejudice the provision of efficient education or the efficient use of resources), no such prejudice shall be taken to arise from the admission to a school in any school year of a number of pupils in any relevant age group which does not exceed –

    (a) the relevant standard number; or

    (b) the number fixed in accordance with this section as the number of pupils in that age group it is intended to admit to the school in that school year;

whichever is the greater.

Education Reform Act 1988: section 26

3.21

Admission of Pupils to County and Voluntary Schools

26. (1) The authority responsible for determining the arrangements for the admission of pupils to any county or voluntary school shall not fix as the number of pupils in any relevant age group it is intended to admit to the school in any school year a number which is less than the relevant standard number.

ibid.: section 26

3.22

38. (1) The provision to be included in a scheme for determining the budget share for any financial year of each school required to be covered by the scheme in that year shall require that share to be

determined (and from time to time revised) by the application of a formula laid down by the scheme for the purpose of dividing among all such schools the aggregated budget for that year of the local education authority concerned.

(2) In this section "formula" includes methods, principles and rules of any description, however expressed; and references in this Chapter, in relation to a scheme, to the allocation formula under the scheme, are references to the formula laid down by the scheme in accordance with subsection (1) above.

(3) The allocation formula under a scheme –

    (a) shall include provision for taking into account, in the case of each school required to be covered by the scheme in any financial year, the number and ages of registered pupils at that school on such date or dates as may be determined by or under the scheme in relation to that year; and

    (b) may include provision for taking into account any other factors affecting the needs of individual schools which are subject to variation from school to school (including, in particular, the number of registered pupils at a school who have special educational needs and the nature of the special educational provision required to be made for them).

ibid.: section 38

3.23

Procedure for acquisition of grant-maintained status

60. (1) Subject to subsection (5) above, in the case of any school which is eligible for grant-maintained status, a ballot of parents on the question of whether grant-maintained status should be sought for the school shall be held in accordance with section 61 of this Act if either

    (a) the governing body decide by a resolution passed at a meeting of that body ("the first resolution") to hold such a ballot and confirm that decision, after the consultations required by sub-section (3) below, by a resolution ("the second resolution") passed at a subsequent meeting of the governing body held not less than twenty-eight days, nor more than forty-two days, after that at which the first resolution was passed; or

> (b) they receive a written request to hold such a ballot which meets the requirements of subsection (2) below.
>
> (2) Those requirements are that the request must be signed (or otherwise endorsed in such manner as the governing body may require) by a number of parents of registered pupils at the school equal to at least twenty per cent of the number of registered pupils at the school on the date on which the request is received.

ibid.: section 60

3.24

Principal provisions

2. (1) The curriculum for every maintained school shall comprise a basic curriculum which includes –
   - (a) provision for religious education for all registered pupils at the school; and
   - (b) a curriculum for all registered pupils at the school of compulsory school age (to be known as "the National Curriculum") which meets the requirements of subsection (2) below.
   (2) The curriculum referred to in subsection (1)(b) above shall comprise the core and other foundation subjects and specify in relation to each of them –
   - (a) the knowledge, skills and understanding which pupils of different abilities and maturities are expected to have by the end of each key stage (in this Chapter referred to as "attainment targets");
   - (b) the matters, skills and processes which are required to be taught to pupils of different abilities and maturities during each key stage (in this Chapter referred to as "programmes of study"); and
   - (c) the arrangements for assessing pupils at or near the end of each key stage for the purpose of ascertaining what they have achieved in relation to attainment targets for that stage (in this Chapter referred to as "assessment arrangements").
   (3) Subsection (1)(a) above shall not apply in the case of a maintained special school.
3. (1) Subject to subsection (94) below, the core subjects are –
   - (a) mathematics, English and science; and

    (b) in relation to schools in Wales which are Welsh-speaking schools, Welsh.

(2) Subject to subsection (4) below, the other foundation subjects are —

    (a) history, geography, technology, music, art and physical education;

    (b) in relation to the third and fourth key stages, a modern foreign language specified in an order of the Secretary of State; and

    (c) in relation to schools in Wales which are not Welsh-speaking schools, Welsh.

ibid.: sections 2–3

3.25

(3) Subject to subsection (4) and (5) below, the key stages in relation to a pupil are as follows —

    (a) the period beginning with his becoming of compulsory school age and ending at the same time as the school year in which the majority of pupils in his class attain the age of seven.

    (b) the period beginning at the same time as the school year in which the majority of pupils in his class attain the age of eight and ending at the same time as the school year in which the majority of pupils in his class attain the age of eleven;

    (c) the period beginning at the same time as the school year in which the majority of pupils in his class attain the age of twelve and ending at the same time as the school year in which the majority of pupils in his class attain the age of fourteen;

    (d) the period beginning at the same time as the school year in which the majority of pupils in his class attain the age of fifteen and ending with the majority of pupils in his class ceasing to be of compulsory school age.

(4) The Secretary of State may by order —

    (a) amend the foregoing provisions of this section; or

    (b) provide that, in relation to any subject specified in the order, subsection (93) above shall have effect as if for the ages of seven and eight there mentioned there were substituted such other ages, less than eleven and twelve respectively, as may be so specified.

(5)   The head teacher of a school may elect, in relation to a particular pupil and a particular subject, that subsection (3) above shall have effect as if any reference to the school year in which the majority of pupils in that pupil's class attained a particular age were a reference to the school year in which that pupil attained that age.

ibid.: sections 3–5

3.26

Every local education authority shall, as respects each school maintained by them other than an aided or special agreement school, and the governors of every aided or special agreement school shall, as respects that school, publish –

(a)   such information as may be required by regulations made by the Secretary of State.

Education Act 1980, section 8 (5) (a)

3.27

From the start of LMS, the Government's policy has been that the bulk of the funding delegates to primary and secondary schools should be allocated on the basis of pupil numbers weighted by age. At present LEAs must distribute at least 80% of the Aggregated Schools Budget for primary and secondary schools on the basis of school's pupil numbers (although only directly for some types of SEN funding). The Government will look again at the scope for simplifying the details. But it remains determined that schools' budgets should be based primarily on their pupil numbers. That gives a clear objective basis for calculating budgets. It also gives schools incentives to ensure that what they offer reflects what parents want, since the size of their budget is directly linked to their success in attracting pupils.

Department for Education and Employment (1996a) *Self-Government for Schools* CM. 3315, para. 33, London: HMSO

3.28

Higher education in the UK is strong and growing

The UK's Higher Education system is already making a powerful contribution to national competitiveness through its range and diversity, and its emphasis on quality and access. Participation in the sector has been transformed in recent years. Since 1988, the proportion of young people enrolling for HE has doubled. Furthermore, 37 per cent of graduates at first degree and sub-degree level have followed science-related courses and over 15 per cent leave with specific professional qualifications.

The Skills Audit shows that, in 1994, 23 per cent of our 25–28 year olds and 19 per cent of the total population were qualified to at least this level. These figures, because they necessarily focus on 25–28 year olds, do not take full account of the increases in achievement at first degree level since 1990. The percentage of young people in the UK labour market with degrees has risen considerably: in 1995, the number of newly qualified first degree graduates in the UK had risen by 50 per cent above the 1992 level.

However, the Skills Audit also shows that our competitors are not standing still either. More young people in France are gaining degree level qualifications and France, with Singapore, has also seen a rise in the proportion of sub-degree higher level qualifications gained. Future success requires UK universities and colleges to continue to develop, whilst preserving quality and standards. The Government has therefore set up a National Committee of Inquiry into Higher Education under Sir Ron Dearing. This has been asked to make recommendations by summer 1997 on how the purpose, shape, structure, size and funding of higher education should develop to meet the needs of the UK over the next 20 years.

Department of Trade and Industry (1996) *Competitiveness: Creating the Enterprise Centre of Europe*, CM. 3300, London: HMSO, paras. 4.29–4.31

3.29

Performance

Table 16 shows that the average GCE A level score of home entrants to full-time higher education has been maintained at a time of greatly increased participation.

Table 16. *Qualifications of home domiciled students on entry to full-time and sandwich first degree courses, England 1989/90 to 1993/94*

Academic year	1989/90 actual	1990/91 actual	1991/92 actual	1992/93 actual	1993/94 provisional
Percentage entrants with					
A level[1]	77	76	73	68	62
BTEC[2]	9	9	10	12	14
Other qualifications[3]	14	15	17	20	24
Total entrants (thousands)[4,5]	**135**	**150**	**169**	**206**	**214**
Average A level point score[6]	18	18	18	18	18

Other measures suggest that quality has been maintained or increased:

- **Table 17** shows that drop-out rates have fluctuated, but they appear low by international standards; and

Table 17. *Full-time and sandwich first degree drop-out rates, 1983/84 to 1992/93*

	percentages								
Academic year	1983/84	84/85	85/86	88/87	87/88	88/89	89/90	90/91	91/92	92/93
Higher education	14	15	14	16	17	14	16	15	17	17

- **Table 18** shows that the proportion of first degree graduates obtaining first and upper second class decrees has increased.

Table 18. *Percentage of students qualifying with full-time and sandwich first degrees achieving 1st and 2nd degrees, England 1988/89 to 1992/93*

	percentage				
Academic year	1988/89 actual	1989/90 actual	1990/91 actual	1991/92 actual	1992/93 provisional
Percentage of students obtaining 1st and 2:1 degrees	46	47	48	49	50

Table 19 shows that graduate unemployment has increased from the levels of the late 1980s, reflecting, in part, the business cycle. The level of graduate unemployment remains significantly below that of the general population. Future levels can be expected to fall.

Table 19. *Destination of first degree graduates from full-time and sandwich courses, England, 1988/89 to 1992/93*

	percentage				
Academic year (in which course completed)	1988/89	1989/90	1990/91	1991/92	1992/93
Permanent employment	58	52	45	42	45
Temporary employment	5	6	6	7	7
Overseas employment[2]	3	3	3	3	2
Teacher training	3	3	4	5	5
Other further education/training	16	17	18	19	18
Overseas graduates leaving UK	5	5	7	7	7
Not available for employment[3]	5	6	5	5	3
Believed unemployed	5	8	12	13	14
Total whose destination[4] was known (thousands)	**85**	**90**	**96**	**104**	**116**
Not known (thousands)	15	15	16	16	19
Total (thousands)[4]	**101**	**106**	**112**	**121**	**134**

Sources: DFE survey Examination Results and First Destination Universities' Statistical Record

Quality assurance

The HEFCE has continued its programme of assessing the quality of teaching and learning in universities and colleges in particular subject areas. Assessments have been published in the following subjects – Chemistry, History, Law, Mechanical Engineering, Applied Social Work, Business and Management, Architecture and Computer Science. There have been 386 published outcomes up to November 1994: the proportion of assessments judged satisfactory, excellent and unsatisfactory are respectively 74%, 25% and 1%. Institutions with subject areas judged to be unsatisfactory are expected to take action to improve the position and receive a follow-up visit within one year of the initial assessment to judge the extent of the improvement. Institutions with subject areas which continue to be assessed as unsatisfactory are at risk of successive withdrawals of funding.

Department for Education and Employment (1996d) *Departmental Report*, London: HMSO, paras. 202; 204–6

4.1

The decision to 'make or buy' goods and services is among the most important facing any commercial or industrial undertaking. One of the keys to success of many Japanese businesses has been the close relation-ship that they have established with, literally, thousands of independent suppliers; exactly the same applies to Marks and Spencer and other leading multiple retailers in the United Kingdom. In every case, a successful relationship allows both the suppliers and the customer to benefit; and in many cases, the design of the final product is influenced by the cost structure and production methods of the component suppliers. (Marks and Spencer even install their own quality assurance procedures – and sometimes people as well – in suppliers' plants).

Local authorities face precisely similar choices between providing services directly or buying them in from outside suppliers. This is nothing new. Every year, authorities spend some £3 billion in bought-in goods or services covering an extraordinarily wide range – from architectural services to pencils for use in schools.

The choice between providing a service directly and buying it in should be based on management's assessment of which route will deliver the most cost competitive service in the long run. Competitiveness is the key: the Commission believes that all local authority services should be subjected regularly to the test of the market place; and Direct Labour Organisations (DLOs) and private suppliers should compete for as much local authority business as possible, on a completely equal footing. It will be evident that the assessment of long run competitiveness will need to be based on the facts of the local situation, rather than on generalised assertions about the relative advantages of the private sector and direct labour:

- The quality of the DLO management will vary from place to place. In some cases, the DLO may be fully cost competitive; in others it may not be
- The capacity of local private sector suppliers to take on additional work will also vary, depending on local market conditions
- The cost structures of individual private suppliers and DLOs will be different, as will their strategic priorities and near-term order books; some will be more 'hungry' for orders and have more scope to reduce their prices than others
- Different levels of risk may be involved. In selecting suppliers, auth-orities will need to evaluate the risk that suppliers will not be able to meet the performance requirements specified in the contract.

The opportunity for local authorities, as major buyers of goods and services, is immense. Purchasing powers should be used constructively to improve competitiveness and to encourage new management approaches within supplying organisations. The result could be improved services at lower cost — because successful competitors will be less wasteful of resources than their would-be rivals. This *Occasional Paper*, therefore, summarises the evidence from the Commission's earlier studies and auditors' experience of the potential for increased competitiveness within local authorities' services. It goes on to identify some of the strategic issues to be taken into account when deciding whether to 'make or buy'. Finally, some practical steps are recommended to assist authorities in putting work out to competitive tender, should they decide to do so.

Audit Commission (1987a) *Competitiveness and Contracting Out of Local Authorities' Services*, London: HMSO, paras. 1–4

4.2

For the purposes of this Part each of the following is a defined authority —

(a) a local authority,
(b) an urban development corporation established by an order under section 135 of the Local Government, Planning and Land Act 1980,
(c) a development corporation established for the purposes of a new town,
(d) the Commission for the New Towns,
(e) a police authority constituted under section 2 of the Police Act 1964 or as mentioned in section 3(1) of that Act, or established by section 24 or 25 of the Local Government Act 1985,
(f) a fire authority constituted by a combination scheme and a metropolitan county fire and civil defence authority,
(g) the London Fire and Civil Defence Authority,
(h) a metropolitan county passenger transport authority,
(i) an authority established by an order under section 10(1) of the Local Government Act 1985 (waste disposal),
(j) a joint education committee established by an order under paragraph 3 of Part II of Schedule 1 to the Education Act 1944 and the Inner London Education Authority,
(k) a water development board in Scotland, and
(l) the Scottish Special Housing Association.

In the application of this Part to England and Wales, "local authority" in subsection (l) above means —

(a) a county council, a district council, a London borough council, a parish council, a community council or the Council of the Isles of Scilly;

(b) the Common Council of the City of London in its capacity as local authority or police authority.

In the application of this Part to Scotland, in subsection (l) above –

(a) "local authority" means a regional, island or district council or any joint board or joint committee within the meaning of the Local Government (Scotland) Act 1973, and

(b) "water development board" has the same meaning as in section 109(1) of the Water (Scotland) Act 1980.

In a case where two or more defined authorities arrange under section 101 of the Local Government Act 1972 for the discharge by a joint committee of theirs of any of their functions, the committee shall itself be treated as a defined authority for the purposes of this Part in its application to England and Wales.

(1) If a defined authority (a bidding authority) propose to enter into a works contract with another person (the other party) and under the contract the bidding authority are to carry out work falling within a defined activity, the bidding authority may not enter into the contract unless –

    (a) the first or second alternative of the first condition is fulfilled, and

    (b) the second condition is fulfilled.

(2) The first alternative of the first condition is that –

    (a) the contract is made by acceptance of the bidding authority's offer to carry out the work,

    (b) the bidding authority made the offer in response to an invitation by the other party to submit such offers, and

    (c) the invitation was made to at least three other persons who are willing to carry out work of the kind concerned, and who are not defined authorities or include at least three persons who are not defined authorities.

(3) The Secretary of State may by regulations vary –

    (a) the number of persons to whom an invitation must be made under subsection 92) (c) above; and

    (b) the minimum number of those persons who are not to be defined authorities.

(4) The second alternative of the first condition is that before entering

into the contract the other party published, in at least one newspaper circulating in the locality in which the work is to be carried out and at least one publication circulating among persons who carry out work of the kind concerned, a notice inviting persons to submit offers to carry out the work.

(5) The second condition is that the other party, in entering into the contract and in doing anything else (whether or not required by this Part) in connection with the contract before entering into it, did not act in a manner having the effect or intended or likely to have the effect of restricting, distorting or preventing competition.

(6) Anything which (apart from this subsection) would amount to a failure to fulfil the first or second alternative of the first condition, or the second condition, shall not do so unless, at the time the contract is proposed to be entered into, the bidding authority are aware of the failure.

(7) This section applies where it is proposed to enter into the works contract on or after 1st April 1989.

Local Government Act 1988: sections 1–7

4.3

2. (1) This section applies for the purposes of this Part.
   (2) Each of the following is a defined activity –
       (a) collection of refuse,
       (b) cleaning of buildings,
       (c) other cleaning,
       (d) catering for purposes of schools and welfare,
       (e) other catering,
       (f) maintenance of ground, and
       (g) repair and maintenance of vehicles;
   (3) The Secretary of State may by order provide for an activity to be a defined activity by adding a paragraph to those for the time being appearing in subsection (2) above.

ibid.: section 2 (1–3)

4.4

17. (1) It is the duty of every public authority to which this section applies, in exercising, in relation to its public supply or works

contracts, any proposed or any subsisting such contract, as the case may be, any function regulated by this section to exercise that function without reference to matters which are non-commercial matters for the purposes of this section.

(5) The following matters are non-commercial matters as regards the public supply or works contracts of a public authority, any proposed or any subsisting such contract, as the case may be, that is to say –

   (a) the terms and conditions of employment by contractors of their workers or the composition of, the arrangements for the promotion, transfer or training of or the other opportunities afforded to, their workforces;

   (b) whether the terms on which contractors contract with their sub-constructors constitute, in the case of contracts with individuals, contracts for the provision by them as self-employed persons of their services only;

   (c) the conduct of contractors or workers in industrial disputes between them or any involvement of the business activities of contractors in industrial disputes between other persons;

ibid.: section 17 (1) and (5)

4.5

In these Regulations – "undertaking" includes any trade or business but does not include any undertaking or part of an undertaking which is not in the nature of a commercial venture.

Transfer of Undertakings (Protection of Employment) Regulations 1981: section 2(1)

4.6

Amendments for transfer of undertaking regulations

(1) The Transfer of Undertaking (Protection of Employment) Regulations 1981 shall be amended as follows.

(2) In Regulation 2(1), in the definition of "undertaking" (which excludes from the Regulations undertakings, and parts of undertakings, not in the nature of a commercial venture), the words from "but does not" to the end shall cease to have effect.

Trade Union Reform and Employment Rights Act 1993: section 33 (1) and (2)

5.1

The Budget represents a further step towards the achievement of the Government's medium-term objectives of bringing down inflation and creating the conditions for sustainable growth of output and employment. In order to permit its monetary objectives to be met at tolerable interest rates, the Government's aim is to contain public sector borrowing to a real level well below that of 1980–81. Within this overriding requirement, the Budget is designed to give some more direct relief to particularly hard-pressed sectors of industry and to provide more opportunities for enterprise, particularly for new and small businesses.

Treasury (1981) *Financial Statement and Budget Report, 1981–82*, London: HMSO, para. 1

Government policies have been directed to achieving a progressive reduction in public sector borrowing over the medium term. Fiscal restraint is essential to the achievement of lower inflation and interest rates. A further reduction in the PSBR over the medium term is required to be consistent with the monetary targets at acceptable interest rates.

Treasury (1984) *Financial Statement and Budget Report, 1984–85*, London: HMSO, para. 2.16

The Government's objective for public spending is to hold its rate of growth below the growth of the economy as a whole and thus to reduce public spending as a proportion of national income. This will enable a low level of borrowing to be combined with reductions in the burden of taxation, so encouraging enterprise and efficiency and thus the growth of output and employment. The ratio of general government expenditure to Gross Domestic Product (GDP) has been falling since 1982–83, and the plans set out in this White Paper will ensure that this downward trend continues.

Treasury (1988) *The Government's Expenditure Plans 1988–89 to 1990–91*, CM. 288-1, London: HMSO, 4

General government spending, excluding privatisation proceeds, has fallen from 46¾ per cent of GDP in 1982–83 to 39½ per cent in 1988–89. The expenditure plans to 1991–92 are consistent with the Government's policy of reducing the share of national income taken by total government spending. The move to Budget surplus has reduced the burden of debt interest, and the fall in unemployment has made savings possible in the social security, employment and training programmes. These savings, together with higher housing receipts and reduced agricultural market support, have made room for increases in priority programmes within the declining trend of total expenditure relative to national income.

Treasury (1989) *Financial Statement and Budget Report, 1989–90*, London: HMSO, para. 5.03

The Budget measures . . .

- keep the PSBR on a downward track
- reduce public spending as a percentage of national income while protecting priority services, developing new partnerships with the private sector, and improving the efficiency of the public sector . . . and encourage enterprise and business.

Treasury (1995) *Financial Statement and Budget Report, 1996–97*, London: HMSO, para. 1.11

5.2

There is no uniquely right way of determining pay but many existing approaches to pay bargaining, beloved of trade unions and employers alike, will need to change if we are to secure the flexibility essential to employment growth. In particular 'the going rate', 'comparability' and 'cost of living increases', are all outmoded concepts – they take no account of differences in performance, ability to pay or difficulties of recruitment, retention or motivation. Pay structures too have to change. National agreements which affect the pay of half the work-force all too often give scant regard to differences in individual circumstances or performance. It is notable that even in areas where the unemployment rate is particularly high, this is not reflected in the levels of earnings. Finally, attachment to an automatic annual round of pay settlements adds yet another inflexibility and upward pressure.

Job growth in the 1990s will depend on replacing these outmoded concepts with pay arrangements which reflect a greater responsiveness to local labour market conditions, changes in product markets and technology, differences in performance, merit and skills: the continuing profitability of the enterprise, and international competitiveness. The importance and relative priority of these factors will vary according to the needs of each individual enterprise at any given time, and employers have to be aware of wider considerations. For example, if all productivity gains are passed to existing workers nothing is left to provide for lower prices and more investment on which profitable output and future jobs depend. Similarly, high earnings growth in sectors with high productivity raises expectations and increases recruitment difficulties in areas with lower productivity such as services. But the development of strategies relating pay more directly to these factors, and more generally to what can be justified and afforded, is essential as the economy moves into the 1990s.

Employment Department (1988) *Employment for the 1990s*, CM. 540, London: HMSO, paras. 3.5–3.6

5.3

The Government will continue to oppose proposals for a national minimum wage. A minimum wage would curtail individual choice and destroy very substantial numbers of jobs. It would also trigger spiralling wage demands as higher paid workers struggled to restore their pay differentials. It would, therefore, price many individuals out of a job, regardless of their own wishes or those of their employers.

Statutory wage fixing also distorts the labour market and reduces the freedom of individuals. The Government has already taken steps to reduce the influence of Wages Councils. The Wages Act 1986 prevented the Councils setting rates of pay for workers under 21 years of age and removed their power to set a whole range of pay minima for different categories of workers. The Act also abolished the Councils' ability to specify minimum holiday pay and entitlements. The Government has made it clear that the Councils can have no permanent place in our system of wage setting. Their operation will continue to be kept under close review.

Employment Department (1992) *People, Jobs and Opportunities*, CM. 1810, London: HMSO, paras. 4.13–4.14

5.4

The Government can and must set an important example in its own role as an employer and as the sponsor of the public sector. The initiatives it has taken in this context so far include:

- the reform of the civil service pay system, introducing more flexible pay regimes to achieve a closer link between performance and rewards, both for individuals and groups of staff. The best performers can now gain extra pay, and at the more senior levels all pay increases will be related to performance;
- development of additional flexibility for Departments and "Next Steps" agencies, to introduce their own, tailor-made grading structures and associated pay arrangements, including performance pay arrangements, separate from the central civil service model;
- the Pay Review Bodies have been invited in this and future years to take individual performance more into account in their recommendations, especially for groups within the National Health Service and for teachers. This message was reinforced recently in the Citizen's Charter;
- greater delegation and flexibility in pay arrangements is being encouraged for teachers through the creation of grant maintained schools and for people in the NHS through the setting up of trusts; and
- support for management's efforts to spread performance related pay in the remaining nationalised industries.

The policies on pay and performance set out in the Citizen's Charter White Paper (CM. 1599) will be a key factor in securing reform in the public sector. To meet the objective of motivating individual employees to improve the quality of public services, the Government will seek: more delegation of decisions on pay; improved rewards for performance and penalties for failure; value for money, by tight cost control; and rewards for performance only when demanding quality of service targets have been met.

ibid.: paras. 4.8–4.9

5.5

Before considering what the principles of pay for the Civil Service should be, we think it is worth while to clear up an ambiguity that tends to arise as to whether there should be one set of principles for the Service as a whole or different principles for different sections of it. It seems to us desirable that there should be one set of principles of pay for the whole Service. This is because it is a unity in that its several parts share a common purpose, admittedly of a very general character, and are linked by a sense of belonging to and forming part of one branch of the public service . . .

First, we do not believe that financial considerations are the sole, or are always the principal, incentive which attracts recruits to the Civil Service or indeed of many other occupations. Tradition, family background and sense of vocation may all play a part so that, except in the very long run and in a very general way, there may be only a tenuous connection between recruitment and rates of pay. This we should consider particularly true of the Civil Service and other employments in which there is a strong element of vocation.

Secondly, we do not regard wastage as a reliable indicator of the fairness or unfairness of rates of pay. It may sometimes be a symptom but the validity of the wastage test must be affected by outside demand for particular skills. In the Civil Service this varies a great deal at different times and for different classes. The skills of some civil service classes (for example the administrative and executive) are not particularly marketable except in very narrow fields; those of others (for example at present some of the specialist classes) may at times be in very high demand. It would not in our view be correct to infer either that where there is little or no wastage the present rates are necessarily fair or that where there is marked wastage rates are necessarily unfair.

Thirdly, we see very considerable danger in the assumption that civil servants are fairly paid and the Service is in a healthy state because its members appear to be carrying out their duties "efficiently". The process of deterioration arising from a sense of grievance on the part of the staff might be a very slow one, particularly in a Service with the high traditions of the British Civil Service; and by the time the tendency manifests itself irreparable damage may have been done.

Royal Commission on the Civil Service 1953–5 (1955), Cmd. 9613, London: HMSO, paras. 87, 90–3

5.6

We do not think that these statements go to the heart of the matter. We believe that the State is under a categorical obligation to remunerate its employees fairly, and that any statement of end which does not explicitly recognise this is not adequate. It may be held that if rates of pay are such as to recruit and retain an efficient staff they must be fair or even that this is what is meant by calling them fair. We do not agree. Such a contention seems to us neither capable of logical demonstration nor to be supported by contemporary facts. We believe that it is true in a general way that if rates of pay for the Civil Service are what we should call fair they will probably, over a period of time and in most classes, enable the Service to recruit and retain an efficient staff, though in conditions of near-full employment many or most employers are likely to be conscious of a recurring, if not a chronic shortage of labour. The converse of this cannot, however, be logically inferred. The proposition that the Civil Service is recruiting and training an efficient staff does not necessarily prove the proposition that the rates of pay are fair. That the analysis of "fairness" in terms solely of recruitment and retention is not supported by the facts . . .

ibid.: para. 90

5.7

We have discussed the main flaws which we see in the system for making comparisons and in the interpretation of the comparisons information. We also think that, twenty-five years after the Priestley Commission reported, the effect of the many social and economic changes which have taken place means that the primary principle of fair comparison no longer appears capable of sustaining virtually by itself a civil service pay determination system. This is not to say that fair comparison has not part to play. It has a part, but not the completely dominating part that it had under the pay research system.

Because fair comparison was the primary principle, civil servants expected that, with the system operating normally, the rates indicated by the comparisons would form the pay settlement. This meant that there was very little room for manoeuvre to take account of factors other than comparisons.

Internal relativities

The Priestley Commission attached only subsidiary importance to internal relativities. The Commission recommended that internal relativities should be used as a supplement to the principle of fair comparison, but should never be allowed to override the primary principle. This appears to us to underestimate the importance of internal relativities to both employer and employee. For management it is essential that the logic of the organisation's structure and of individuals' contribution within it should be reflected in the pay structure. Employees often see it as more important that their pay should be compared fairly with that of other employees in their organisation than with that of outside employees.

Recruitment and retention

While it had been generally agreed until then that the Civil Service should pay what was necessary to recruit and retain an efficient staff, the Priestley Commission did not admit this criterion as an overall aim. They said (paragraph 90) "We believe that . . . if rates of pay for the Civil Service are what we should call fair they will probably, over a period of time and in most cases, enable the Service to recruit and retain an efficient staff." Experience shows, however, that the Priestley Commission's system failed to provide a good enough response to short term fluctuations in "market" rates of pay.

There have been occasions when the Civil Service has been slow in adjusting its pay rates to enable it to recruit and retain staff in occupations where there is a shortage of qualified persons available. At such times the relevant pay rates offered have been less than necessary for an efficient, properly motivated and adequately staffed Civil Service. More recently, a case could be made out – and indeed the Government has done so – that there are some areas of the Service where pay levels do not need to be increased to recruit and retain adequate staff. In times of high unemployment, in particular, there are fewer recruitment and retention problems in many areas of the Service. At such times there is a fine balance to be struck between levels of remuneration fair to civil servants many of whom, because of the career structure of much of the Civil Service, have developed skills and expertise peculiar to Government service; and levels fair to Government and taxpayer, who should not be asked to pay more than necessary for an efficient, properly motivated and adequately staffed Civil Service.

In many organisations pay systems contain specific provision, over and above the general level of pay, for motivating employees, encouraging them to improve their performance, and rewarding increased efficiency and productivity. This need is no less acute in the Civil Service than elsewhere. But the only equivalent provisions in the civil service pay system are proficiency payments in a very few grades. The annual pay increments (up to maxima for each grade) are intended to reward growing experience and competence in the grade, and are in practice, though not in theory, virtually automatic. This system applies widely in the public sector but it appears increasingly anachronistic compared with the pay structures used effectively by private sector employers.

Report of an Inquiry into Civil Service Pay (1982) Volume 1, Cmd. 8590, London: HMSO (Megaw Report), paras. 78–84

5.8

The Health Departments repeated their belief that the pay of nursing staff should not be governed primarily by comparisons with the pay of staff in other employments, still less with their own at some date.

Review Body for Nursing Staff, Midwives and Health Visitors (1987) *Fourth Report*, CM. 129, London: HMSO, para. 67

Direct comparability with other groups should not be the basis for determining the pay of public sector employees. Pay should be set rather at the appropriate level to ensure that sufficient employees of the right standard could be recruited and retained.

Review Body for Nursing Staff, Midwives and Health Visitors (1988) *Fifth Report*, CM. 360, London: HMSO, para. 63

Data about pay settlements and earnings movements should inform pay determination only to the extent that they were relevant to recruitment and retention.

Review Board for Nursing Staff, Midwives and Health Visitors (1991) *Eighth Report*, CM. 1410, London: HMSO, para. 40

The Health Departments . . . also reaffirmed their view that data on pay settlements and earnings movements elsewhere in the NHS and in the economy generally should inform pay determination only to the extent that they were relevant to the recruitment and retention of nursing staff in the NHS.

Review Body for Nursing Staff, Midwives and Health Visitors (1994) *Eleventh Report*, CM. 2462, London: HMSO, para. 38

The Health Departments commented that rates of pay for staff within our remit should be no more than were necessary to recruit, retain and motivate sufficient numbers of suitably qualified staff.

Review Body for Nursing Staff, Midwives and Health Visitors (1996) *Thirteenth Report*, CM. 3093, London: HMSO, para. 55

That when considering pay levels the main determinant should be what was sufficient to recruit, retain and motivate staff of the right quality and in the right numbers within the limits of affordability.

Review Body on Doctors' and Dentists' Remuneration (1991) *Twenty First Report*, CM. 1412, London: HMSO, para. 18

The Departments pointed out that they did not consider it appropriate to determine pay rates for the professions solely or substantially by comparisons with the earnings of other professional groups . . . data on pay settlements and earnings movements . . . should inform pay determination only to the extent that they were relevant to recruitment and retention.

Review Body on Doctors' and Dentists' Remuneration (1994) Twenty *Third Report*, CM. 2460, London: HMSO, para. 33

The Departments said that data on pay settlements and earnings movements in the NHS, elsewhere in the public sector and in the economy generally should inform pay determination only to the extent that they were relevant to motivation, recruitment and retention.

Review Body on Doctors' and Dentists' Remuneration (1996) *Twenty Fifth Report*, CM. 3090, London: HMSO, para. 1.21

5.9

The arguments for a measure of decentralisation were put to us by the Ministry of Defence. It has contended that it employs large numbers of professional staff on a wide variety of functions unique to the Ministry, without close affinity to the rest of the Service, such as the running of dockyards and ordnance factories. The Ministry (and the Property Services Agency) are associated with the main pay negotiations for industrial civil servants and have a degree of delegated authority in respect of certain areas such as productivity schemes and allowances within agreed principles. In the non-industrial pay field (the field with which we are concerned) individual departments have since a centralisation programme in the early 1970s, been only indirectly involved. The Ministry of Defence has now indicated that it would in general welcome changes in the pay system, and in delegated authority within it which enabled its management requirements to be reflected more directly in the fixing of pay for its non-industrial staff.

We were attracted to the concept of decentralisation, because we believe that the transfer of responsibility for pay to the centre has tended to undermine the ability of managers in the Civil Service to respond to management needs, and has in some cases led them to take less interest in important management issues than they should. Rather than pursue matters with central departments, over whom they have sometimes felt it was difficult to have much influence, they have tended to become spectators in the face of pressing problems. They have not always felt in a position to share the responsibility for avoiding or dealing with these problems. To give departments a larger measure of responsibility for the determination and structure of the pay of their staff might well effect a positive and valuable change in civil service management style.

Report of an Inquiry into Civil Service Pay (1982), paras. 278 and 281

5.10

The main arguments for introducing greater geographical variation in pay rates than at present are threefold. First, the Civil Service is probably paying more than it needs to do in some areas to recruit and retain staff of adequate quality. As a large employer it may accordingly force up other employers' pay rates in the locality unnecessarily, or alternatively cream off the best available staff.

Secondly, the Civil Service may be paying too little in other areas. Particular difficulties have arisen in recent years in some areas, especially London, in recruiting enough staff of adequate quality for some grades although in current economic circumstances these difficulties have eased. Examples of the difficulties which have been encountered in the past have been given in evidence by individual Departments, including Inland Revenue, Customs and Excise and the Department of Health and Social Security.

Thirdly, if a new pay system were to include comparisons with outside rates these should in principle reflect geographical differences where they are significant.

ibid.: paras. 292–4

5.11

Each year since 1987 the Health Departments have expressed a wish to introduce more flexible remuneration arrangements in order to enable the

Documents

NHS to adjust to differences in local labour market conditions. In 1988, in evidence for our sixth review, the Departments proposed a pilot scheme whereby national pay rates for nursing staff could be selectively supplemented where this was deemed appropriate on recruitment and retention grounds. They asked us to support these proposals and we did so, but subject to a number of conditions which in the event were not met. In our 1991 (eighth) report we were critical of the way in which the pilot scheme for selective pay supplements had been monitored and in our 1992 (ninth) report we said that the data from the second year of monitoring did not provide us with an adequate basis on which to reach any worthwhile conclusion on the efficacy of the supplements, given all the other changes that were happening within units at the same time.

The White Paper "The Citizen's Charter" published in 1991 urged the Review Bodies for the health professions to ". . . take performance more into account in their recommendations over successive reports . . .", and the Patient's Charters later that year implied continuing commitment to measuring and improving the performance of the NHS.

In November 1991 the Health Departments, as part of their evidence for the ninth review, proposed that in future the Review Body would be invited to recommend a "target average percentage pay increase" (TAPPI) for nursing staff, of which a proportion would be recommended as a basic increase payable automatically to all staff, and the balance would be available for local flexibility including performance pay. We were critical of the TAPPI approach because we felt that in the circumstances at the time it could not simultaneously deliver "local labour market" flexibility and pay for performance. The Departments subsequently withdrew the TAPPI proposal and said they would be considering a broader approach to pay flexibility.

During 1992 and 1993 the two Sides of the Nursing and Midwifery Staffs Negotiating Council discussed pay flexibility but the Departments did not put forward any specific proposals. Meanwhile the Prime Minister re-emphasised the Government's commitment to the development of performance pay and more decentralised pay arrangements in his letter to us on 12 November 1992.

In late November 1993 the Departments presented a new proposal to the Staff Side and to the Review Body for pay determination in 1994–95 intended to accelerate the introduction of pay flexibility and local bargaining. The proposal was to insert into the Whitley Council agreement the following clause:

"That employing authorities may make performance related payments to employees under locally devised schemes based on achievement of increased productivity and/or improved efficiency".

This approach linked the Departments' commitment to local pay determination with their commitment to pay related to performance and to improving the productivity of the National Health Service. As the Staff Side predicted, the Sides did not reach agreement on the proposal within the timescale envisaged by the Departments.

We had to consider whether the Departments' call for an "exceptionally modest" increase in national rates of pay, coupled with their initiative, provided a realistic basis for remuneration in 1994–95, given the state of development of pay determination in the NHS at the time. We concluded that local managements were at best at early stages of preparedness for determining pay at local level and we were not able to support the proposal. We said that we did not want to put any pressure on Trusts to commence local negotiations when they were not ready. That would have resulted in ill thought out schemes and therefore we considered how we could make suitable pay recommendations for what we hoped would be a transitional year.

We therefore said in our 1994 (eleventh) report "Had the discussions between the parties at national level, and the preparations at local level, been more advanced, we would have recommended an increase of 2 per cent in national pay rates with strong encouragement for local determination of increases beyond that, while providing safeguards for staff denied any access to productivity deals. On this basis, all staff within our remit would have received that 2 per cent increase as a minimum". Staff in units where local productivity-related arrangements proved capable of achievement could have received an additional increase reflecting the productivity gain of their unit and local agreement on its distribution.

However we concluded that the Departments and the Staff Side and, for the most part, local managers and staff representatives needed more time to develop arrangements for local negotiations of the type envisaged in the draft enabling clause and that is why we made the recommendations described in paragraph 1. We said that we were pleased that both parties had told us that they were prepared to enter into early negotiations about the introduction of local pay determination. We encouraged them to come back to us in September 1994 with joint evidence on the way ahead that would enable us to consider what form of recommendations would then be appropriate for 1995–96. In the event negotiations have not progressed sufficiently and they have been unable to do so.

Review Body for Nurses, Midwives and Health Visitors (1995) *Twelfth Report*, CM. 2762, London: HMSO, paras. 51–8

5.12

The main arguments put to us in evidence in favour of performance related pay were:–

(a) it would be desirable to have a more effective means of rewarding good performance and penalising poor performance than promotion on the one hand and downgrading and dismissal on the other. Staff who work hard and are valuable to their departments will not always have the right qualities for promotion. There is a need for ways of acknowledging their contribution and maintaining their motivation and morale;

(b) it is inequitable to reward competent and hard-working staff equally in financial terms with those who are less capable and hard-working; a financial reward for good performance would make the Service more attractive to more able staff;

(c) as the size of the Civil Service is reduced there will be proportionately fewer promotions. There will therefore be a greater need for other incentives;

(d) outside organisations have successfully introduced merit pay schemes.

A number of problems were, however, mentioned to us which would need to be overcome if a successful merit pay scheme was to be launched in a non-industrial Civil Service:

(a) the nature of public service work creates a particular need for co-operation and shared objectives. In the private sector it may be easier to establish a clear link between merit pay and contribution to profit as a basis for a more objective assessment;

(b) judgements can, and are, made of the performance of staff in the Civil Service but they are necessarily more subjective than those which can be made in many other organisations. For the most part civil service work does not lend itself to the clear measurement of individual performance, nor can performance be judged by quantitative criteria such as a profit and loss account or sales figures. In a very large organisation it is difficult to ensure complete consistency of standards;

(c) the opportunities for demonstrating merit vary from job to job and there could be reluctance to accept moves to less "eye-catching", but none the less essential jobs;

(d) there could be significant additional administrative costs with extra staff required in personnel areas and more time required in line management for dealing with staff assessment issues;

(e) there is a danger that a merit pay scheme would not in practice lead to sufficient improvement in the performance of those who are highly rated (and are probably already more highly motivated) to offset the danger of demotivating those who do not benefit from it.

Report of an Inquiry into Civil Service Pay (1982), para. 326

5.13

The ways in which people are paid can have a powerful effect on improving performance. Pay systems in the public sector need to make a regular and direct link between a person's contribution to the standards of service provided and his or her reward. But of course the label of 'performance pay' must not be used, as has sometimes happened in the past, as a way of dressing up what would otherwise be unacceptable pay increases.

Action to achieve this objective has been taken across the public sector, including:

- new contracts for family doctors, including payments for hitting targets;
- general managers in the NHS paid according to performance, including success in tackling waiting lists;
- in schools, heads and deputies receiving more pay for improved performance;
- extra payments available for the best classroom teachers;
- in the Civil Service, performance pay related to individual performance for most staff;
- in the new agencies of government, the chief executives' pay related directly to performance and many chief executives on short term performance-related contracts;
- nationalised industry directors eligible for bonuses which depend on the industry meeting its service targets.

But much more is required to make the links between pay, performance, and quality of service tighter and more effective. We want to see:

- more **delegation** of decisions on pay – the system of reward must be closer to the responsibility for the delivery of a service;
- **extending rewards** for performance – and, equally important, penalties for failure – as part of the normal package of pay and conditions;
- securing **value for money** for the taxpayer by tight cost control, with the net cost of performance rewards paid for by real productivity increases;
- ensuring that rewards for performance are only given when demanding **quality of service targets** have been met.

Over the coming months we want to see these principles advanced:

- we will urge the Pay Review Bodies to take performance more into account in their recommendations over successive reports, especially for those in the NHS and for teachers. This does not mean that the Review Bodies should recommend a higher increase in the pay bill than they otherwise would.

But we will expect the composition of the recommendations to change so that a larger proportion of pay would be linked to performance;

- we will encourage the drive towards greater delegation and flexibility in the Civil Service (to departments and agencies); in the NHS (through trusts); and in education (to grant-maintained schools);
- in the remaining nationalised industries we will support management's efforts to spread performance-related pay; we want to see the rewards of the top management of, for example, British Rail and the London Underground more closely linked to the delivery of improved services to the travelling public.

Prime Minister's Office (1991) *The Citizen's Charter: Raising the Standard*, CM. 1599, London: HMSO, 35

5.14

Experience has shown that delegated pay and grading systems have a number of advantages. They can be more flexible and more closely tailored to the needs of the organisation. No two Civil Service organisations are identical, any more than two organisations elsewhere in the public or private sector. It is right that pay and grading systems, like other management arrangements, should be attuned to individual circumstances and relevant labour markets. In that way an organisation is able to focus more closely on the delivery of its objectives, to exercise direct control over the costs and quality of staff, to maximise value for money from its paybill, and to ensure that business needs are fully reflected in the management of staff. An example of the latter is performance-related pay; it is right that there should be a clear link between an individual's pay and their contribution to the achievement of the organisation's objectives.

The Government proposed to extend this policy, so that by April 1996 responsibility for the pay and grading of staff below senior levels should be delegated to all departments and the existing national pay arrangements replaced. This will remove the rigidities inherent in the current system. The existing consultation arrangements for delegation made under the Civil Service (Management Functions) Act will apply in each case. The Government is keen, in addition, for each agency within a department to be responsible for its own pay and grading.

Such delegation will be a very important step, assisting departments and agencies to achieve additional efficiencies, to improve delivery of services in accordance with the principles of the Citizen's Charter, and to establish pay and grading arrangements which reflect the proper interests of staff. It will be a valuable mechanism to help departments to achieve the efficiencies necessary properly to reward staff within agreed running costs. It should also enable departments and agencies, in consultation with staff and trade unions, to re-examine the old-fashioned distinction between 'industrial' and 'non-industrial' staff.

The Government believes that the pay of civil servants should be set on a fair basis which reflects the need to recruit, retain, and motivate staff of the right quality and recognises good performance. This applies at all levels. It is also the Government's policy, as the Chancellor of the Exchequer announced on 14 September 1993 and reiterated in his Budget statement on 30 November, that pay increases have to be covered from efficiency savings and other economies.

Prime Minister's Office (1994) *The Civil Service: Continuity and Change*, CM. 2627, London: HMSO, paras. 3.25–3.28

5.15

We agree that pay comparisons are relevant to recruitment and retention but we believe that they also influence motivation and morale. Remuneration is not the main factor in inducing people to enter or leave the NHS or the professions themselves (although the long lead times make this difficult to judge), but if those that remain in the NHS feel that they are treated unfairly compared with people of similar education, training and commitment, we believe they will be less motivated to give of their best and will become demoralised. We have looked at a range of the professions with which doctors and dentists compare themselves, as well as other professions and self-employed people – comparing their hours of work as well as their pay. We do not believe that the comparative remuneration of doctors and dentists has so deteriorated in recent years as to make this a significant issue in determining pay for 1994–95.

We also accept the Departments' point that it is necessary to compare the whole package of remuneration and other opportunities offered by different professions and occupations. We have continued to keep under review the values of pensions and benefits for doctors and dentists in relation to those of other comparable groups of employees. We have looked carefully at a range of other occupations and have concluded that there has been no substantial change since the position was last reviewed in 1991.

Morale and motivation are not primarily a matter of earnings or earnings comparisons. Any current problems of morale and motivation (the extent of which we find it difficult to judge) seem more likely to be related to workload and the organisational changes of recent years. However, we do think it is important that doctors and dentists should not feel under-valued by a community which would allow their remuneration to be eroded by inflation and their increases to be kept, year after year, well below the rate of increase obtained by comparable occupations.

Review Body on Doctors' and Dentists' Remuneration (1994) *Twenty-Third Report*, Cm. 2460, London: HMSO, paras. 34–6

5.16

We compared the typical career progression for hospital doctors with that of a number of other public sector professions, including senior civil servants, members of the armed forces, schoolteachers, university lecturers and top management grades in the police. Comparability with the private sector was more difficult as there are no definitive comparators with easily identified progression. Historically, doctors have tended to compare themselves with other (largely self-employed) professionals such as solicitors, accountants and actuaries, but we believe the range of jobs that can be considered 'professional' is significantly wider and includes personnel such as architects, computer specialists, personnel specialists, engineers and so on. Survey information on remuneration levels for these occupations in the private sector is available from a number of sources, and we looked at them for the purpose of our evaluations.

In our assessment of pay movements, both in terms of relativity with other comparable professions and with movements in prices, we concluded that over the last ten years doctors' and dentists' pay has risen more than inflation but slightly less than average earnings, and has broadly kept pace with that of other Review Body groups. Their settlements have been higher than those for many other public sector employees. Our analysis of data from the New Earnings Survey implied that doctors and dentists have lost out against higher earners in the economy since 1985, a result of the widening of earnings differentials in the private sector. This finding was borne out by data from Remuneration Economics' National Management Salary Survey.

Review Body on Doctors' and Dentists' Remuneration (1996) *Twenty-Fifth Report*, CM. 3090, London: HMSO, paras. 1.27–1.28

5.17

The logic of the argument about market forces would, if applied to this situation suggest that pay levels need be set only marginally above the point at which significant losses would occur from nurses abandoning their profession altogether and seeking other forms of employment. Those who commit themselves to a professional career such as nursing, and eschew industrial action, may reasonably expect that wider considerations than this will be taken into account in settling their pay. Moreover, the NHS controls the number of training places and therefore the supply of trained staff as well as the demand for them; in such a near monopoly situation, the sufficiency of applicants at any time is an inconclusive test of the adequacy of existing levels.

Review Body for Nursing Staff, Midwives and Health Visitors (1991) *Eighth Report*, CM. 1410, London: HMSO, para. 30

5.18

We take the view that recruitment and retention are the main considerations in looking at comparability. If the levels of pay for nursing staff fall too far out of line with the pay of those in comparable or 'competitor' occupations the motivation and morale of the existing workforce may fall because of a feeling of unfairness, and recruitment will be made more difficult as a result. But there is also a wider sense in which the pay of nursing staff should, in general, be 'felt fair', both by the staff themselves and by the community as a whole.

Review Body for Nursing Staff, Midwives and Health Visitors (1994) *Eleventh Report*, CM. 2462, London: HMSO, para. 39

It is apparent that the concepts of fairness and comparability can be interpreted in a number of ways and that local pay determination adds a further dimension. The common thread is that pay levels should be sufficient to recruit, retain and motivate staff: but we again recognise the wider sense in which pay for nursing staff should be "felt fair". We accept that nurses perceive the Review Body's recommendations as representing society's valuation of their role. We have borne these points in mind when formulating our recommendations, but would make the following observations. Firstly, in 1995–96, according to the OME survey, over 86 per cent of nursing staff will have received pay offers of 3 per cent or more: this compares favourably with many of the awards elsewhere in the public sector, and is broadly in line with those in the private sector. Secondly, the annual uprating provision in the framework agreement provides a mechanism to ensure that pay rates between Trusts and in different areas of the country do not get too far out of line. Thirdly, while it is helpful to consider information on the pay of comparator groups, pay comparability is difficult to assess and cannot on its own form a basis for determining our recommendations. On the last point we have borne in mind that basic pay scales for nursing staff do not provide a complete picture since enhancements to pay can form a significant proportion of earnings, especially for lower paid staff. We are aware that not all staff receive such enhancements and that some 'competitor' groups can also earn significant amounts in excess of basic pay and we have taken all of this into account in considering the evidence before us.

Review Body for Nursing, Midwives and Health Visitors (1996) *Thirteenth Report*, CM. 3092 London: HMSO, para. 58

5.19

There are strong reasons against introducing greater regional variations in pay rates. These include the difficulty of establishing reliably the extent to which there are geographical variations in the pay rates of comparable employees; the complexity and cost of administering a more regionalised system; and the difficulty of establishing functional boundaries.

A major difficulty in making an accurate assessment of the case for change is the lack of detailed and reliable information on regional variations in pay for comparable groups of employees. The Treasury has provided the Committee with useful information on geographical variations in earnings among non-manual employees from the Department of Employment's New Earnings Survey . . . The main conclusions were that at regional level there was, London apart, relatively little variation between regions, but earnings in a few counties, as well as London, varied substantially. Even at county level, however, earnings in the majority of counties were broadly similar.

The reasons for geographical variations in pay rates are not clear: possible factors involved include local living costs, local differences in the ease with which staff can be recruited, or the presence within an area of large high-paying or low-paying organisations. Nor is it clear how far geographical variations apply in the same way to different groups of staff. The pattern of market rates for specialist staff, for example, may be very different from that of general clerical and administrative staff. Simple statistical evidence of geographical variation cannot therefore be considered sufficient evidence that civil service pay rates should reflect such variation.

We conclude from the statistical evidence that there are indications of substantial variations in clerical earnings in certain localities outside London, but the evidence is not clear enough to serve as a solid basis for delineating pay regions. To establish firmly on a statistical basis whether there is a real case for regional pay rates outside London, enquiries with much larger samples for different localities and occupations would need to be conducted: this would be very expensive. We do not regard the option of a "regional index" to determine civil service regional rates as a practicable one.

Cost and complexity

Both the Government and the Civil Service unions have pointed out that regional pay would inevitably add to the cost and complexity of the pay system. As was found to be the case with the earlier system of provincial differentiation, the pay negotiating process would itself become more complex and probably more lengthy too. There could also be a considerable extra load on departmental personnel units, pay offices and computer centres where the greatly increased number of pay scales and disputes about the boundaries stemming from pay variation would have to be handled. The costs of administration would increase in proportion to the number of separate pay zones or large town allowances.

Boundaries

Where departments are organised regionally their regional boundaries do not necessarily coincide either with each other or with other common boundaries such as the boundaries used for regional planning purposes. At both the regional and more local levels it would be difficult to find boundaries which met the management requirements of all departments. The smaller the unit of variation which was adopted in any scheme the greater the number of boundaries and therefore the greater the problems stemming from staff crossing boundaries. Unless agreement could be reached on boundary alignment serious difficulties would occur for departments which need to move staff within a departmental region across a pay boundary. Staff would be reluctant to move from a high paying area to a lower paying one, especially if there is no noticeable difference in living costs between the two.

It has been suggested that this problem would be less difficult to manage in the case of non-mobile staff (below Executive Officer and equivalent) since it is unlikely that many of them will be asked – and none of them could be required – to move to an office outside their own area. However, if local pay applied to non-mobile staff only, this would give rise to difficulties at the "interface" between grades whose pay was determined regionally and those whose pay was determined nationally. There could be excessive squeezing or widening of differentials, with consequent pressure to increase rates to restore differentials.

Report of an Inquiry into Civil Service Pay (1982): paras. 297–303

5.20

We then considered the extent to which pay variations were likely to contribute towards redressing these imbalances (in geographical distribution of teachers).

Teaching has traditionally been a collegiate enterprise, with teachers operating broadly as a team and expecting broadly the same opportunities to gain career rewards. But there has always been a certain measure of informal pay differentiation on the basis of recruitment and retention needs. Some of this has been explicit: the London area allowance and social priority allowance (discussed in sections 5.3 and 5.4) are examples. Other elements of pay differentiation are disguised: it has long been accepted that to recruit a teacher of, say, CDT might require the offer of pay one scale higher (or now, one level of incentive allowance higher) than an equivalently-qualified teacher in some secondary subject in greater supply. The facility to offer new entrants "in an urban area" up to two additional increments, as well as up to one increment for each year of useful experience beyond age 23, is also used differentially by authorities according to their recruitment and retention needs. We have found that teachers and employers are comfortable with this arrangement, which provides for enhancement or "topping-up" of basic salaries at managerial discretion, within an agreed national framework. The employers asked for slightly greater flexibility in applying the system, but sought no fundamental change at this stage. In oral evidence we learned that the DES too favoured continuation of a system of national determination of teachers' pay, with local variations restricted to discretionary application of nationally-agreed supplements.

We can see no reason to challenge this consensus between the parties. Education is a national service, locally delivered. The reforms in train are intended to introduce a greater degree of uniformity in the national curriculum; examples of good teaching practice in one part of the country will become even more relevant in other parts. Within obvious limits, we should therefore seek to encourage teacher mobility. If basic pay were substantially lower in one area simply because recruitment and retention were for the time being easier, teachers from elsewhere would be discouraged from moving in, and the local schools would tend to lose any influx of new blood and fresh ideas. Equally, to restrict pay everywhere to the basic national salary scale or level, without supplements of any kind, would result in severe difficulties in high-cost areas where there is fierce competition for qualified personnel. The present system of nationally-determined basic rates of pay enhanced by local additions as necessary seems the one most likely to produce the desired result.

In any case, we see other arguments against explicit regional/local or subject differentiation of teachers' pay. First, it would be likely to be inflexible. Today's shortage subject may next year be in adequate supply; today's depressed area could be a prosperous region in the 1990s; yet teachers need some assurance about their likely career and pay prospects over several years, and will not easily relinquish supplements once promised, merely because the recruitment market has changed. (Our comments on the anachronistic nature of both the London area and social priority allowances are relevant.) Secondly, it would undoubtedly be perceived as unfair; it is argued that a teacher works as hard whatever his specialism, and equally that a teacher faces the same cost-of-living expenses in a "good" urban area as in a neighbouring "bad" area with severe recruitment problems. Third, it might only redistribute shortages, since – in the short term at least – the supply of qualified teachers is relatively inelastic, and local authorities are not in a position to engage in a free-market auction. Finally, and decisively, the evidence suggests that this approach would be ineffective. Very large sums would be needed to keep in the profession all those teachers – relatively few in number – who leave to take up highly-paid jobs in expanding areas like computing; the private sector would always be able to outbid local authorities.

Given the rate at which the needs of the education system are changing, it will be essential that any system designed to cope with current shortages should incorporate sufficient flexibility to allow for changes in future years.

We therefore **recommend** that teachers' **basic** rates of pay should continue to be the same for all parts of the country, and for all subjects in the curriculum.

Interim Advisory Committee on School Teachers' Pay and Conditions (1988). *First Report*, CM. 363, London: HMSO paras. 5.2.5 – 5.2.10

5.21

There are, however, a number of weighty arguments against giving departments more discretion to determine pay. The main one is that we do not think it possible for widespread authority over pay to be delegated to departments without widespread delegation of financial authority to match. We are not clear that the necessary mechanisms for financial and budgetary controls are available to enable greater decentralisation of financial authority.

Measures of departments' performance would be needed so that departments could be made accountable for their results. To devise suitable measures over the whole Civil Service might be a difficult, lengthy and perhaps even impossible process. It raises problems well outside our terms of reference.

There are other important arguments against decentralising responsibility for pay. A high proportion of the Civil Service is to be found in grades which exist service-wide, and flexible movement of staff between departments and between different areas of staff within departments is made easier by common pay-scales for the grades. Giving departments the possibility of raising pay to meet shortages might result in "bidding-up" between departments who are often competitors for very similar labour in the same area. This would be costly to the taxpayer and cause a general rise in pay for the occupations in question with little management gain. Relaxation of central control and creation of departmental negotiations would be very difficult to reconcile with the political sensitivity of the overall result of negotiations and would be very hard to keep within bounds; in a Civil Service which boasts a wide measure of central cohesion and co-operation such decentralisation would spread the seeds of friction between departments and for sectional disputes between unions and groups of staff. It could be more costly to administer a fragmented bargaining system. Neither departments nor unions are at present organised to provide quickly a sufficient pool of expertise for pay negotiations at departmental level. There are good arguments for concentrating negotiations in the hands of those with a high degree of knowledge and experience in industrial relations and pay bargaining.

Report of an Inquiry into Civil Service Pay (1982), paras. 283–4

5.22

Had the discussions between the parties at national level, and the preparations at local level, been more advanced, we would have recommended an increase of 2 per cent in national pay rates with strong encouragement for local determination of increases beyond that, while providing safeguards for staff denied any access to productivity deals. On this basis, all staff within our remit would have received that 2 per cent increase as a minimum. Those in units where local productivity-related arrangements proved capable of achievement could have received an additional increase reflecting the productivity gain and the local agreement on its distribution.

However, we have come to the conclusion that the Departments and the Staff Side, and for the most part, local managers and staff representatives, need more time to develop the arrangements for local negotiations which would be necessary to conduct the sort of productivity bargaining which the Departments proposed on 29 November, or to deal more generally with performance-related pay and local factors such as labour market pressures and different working arrangements. We are pleased that both parties have told us that they are prepared to enter into early negotiations about the introduction of local pay determination. We hope they will come back to us in September 1994 with joint evidence on the way ahead. That would enable us to consider what form of recommendations would then be appropriate. Meanwhile we urge all local units that feel they are ready for local productivity pay bargaining to go ahead with discussions at local level.

Review Body for Nursing Staff, Midwives and Health Visitors (1994) *Eleventh Report*, CM. 2462, London: HMSO, paras 66 and 68

A very small number of Trusts have introduced their own comprehensive locally determined pay structures which represent a radical departure from nationally agreed Whitley terms and conditions. The Departments' assumption, and that of the organisations representing Trusts, appears to be that all Trusts will move in due course to this position. However, the Departments made clear to us in oral evidence that they did not expect a significant additional number of Trusts to introduce their own comprehensive pay structures in 1995–96, though some might choose to do so. The Departments believed that many Trusts might prefer to award across-the-board increases related to their own particular circumstances. In any case the effect would be for Trusts which had not already done so to begin to take ownership of their own pay and conditions of employment.

Review Body for Nursing Staff, Midwives and Health Visitors (1995) *Twelfth Report*, CM. 2762, London: HMSO, para. 63

There are significant differences in the parties' perceptions of the extent to which Trusts were prepared for local pay negotiations in 1995–96, and on the degree of progress that has now been made. On the one hand, the Staff Side pointed to the relatively low proportion of staff on distinct Trust contracts (estimated by the Health Departments at some 5 per cent), and the time it took for Trusts to make pay offers in 1995. On the other, the Departments and the employers' organisations maintained that significant progress had been made, citing as evidence managers' attempts to use local pay negotiation to tackle issues like sickness absence and progress towards concluding recognition agreements. Judgements on progress are not helped by the fact that, for various reasons, the vast majority of Trusts have in the end made pay awards of 3 per cent with few, if any, conditions attached. **Our view is that, while we are not convinced that all Trusts are as committed to the concept of local pay determination as the evidence from the employers' organisations might suggest, many Trusts have made significant progress in developing their thinking about local pay this year and in some instances are devising attractive local pay packages** (emphasis in the original).

Review Body for Nursing Staff, Midwives and Health Visitors (1996)
Thirteenth Report, CM. 3092, London: HMSO, para. 47

Our 1996 report also described a number of further criteria against
which progress would be judged. These included: the need for Trusts and
purchasers to work constructively together to achieve a beneficial outcome
for both nursing staff and patients; that efficiency gains arising from local
pay determination should benefit Professions Allied to Medicine staff
directly, as well as the Trust as a whole; that Trusts should develop
attractive pay strategies; and that staff should be persuaded of the benefits
of local pay determination. In our view, these criteria have not been widely
met.

Review Body for Nursing Staff, Midwives and Health Visitors (1997)
Fourteenth Report, CM. 3538, London: HMSO, para. 23

5.23

The **Staff Side's** evidence stated clearly its objections to local pay determination. Its main argument was that a National Health Service required
a national pay system to reflect common values, standards and measures
of quality. Local pay determination was unfair; it undermined the role of
the Review Body as guardian of fair pay in nursing; and could lead to a
resurgence of industrial conflict. It would generally result in lower pay
for nurses and a wide variation of standards; could discriminate against
women; was likely to limit training opportunities; and would be expensive
to implement and operate. Trusts would need to employ extra staff to
negotiate and implement local arrangements, and there would be additional
costs to cover clinical staff who took part in local negotiations. Moves to
local pay determination for nursing staff in other countries had not worked
well and existing national arrangements provided sufficient flexibility to
recruit and retain staff. Many managers were neither enthusiastic nor
prepared for local pay negotiation.

Review Body for Nursing Staff, Midwives and Health Visitors (1996)
Thirteenth Report, CM. 3092, London: HMSO, para. 40

The Staff Side's evidence, by contrast, maintained that local pay determination did not work and was not wanted. It argued that very few Trusts
had implemented local pay schemes and that most Trusts had little real
enthusiasm for the process. It felt that where such schemes had been

introduced they had generally led to lower pay and poor conditions of service. Local pay determination had also led to Trusts introducing what the Staff Side believed to be undesirable practices which it urged us to discourage. These included the linking of pay increases to performance, productivity, local labour markets and absence rates.

Review Body for Nursing Staff, Midwives and Health Visitors (1997) *Fourteenth Report*, CM. 3538, London: HMSO, para. 50

5.24

The evidence presented to us in relation to pay flexibility and performance-related pay tended to conflate those two issues but we think that they should be clearly distinguished. We regard **pay flexibility** as the flexibility needed to accommodate differences in particular labour markets, its purpose being to assist in the recruitment and retention of suitable staff in sufficient numbers in a particular occupation or locality. **Performance-related pay** is different in that it provides motivation for people already employed in the organisation to improve their effectiveness in the job, whether as individuals or as part of a team.

The Departments' outline does not separate the concepts of pay flexibility and performance-related pay. We believe they have very different managerial, motivational and financial implications and we suggest that when the parties begin their discussions they should consider pay flexibility and performance-related pay as separate issues.

Review Body for Nurses, Midwives and Health Visitors (1992) *Ninth Report*, CM. 1811, London: HMSO, paras. 15 and 29

The changes of approach over the years on "local pay" have ensured a period of continuing uncertainty in the NHS about what is meant by that term. Last year the Departments were emphasising the value of performance-related pay, and seeking to encourage local schemes based on increased individual productivity or improved efficiency. In their 1994 evidence the Departments have not encouraged linking pay and individual performance but proposed that local payments should be linked to the performance of each employing unit in relation to its objectives. They have emphasised that it would be up to each Trust to specify the form of its own local pay arrangements, but suggested that performance might be assessed against a number of factors including for example, the achievement of quality standards and target case volumes, as well as Trusts' financial targets. In the context of moving to local pay arrangements they have urged the Review Body "not to recommend an across-the-board increase but instead to give a strong steer to the continued development and implementation of local arrangements by leaving employers with maximum scope for local action".

Review Body for Nurses, Midwives and Health Visitors, (1995) *Twelfth Report*, CM. 2762, London: HMSO, para. 62

5.25

We simply do not accept that there are sufficient differences between the public and private sectors to justify the difference in practice over performance pay. In the private sector there can be equal difficulties in many areas in finding objective measures of achievement. There can also be just as much need to pay attention to quality as to quantity of output. Private sector staff have to work together as colleagues in teams, live with judgement on their relative contributions, and defend the judgements they make of others against criticism about their relative fairness.

Report of an Inquiry into Civil Service Pay (1982), para. 330

5.26

Paragraph 4.4 of the *School Teachers' Pay and Conditions Document 1996* requires that when determining the salary of the head and any deputies the relevant body shall have regard in particular, but not exclusively, to the following criteria:

(i)   the responsibilities of the post;
(ii) the social, economic and cultural background of the pupils attending the school;
(iii) whether the post is difficult to fill; and
(iv) whether there has been a sustained high quality of performance by the headteacher or deputy headteacher (*to which will be added from 1 September 1997:* in the light of performance criteria previously agreed between the relevant body and the headteacher or deputy headteacher as the case may be).

As at 1 September 1997

- Carry out performance review against the previously agreed performance criteria.
- Review salary in the same way as at 1 September 1996 except that the *Document* will have been amended to refer to previously agreed performance criteria.
- Award any additional spine points only after completion of a performance review.
- Notify in writing the outcome of the annual salary review, in the same way as at 1 September 1996.

School Teachers' Review Body (1997) *Sixth Report*, CM. 3536, London: HMSO, pp. 29–30

Bibliography

ACC/AMA (Association of County Councils/Association of Metro-
politan Authorities) (1995) *Who Gets Community Care? A Survey of
Community Care Eligibility Criteria*, London: Association of County
Councils/Association of Metropolitan Authorities

Allen, P. (1995) *A Legal Perspective on Contracts in the NHS Internal
Market*, Bristol: School of Advanced Urban Studies (Studies in
Decentralisation and Quasi-Markets no. 22)

Ascher, K. (1987) *The Politics of Privatisation: Contracting Out Public
Services*, London: Macmillan

Association of London Authorities (1987) *London's Financial Problems:
A Response to the Audit Commission*, London: Association of London
Authorities

Audit Commission (1983) *Performance Review in Local Government: A
Handbook for Auditors and Local Authorities*, London: HMSO

—— (1985) *Capital Expenditure Controls in Local Government in
England*, London: HMSO

—— (1986) *Making a Reality of Community Care*, London: HMSO

—— (1987a) *Competitiveness and Contracting Out of Local Authorities'
Services*, London: HMSO

—— (1987b) *The Management of London's Authorities: Preventing the
Breakdown of Services*, London, HMSO

—— (1988) *The Competitive Council*, London: HMSO

—— (1992) *Lying in Wait*, London: HMSO

—— (1993a) *Practice Makes Perfect: The Role of the Family Health
Services Authority*, London: HMSO

—— (1993b) *Unfinished Business: Full-Time Education Courses for
16–19 Year Olds*, London: HMSO

—— (1994) *Watching Their Figures*, London: HMSO

—— (1995) *Paying the Piper: People and Pay in Local Government*,
London: HMSO

—— (1996) *Balancing the Care Equation: Progress with Community
Care*, Community Care Bulletin, Number 3, London: HMSO

Bacon, R. and Eltis, W. (1978) *Britain's Economic Problem: Too Few
Producers*, Basingstoke: Macmillan

Bailey, R. and Trinder, C. (1989) *Under Attack? Public Sector Pay over Two Decades*, London: Public Finance Foundation

Bargaining Report (1990) 'Compulsory Competitive Tendering – The Effect on Wages and Conditions', May, pp. 5–11

Basford, P. and Downie, C. (1991) 'How to Prepare a Business Plan', *Nursing Times*, 5 June, p. 63

Bootle, R. (1981) 'How Important is it to Defeat Inflation? – The Evidence', *Three Banks Review* 132, pp. 23–47

Bosanquet, N. (1984) 'Social Policy and the Welfare State', in R. Jowell and C. Airey (eds), *British Social Attitudes: the 1984 Report*, London: Social and Community Planning Research

Bowe, R. and Ball, S. J. with Gold, A. (1992) *Reforming Education and Changing Schools: Case Studies in Policy Sociology*, London: Routledge

Bragg, C. (1988) 'Tendering Makes a Clean Sweep', *Health Services Journal*, 24 March, pp. 336–7

Brook, L., Hall, J. and Preston, I. (1996) 'Public Spending and Taxation', in R. Jowell (ed.), *British Social Attitudes: The 13th Report*, London: Social and Community Research, pp. 185–202

Brown, G. (1994) *Fair is Efficient: a Socialist Agenda for Fairness*, Fabian Pamphlet 563, London: Fabian Society

Brown, J. and Fraser, R. (1996) 'First-Round Win for Housing DSOs', *Local Government Chronicle*, 19 April, pp. 14–15

Brown, W. (1991) 'Industrial Relations', in M. Artis and D. Cobham (eds), *Labour's Economic Policy 1974–79*, Manchester: Manchester University Press

—— and Rowthorn, R. (1990) *A Public Services Pay Policy*, London: Fabian Society (Fabian Tract 542)

—— and Walsh, J. (1991) 'Pay Determination in Britain in the 1980s: the Anatomy of Decentralisation', *Oxford Review of Economic Policy*, 7:1, pp. 44–59

Burton, J. (1984) *Why No Cuts?*, London: Institute of Economic Affairs

Butler, D. (1989) *British General Elections Since 1945*, Oxford: Basil Blackwell

—— and Kavanagh, D.(1992) *The British General Election of 1992*, Basingstoke: Macmillan

Butler, J. (1992) *Patients, Policies and Politics: Before and After "Working for Patients"*, Buckingham: Open University Press

Butler, R. (1993) 'The Evolution of The Civil Service', *Public Administration* 71, pp. 395–406

Carroll, D. (1983) 'Review' of 'In Search of Excellence', *Harvard Business Review*, 61: 6

Bibliography

Carter, J. and Rayner, M. (1996) 'The Curious Case of Post-Fordism and Welfare', *Journal of Social Policy*, 25:3, pp. 347–68

Carter, N., Klein, R. and Day, P. (1992) *How Organisations Measure Success: The Use of Performance Indicators in Government*, London: Routledge

Cave, M., Hanney, S. and Kogan, M. (1991) *The Use of Performance Indicators in Higher Education: A Critical Analysis of Developing Practice*, London: Jessica Kingsley (2nd Edition)

Chandler, T. and Feuille, P. (1991) 'Municipal Unions and Privatization', *Public Administration Review*, 51:1, pp. 15–22

Chubb, J. and Moe, T. (1990) *Politics, Markets and America's Schools*, Washington, DC: Brookings Institution

CIPFA (1995) *Education Statistics 1995–96, Estimates*, London: CIPFA

Clapham, D. (1992) 'The Effectiveness of Housing Indicators', *Social Policy and Administration*, 26:3, pp. 209–25

Clarke, A. (1996) 'Why Are We Trying to Reduce Length of Stay? Evaluation of the Costs and Benefits of Reducing Time in Hospital Must Start from the Objectives that Govern the Change', *Quality in Health Care*, 5:3, pp. 172–9

—— and Mckee, M. (1992) 'The Consultant Episode: An Unhelpful Measure', *British Medical Journal*, 305 (28 November), pp. 1307–8

Committee of Inquiry into Local Government Finance (Layfield Committee) (1976) *Report*, CMND. 6453, London: HMSO

Community Care (1992) 'Facing a Trickle or Flood?, 5 November, pp. 14–15

Community Care (1996) 'Judicial Review Follows Refusal', 1–7 February, p.1

Convery, P. (1995/6) 'The Real Cost of Unemployment', *Working Brief*, 70, pp. 16–17

Conway, M. and Knox, C. (1990) 'Measuring Housing Effectiveness: A Case Study in Customer Evaluation', *Housing Studies*, 5:4, pp. 257–72

Cragg, S. (1996) 'Sliding Scale', *Community Care*, 1–7 August, p. 19

Cubbin, J., Domberger, S. and Meadowcroft, S. (1987) 'Competitive Tendering and Refuse Collection: Identifying the Sources of Efficiency Gains', *Fiscal Studies*, 8:3, pp. 49–58

Cully, M. and Woodland, S. (1996) 'Trade Union Membership and Recognition: An Analysis of Data from the 1995 Labour Force Survey', *Labour Market Trends*, May, pp. 215–25

Cunningham, I. and Hyman, J. (1996) 'Empowerment: the Right Medicine for Improving Employee Commitment and Morale in the NHS?', *Health Manpower Management*, 22:6, pp. 14–24

Cutler, T. (1992a) *Numbers in a Time of Dearth: Using Performance Indicators to 'Manage' Higher Education*, paper presented at the 10th Annual Conference on the Organisation and Control of the Labour Process, University of Aston, April

—— (1992b) 'Vocational Training and British Economic Performance: a Further Instalment of the "British Labour Problem"?', *Work, Employment and Society*, 6:2, pp. 161–83

—— (1993) *Sunlight Later? The Audit Commission and the Management of Acute Hospitals*, paper presented at the 11th Annual Conference on the Organisation and Control of the Labour Process, University of Central Lancashire

——, James, P. and Waine, B. (1997) 'Atypical Employment and the New Universities: the Case of Part-time Staff', *Higher Education Review*, pp. 34–51

—— and Waine, B. (1994) *Managing the Welfare State: The Politics of Public Sector Management*, Oxford: Berg

—— and Waine, B. (1997) 'The Politics of Quasi-Markets: How Quasi-Markets Have been Analysed and How They Might be Analysed', *Critical Social Policy*, 17: 2, pp. 3–26

—— Williams, K. and Williams, J. (1986) *Keynes, Beveridge and Beyond*, London: Routledge and Kegan Paul

Department for Education (1992) *Choice and Diversity: a New Framework for Schools*, London: HMSO

—— (1994) *Our Children's Education: The Updated Parent's Charter*, London: Department for Education

—— (1995) *Departmental Report: The Government's Expenditure Plans 1995–96 to 1997–98*, London: HMSO

Department for Education and Employment (1996a) *Self-Government for Schools*, CM. 3315, London, HMSO

—— (1996b) *Statistics of Education: Schools in England 1995*, London: HMSO

—— (1996c) *Statistics of Education: Public Examinations: GCSE and GCE in England 1995*, London: HMSO

—— (1996d) *Departmental Report: The Government's Expenditure Plans 1996–97 to 1998–99*, CM. 3210, London: HMSO

Department of Education and Science (1988) *Education Reform Act: Local Management of Schools*, Circular No. 7/88, London: Department of Education and Science

—— (1991) *Higher Education: A New Framework*, CM. 1541, London: HMSO

—— (Undated) *Statistics of Education, Further Education, Higher Education in Polytechnics and Colleges*, London: Department of Education and Science

Department of Employment (1985) *Employment: The Challenge for the Nation*, CMND. 9474, London: HMSO

Department of Health (1989a) *Working for Patients*, CM. 555, London: HMSO

——(1989b) *Self Governing Hospitals*: Working Paper 1, London: HMSO

—— (1989c) *Caring for People: Community Care in the Next Decade and Beyond*, CM. 849, London: HMSO

—— (1992a) *Memorandum on the Financing of Community Care Arrangements after April 1993 and on Individual Choice of Residential Accommodation*, London: Department of Health

——(1992b) *Report of the Inquiry into London's Health Service, Medical Education and Research*, London: HMSO

—— (1993a) *Making London Better*, London: HMSO

——(1993b) *Managing the New NHS: A Background Document*, London: Department of Health

—— (1995a) *NHS Responsibilities for Meeting Continuing Care Needs* (HSG (95/8 LAC (95) 5), London: Department of Health

—— (1995b) *NHS Responsibilities for Meeting Continuing Care Needs – NHS Executive/SSI Monitoring*, EL (95) 88, 17th August, London: Department of Health

—— (1996) *The Government's Expenditure Plans 1996–97 to 1998–99, Departmental Report*, CM. 3212, London: HMSO

—— (1997) *Social Services – Achievement and Challenge*, London: HMSO

Department of Health and Social Security (1983) *Health Service Management: Competitive Tendering in the Provision of Domestic, Catering and Laundry Services*, HC (83) 18, London: DHSS

Department of Social Security (1993) *Annual Report: The Government's Expenditure Plans 1993–94 to 1995–96*, CM. 2213, London: HMSO

Department of Trade and Industry (1996) *Competitiveness: Creating the Enterprise Centre of Europe*, CM. 3300, London: HMSO

Dixon, R. (1991) 'Repercussions of LMS', *Educational Management and Administration*, 19:1, pp. 52–61

Domberger, S., Meadowcroft, S. and Thompson, D. (1988) 'Competition and Efficiency in Refuse Collection: A Reply', *Fiscal Studies*, 9:2, pp. 86–90

Donahue, J. (1989) *The Privatization Decision*, New York: Basic Books

Eccleshall, R. (1990) *English Conservatism since the Restoration: An Introduction and Anthology*, London: Unwin-Hyman

Echols, F., Mcpherson, A. and Willns, J. (1990) 'Parental Choice in Scotland', *Journal of Education Policy*, 5:3, pp. 207–22

Elliott, R. F. and Duffus, K. (1996) 'What Has Been Happening to Pay in the Public Sector of the British Economy? Developments over the Period 1970– 1992', *British Journal of Industrial Relations*, 34:1, pp. 51–85

Employment Department (1988) *Employment for the 1990s*, CM. 540, London: HMSO

Employment Department (1992) *People, Jobs and Opportunities*, CM. 1810, London: HMSO

Enthoven, A. (1985) *Reflections on the Management of the National Health Service*, London: Nuffield Provincial Hospitals Trust

Escott, K. and Whitfield, D. (1995) *The Gender Impact of CCT in Local Government*, Manchester: Equal Opportunities Commission

Fitz-Gibbon, C. (1996a) 'Discussion' of Goldstein and Spiegelhalter, *Journal of the Royal Statistical Society*, 159:3, pp. 410–12

—— (1996b) *Monitoring Education: Indicators, Quality and Effectiveness*, London: Cassell

Flemming, J. and Oppenheimer, P. (1996) 'Are Government Spending and Taxes Too High (or Too Low)?', *National Institute Economic Review*, pp. 58–76

Flynn, N. (1986) 'Performance Measurement in Public Sector Services', *Policy and Politics*, 4:3, pp. 389–404

—— (1990) *Public Sector Management*, London: Harvester-Wheatsheaf

—— and Strehl, F. (eds) (1996) *Public Sector Management in Europe*, London: Prentice Hall

Foreman, D. (1991) 'Pricing up Performance', *Managing Schools Today*, 1:4, pp. 8–9

Freeman, R. (1995) 'The Limits of Wage Flexibility to Curing Unemployment', *Oxford Review of Economic Policy*, 11:1, pp. 63–72

Fretwell, L.(1988) 'Contracting Out Gets a Boost', *Local Government Chronicle*, 8 July (Supplement), pp. 3–33

Froud, J., Haslam, C., Johal, S. and Williams, K. (1997) *Notes on Efficiency and Productivity*, mimeo, University of Manchester/Royal Holloway College, University of London

Fulton, Lord (1968) *The Civil Service: Report of the Committee*, CMND. 3638, London: HMSO

Ganley, J. and Grahl, J. (1988) 'Competition and Efficiency in Refuse Collection: A Critical Comment', *Fiscal Studies*, 9:2, pp. 80–5

Gewirtz, S., Ball, S. and Bowe, R. (1995) *Markets, Equity and Choice in Education*, Buckingham: Open University Press

Gilmour, I. (1994) 'The Thatcher Memoirs', *Twentieth Century British History*, 5:2, pp. 257–77

Glennester, H. (1997) 'Bound to Have Regrets', *The Guardian* (Society), pp. 2–3

Godley, W. (1996) 'America's Unaccountable Admiration for Mrs Thatcher's Economics', in J. Eatwell (ed.), *Global Unemployment: Loss of Jobs in the 90s*, New York: M. E. Sharpe

Gosling, P. (1995) 'It Pays to Join the Club', *The Independent*, 24 May, p. 28

Government Statistical Service (1996) *Civil Service Statistics*, London: Government Statistical Service

Green, D. (1990) 'A Missed Opportunity', in D. Green, J. Neuberger, M. Young and M. Burstall, *The NHS Reforms: Whatever Happened to Consumer Choice?*, London: Institute of Economic Affairs

Green, J. and Wintfield, N. (1995) 'Report Cards on Cardiac Surgeons: Assessing New York State's Approach', *New England Journal of Medicine*, 332:18, pp. 1229–32

Greer, P. (1994) *Transforming Central Government: The Next Steps Initiative*, Buckingham: Open University Press

Griffiths, R. (1983) *NHS Management Inquiry*, London: DHSS

—— (1988) *Community Care: Agenda for Action*, London: HMSO

Halpin, D., Power, S. and Fitz, J. (1993) 'Opting into State Control? Headteachers and the Paradoxes of Grant-Maintained Status', *International Studies in Sociology of Education*, 3:1, pp. 3–23

Halsey, A. H. (1995) *The Decline of Donnish Dominion: The British Academic Profession in the Twentieth Century*, Oxford: Clarendon Press

Harris, R. and Seldon, A. (1987) *Welfare Without the State: A Quarter of a Century of Suppressed Public Choice*, London: Institute of Economic Affairs

Harrison, S. (1988) *Managing the National Health Service: Shifting the Frontier*, London: Chapman and Hall

Harrison, S. and Choudhry, N. (1996) 'General Practice Fundholding in the U.K. National Health Service: Evidence to Date', *Journal of Public Health Policy*, 17:3, pp. 331–50

Hayek, F. (1960) *The Constitution of Liberty*, London: Routledge and Kegan Paul

—— (1967) *Studies in Philosophy, Politics and Economics*, London: Routledge and Kegan Paul

—— (1976) *Law, Legislation and Liberty: A New Statement of the Liberal Principles of Justice and Political Economy*, Volume 2. *The Mirage of Social Justice*, London: Routledge and Kegan Paul

—— (1978) *New Studies in Philosophy, Politics, Economics and the History of Ideas*, London: Routledge and Kegan Paul

HEFCE (Higher Education Funding Council (England)) (1995a) *Recurrent Grant for Academic Year 1995–6* (Circular 6/95), Bristol: HEFCE

—— (1995b) *A Guide to Funding Higher Education in England*, Bristol: HEFCE

—— (1996) *Teaching Quality Assessment: Guidance for Assessors 1996–98*, Bristol: HEFCE

Heyes, J. and Stuart, M. (1994) 'Placing Symbols Before Reality: Re-Evaluating the Low Skills Equilibrium', *Personnel Review*, 23:5, pp. 34–49

Hibberd, J. (1993) 'Trends in Public Expenditure 1978–79 to 1992–93', *Treasury Bulletin*, Summer, pp. 20–32

Higher Education Statistics Agency (1995) *Higher Education Statistics 1992/93*, Cheltenham: Higher Education Statistics Agency

Hoggett, P. (1987) 'A Farewell to Mass Production? Decentralisation as an Emergent Private and Public Sector Paradigm', in P. Hoggett and R. Hambleton (eds), *Decentralisation and Democracy: Localising Public Services*, Bristol: School of Advanced Urban Studies

Hughes, A. (1996) 'Employment in the Public and Private Sectors', *Labour Market Trends*, 104:8, pp. 373–9

Hughes, D. (1991) 'The Reorganisation of the National Health Service: The Rhetoric and Reality of the Internal Market', *Modern Law Review*, 54:1, pp. 88–103

Income Data Services (1991) *Pay in the Public Sector*, London: Income Data Services

—— (1996) *Pay in the Public Services: Review of 1995: Prospects for 1996*, London: Income Data Services

Income Data Services Report (1992) 'The Government Seeks to Clarify its Public Sector Pay Limit', 631, December, p. 6

Income Data Services Report (1993) 'Public Sector Pay in 1994', 650, October, pp. 25–8

Income Data Services Report (1995) 'Public Sector Pay in 1996', 698, October, pp. 25–7

Income Data Services Report (1996a) 'Public Sector Pay in 1997', 723, October, pp. 25–7

Income Data Services Report (1996b) 'Public Sector Labour Market Survey Part 1', 725, November, pp. 25–32

Income Data Services Report (1996c) 'Public Sector Labour Market Survey Part 2', 726, December, pp. 28–31

Interim Advisory Committee on School Teachers' Pay and Conditions (1988) *First Report*, CM. 363, London: HMSO
—— (1989) *Second Report*, CM. 625, London: HMSO
—— (1990) *Third Report*, CM. 973, London: HMSO
—— (1991) *Fourth Report*, CM. 1415, London: HMSO
James, J. (1995) 'Reforming the British National Health Service: Implementation Problems in London', *Journal of Health Politics, Policy and Law*, 20:1, pp. 191–210
Jencks, S., Williams, D. and Kay, T. (1988) 'Assessing Hospital Associated Deaths from Discharge Data: The Role of Length of Stay and Comorbidities', *Journal of the American Medical Association*, 260 (15), pp. 2240–6
Jenkins, K., Caines, K. and Jackson, A. (1988) *Improving Management in Government: The Next Steps: Report to the Prime Minister*, London: HMSO
Jesson, D. (1996) *Value Added Measures of School Performance* (Department for Education and Employment Research Studies No. 14), London: HMSO
Jessop, B. (1991) *Fordism and Post-Fordism: A Critical Reformulation*, Lancaster: Lancaster Regionalism Group
—— (1994) 'The Transition to Post-Fordism and the Schumpeterian Workfare State', in R. Burrows and B. Loader (eds), *Towards a Post-Fordist Welfare State*, London: Routledge
Keep, E. and Mayhew, K. (1996) 'Economic Demand for Higher Education – A Sound Basis for Further Expansion?', *Higher Education Quarterly*, 50:2, pp. 89–109
Kenny, D. and Edwards, P. (1996) *Community Care Trends: The Impact of Funding on Local Authorities. Report for January 1995 – September 1995*, London: Association of Directors of Social Services
Kerley, L. and Wynn, D. (1991) 'Competitive Tendering – The Transition to Contracting in Scottish Local Authorities', *Local Government Studies*, 17:5, pp. 33–51
Kessler, I. (1993) 'Pay Determination in the British Civil Service since 1979', *Public Administration*, 71, pp. 323–40
—— (1994) 'Performance Related Pay; Contrasting Approaches', *Industrial Relations Journal*, 25:2, pp. 122–35
—— and Purcell, J. (1992) 'Performance Related Pay: Objectives and Application', *Human Resource Management Journal*, 2:3, pp. 16–33
King's Fund (1994) *London Monitor*, London: King's Fund Institute
Knapp, M. and Missiakoulis, S. (1982) 'Inter-Sectoral Cost Comparisons: Day Care for the Elderly', *Journal of Social Policy*, 11:3, pp. 335–54

Labour Party (1987) *Britain Will Win*, London: The Labour Party

—— (1992) *It's Time to Get Britain Working Again*, London: The Labour Party

—— (1995a) *Renewing the NHS: Labour's Agenda for a Healthier Britain*, London: The Labour Party

—— (1995b) *Excellence for Everyone: Labour's Crusade to Raise Standards*, London: The Labour Party

Laming, H. (1992) *Implementing Caring for People: Assessment*, CI (92) 34, London: HMSO

Le Grand, J. (1990) *Quasi-Markets and Social Policy*, Bristol: School of Advanced Urban Studies

Lewis, J. and Glennester, H. (1996) *Implementing the New Community Care*, Buckingham: Open University Press

Lipsey, D. (1994) 'Do We Really Want More Public Spending?', in R. Jowell *et al.*, *British Social Attitudes: The 11th Report*, London: Social and Community Planning Research

Local Government Management Board (1992) *CCT Information Service Report No. 5*, London: Local Government Management Board

—— (1996a) *Notices for Anti-Competitive Behaviour*, mimeo, Local Government Management Board

—— (1996b) *CCT Information Service Survey Report No. 14*, London, Local Government Management Board

London Region Social Services Research Group (1989) 'Performance Indicators: Services for Children', *Research Policy and Planning*, 7:2, pp. 1–15

Macfarlane, A. (1994) 'Statistical Information about the NHS – An Update', *Radical Statistics*, 57, pp. 21–33

Macgregor, J. (1991) 'Spare Capacity', *Municipal Review and AMA News*, June, pp. 60–1

Machin, S. (1996) 'Wage Inequality in the U.K.', *Oxford Review of Economic Policy*, 12:1, pp. 47–64

Mandelson, P. and Liddle, R. (1996) *The Blair Revolution: Can New Labour Deliver?*, London: Faber and Faber

Marchant, C. (1992) 'Care Funds Breakdown Shows Major Shortfall', *Community Care*, 22 October, p. 5

Marsden, D. (1993) 'Reforming Public Sector Pay', in OECD, *Pay Flexibility in the Public Sector*, Paris: OECD

Marsden, D. and Richardson, R. (1994) 'Performing for Pay? The Effects of "Merit Pay" in a Public Service', *British Journal of Industrial Relations*, 32:2, pp. 243–61

Marsh, D. (1991) 'Privatization under Mrs Thatcher: A Review of the

Literature', *Public Administration*, 69:4, pp. 459–80

Mason, G. (1995) *The New Graduate Supply-Shock: Recruitment and Utilisation of Graduates in British Industry*, London: National Institute for Economic and Social Research

Mays, N. (1987) 'Measuring Needs in the National Health Service Resource Allocation Formula: Standardised Mortality Ratios or Social Deprivation?', *Public Administration*, 65:1, pp. 45–60

Mayston, D. (1992) *School Performance Indicators and Performance Related Pay*, York: Centre for Health Economics, University of York

McGuirk, T. (1991) 'Is the Private Sector Cleaning up on CCT?', *Public Finance and Accountancy*, 30 August, pp. 15–17

Mckee, M. and Hunter, D. (1994) 'What Can Comparisons of Hospital Death Rates Tell Us About Quality of Care?', in T. Delamothe (ed.), *Outcomes into Clinical Practice*, London: BMJ Books

McPherson, A. (1992) *Measuring Added Value in Schools*, London: National Commission on Education (NCE Briefing No. 1)

McSweeney, B. (1988) 'Accounting for the Audit Commission', *Political Quarterly*, 59:1, pp. 28–43

Megaw (1982), see *Report of an Inquiry into Civil Service Pay*

Milne, R. (1987) 'Competitive Tendering in the NHS: An Economic Analysis of the Early Implementation of HC (83) 18', *Public Administration*, 65:2

—— (1993) 'Contractors' Experience of Compulsory Competitive Tendering: A Case Study of Contract Cleaners', *Public Administration*, 71, pp. 301–21

Ministry of Health (1953) *On the State of Public Health: Annual Report of the Chief Medical Officer 1952*, CMD. 9009, London: HMSO

Minogue, K. (1986) 'Politics and the Gross Intellectual Product', *Government and Opposition*, 21:4, pp. 396–405

Morgan, J. (1996) 'Labour Market Recoveries in the U.K. and Other OECD Countries', *Labour Market Trends*, December, pp. 529–39

Morrell, D. (1991) 'Role of Research in the Development and Organisation of General Practice', *British Medical Journal*, 302, 1 June, pp. 1313–16

Morrison, H. and Cowan, P. (1996) 'The State Schools Book: A Critique of a League Table', *British Educational Research Journal*, 22:2, pp. 241–9

Murlis, H. (1987) 'Performance Related Pay in the Public Sector', *Public Money*, 6:4, pp. 29–33

Murray, I. (1995) *Desparately Seeking . . . a Job: A Critical Guide to the 1996 Jobseeker's Allowance*, London: Unemployment Unit

Napier, B. (1994) 'Using Community Law to Protect Workers' Rights', in K. Ewing, C. Gearty and B. Hepple (eds), *Human Rights and Labour Law*, London: Mansell

National Audit Office (1994) *The Financial Health of Higher Education Institutions in England*, London: HMSO

National Health Service and Community Care Act 1990, reprinted 1994, London: HMSO

NBPI (National Board for Prices and Incomes) (1968) *Payment by Results Systems*, Report No. 65, CMND. 3627, London: HMSO

—— (1969) *Salary Structures*, CMND. 4187, London: HMSO

Neale, A. (1992) 'Are British Workers Pricing Themselves out of Jobs?', *Work, Employment and Society*, 6:2, pp. 271–87

NHS Executive (1992) *The NHS Reforms: The First Six Months*, London, NHS Executive

—— (1995a) *Developing NHS Purchasing and GP Fundholding: Towards a Primary Care-led NHS*, London: Department of Health

—— (1995b) *An Accountability Framework for GP Fundholding: Towards a Primary Care-led NHS*, London: Department of Health

—— (1996a) *Priorities and Planning Guidance for the NHS 1997/98*, London: Department of Health

—— (1996b) *The NHS Performance Guide 1995–96*, London: HMSO

Nichols, T. (1986) *The British Worker Question*, London: Routledge and Kegan Paul

OECD (Organisation for Economic Cooperation and Development) (1987) *Historical Statistics 1960–1985*, Paris: OECD

—— (1994) *Trends in Public Sector Pay: A Study of Nine OECD Countries 1985–1990*, Public Management Occasional Papers, Paris: OECD

Orchard, C. (1994) 'Comparing Healthcare Outcomes', *British Medical Journal*, 308 (4 June), pp. 1493–6

Oxley, H., Maher, J. and Nicoletti, G. (1991) *The Public Sector: Issues for the 1990s*, OECD, Economics and Statistics Department, Working Paper No. 90, Paris: OECD

Painter, J. (1991) 'Compulsory Competitive Tendering in Local Government: The First Round', *Public Administration*, 69:2, pp. 191–210

Parker, D. and Hartley, K. (1990) 'Competitive Tendering: Issues and Evidence', *Public Money and Management*, 10:3, pp. 9–14

Paton, C. (1992) *Competition and Planning in the National Health Service: The Danger of Unplanned Markets*, London: Chapman and Hall

—— and Bach, S. (1990) *Case Studies in Health Policy and Management*, London: Nuffield Provincial Hospitals Trust

Pay and Benefits Bulletin (1989) 'Performance-Related Pay Extends to NHS "Middle" Managers', 245, 5 December, p. 12

Pay and Benefits Bulletin (1996) 'Agency Awards Worth 2.5% to 3%', 398, April, pp. 2–5

Peters, T. and Waterman, R. (1982) *In Search of Excellence: Lessons from America's Best-Run Companies*, New York: Harper and Row

Pierson, P. (1994) *Dismantling the Welfare State: Reagan, Thatcher and the Politics of Retrenchment*, Cambridge: Cambridge University Press

Piore, M. and Sabel, C. (1984) *The Second Industrial Divide: Possibilities for Prosperity*, New York: Basic Books

Pollitt, C. (1986) 'Beyond the Managerial Model: The Case for Broadening Assessment in Government and Public Services', *Financial Accountability and Management*, 2:3, pp. 155–70

Pollitt, C. (1990a) *Managerialism and the Public Services: The Anglo-American Experience*, Oxford: Basil Blackwell

Pollitt, C. (1990b) 'Measuring University Performance: Never Mind the Quality: Never Mind the Width', *Higher Education Quarterly*, 44:1, pp. 60–81

Pollitt, C. (1990c) 'Performance Indicators, Root and Branch', in M. Cave, M. Kogan and R. Smith (eds), *Output and Performance Measurement in Government: The State of the Art*, London: J. Kingsley

Pollitt, C., Harrison, S. and Marmoch, P. (1991) 'General Management in the NHS: The Initial Impact 1983–88', *Public Administration*, 69:1, pp. 61–85

Priestley Commission, see *Royal Commission on the Civil Service* (1955)

Prime Minister's Office (1991) *The Citizen's Charter: Raising the Standard*, CM. 1599, London: HMSO

—— (1994) *The Civil Service: Continuity and Change*, CM. 2627, London: HMSO

—— (1995) *The Citizen's Charter: The Facts and Figures*, CM. 2970, London: HMSO

Purcell, J. and Ahlstrand, B. (1994) *Human Resource Management in the Multi-Divisional Company*, Oxford: Oxford University Press

Radical Statistics Health Group (1992) 'NHS Reforms: the First Six Months – Proof of Progress or a Statistical Smokescreen?', *British Medical Journal*, 304 (14 March), pp. 705–9

—— (1995) 'NHS "Indicators of Success": What Do They Tell Us?', *British Medical Journal*, 310 (22 April), pp. 1045–50

Report of an Inquiry into Civil Service Pay (1982) Volume 1, CMD. 8590, London: HMSO (Megaw Report)

Review Body for Nursing Staff, Midwives and Health Visitors (1984) *First Report*, CMD. 9258, London: HMSO
—— (1985) *Second Report*, CMD. 9529, London: HMSO
—— (1987) *Fourth Report*, CM. 129, London: HMSO
—— (1988) *Fifth Report*, CM. 360, London: HMSO
—— (1989) *Sixth Report*, CM. 577, London: HMSO
—— (1991) *Eighth Report*, CM. 1410, London: HMSO
—— (1992) *Ninth Report*, CM. 1811, London: HMSO
—— (1994) *Eleventh Report*, CM. 2462, London: HMSO
—— (1995) *Twelfth Report*, CM. 2762, London: HMSO
—— (1996) *Thirteenth Report*, CM. 3092, London: HMSO
—— (1997) *Fourteenth Report*, CM. 3538, London: HMSO
Review Body on Doctors' and Dentists' Remuneration (1983) *Thirteenth Report*, CMD. 8878, London: HMSO
—— (1984) *Fourteenth Report*, CMD. 9256, London: HMSO
—— (1987) *Seventeenth Report*, CM. 127, London: HMSO
—— (1991) *Twenty First Report*, CM. 1412, London: HMSO
—— (1994) *Twenty-Third Report*, CM. 2460, London: HMSO
—— (1995) *Twenty-Fourth Report*, CM. 2760, London: HMSO
—— (1996) *Twenty-Fifth Report*, CM. 3090, London: HMSO
Roberts, H. (1990) *Outcome and Performance in Health Care*, London: Public Finance Foundation
Rogers, M. (1992) *Opting Out: Choice and the Future of Schools*, London: Lawrence and Wishart
Rowthorne, B. (1992) 'Government Spending and Taxation in the Thatcher Era', in J. Michie (ed.) *The Economic Legacy 1979–1992*, London: Academic Press
Royal Commission on the Civil Service 1953–55 (1955), Cmd 9613, London: HMSO (Priestley Commission)
Rubery, J. (1995) 'Performance Related Pay and the Prospects for Gender Pay Equity', *Journal of Management Studies*, 32:5, pp. 637–54
Sabel, C. (1994) 'Flexible Specialisation and the Re-Emergence of Regional Economies', in A. Amin (ed.), *Post-Fordism: A Reader*, Oxford: Blackwell
Saran, R. and Sheldrake, J. (eds) (1988) *Public Sector Bargaining in the 1980s*, Avebury: Gower
Shaoul, J. (1996) *NHS Trusts – A Capital Way of Operating*, Mimeo, Department of Accounting and Finance, Manchester University
Shaw, K., Fenwick, J. and Foreman, A. (1994) 'Compulsory Competitive Tendering: The Experience of Local Authorities in the North of England 1988–1992', *Public Administration*, 72 (summer), pp. 201–17

Bibliography

Sherman, J. (1985) 'Waiting for the Big Bite', *Health and Social Service Journal*, 27 June, pp. 806–7

Sloan, A. (1986) *My Years With General Motors*, Harmondsworth: Penguin

Social Services Committee (1990) *Community Care Funding for Local Authorities, Session 1989/90*, HC 277, London: HMSO

Stevens, B. (1984) 'Comparing Public and Private Sector Productive Efficiency: An Analysis of Eight Activities', *National Productivity Review*, 3:3, pp. 395–406

Stott, N. (1992) 'Day Case Surgery Generates No Increased Workload for Community Based Staff. True or False?', *British Medical Journal*, 304, 28 March, pp. 825–6

STRB (School Teachers' Review Body)(1992) *First Report*, Cm. 1806, London: HMSO

—— (1993) *Second Report*, CM. 2151, London: HMSO

—— (1994) *Third Report*, CM. 2466, London: HMSO

—— (1995) *Fourth Report*, CM. 2765, London: HMSO

—— (1996) *Fifth Report*, CM. 3095, London: HMSO

—— (1997) *Sixth Report*, CM. 3536, London: HMSO

Szykmanksi, S. (1996) 'The Impact of Compulsory Competitive Tendering on Refuse Collection Services', *Fiscal Studies*, 17:3, pp. 1–19

Taylor-Gooby, P. (1991) 'Attachment to the Welfare State', in R. Jowell, L. Brook and B. Taylor, with P. Prior (eds), *British Social Attitudes: The Eighth Report*, London: Social and Community Planning Research

Thatcher, M. (1993) *Downing Street Years*, London: HarperCollins

Thirlwall, A. (1981) 'Keynesian Employment Theory is not Defunct', *Three Banks Review*, 132, pp. 14–29

Thomson, A. W. J. and Beaumont, P.B. (1978) *Public Sector Bargaining: A Study of Relative Gain*, Farnborough: Saxon House

Thompson, M. (1993) *Pay and Performance: The Employee Experience*, Brighton: Institute of Manpower Studies, University of Sussex (IMS Report No. 258)

Thompson, N. (1996) *Political Economy and the Labour Party*, London: UCL Press

Thornley, C. (1994) *Back to the Future: Learning the Lessons from the 1930s, Local Pay Determination for Nurses*, London: Unison Health Care

Timmins, N. (1995) *The Five Giants: A Biography of the Welfare State*, London: HarperCollins

Tomlinson, J. (1990) *Hayek and the Market*, London: Pluto

Tomlinson, R. and Warde, A. (1993) 'Social Class and Change in Eating Habits', *British Food Journal*, 95:1, pp. 3–10

Trade Union Research Unit (1992) *Performance Related Pay*, London: NASUWT/NUT

Treasury (1979) *Government Expenditure Plans 1980–81*, CMND. 1746, London: HMSO

—— (1981) *Financial Statement and Budget Report 1981–82*, London: HMSO

—— (1984) *Financial Statement and Budget Report 1984–85*, London: HMSO

—— (1986) *Using Private Enterprise in Government: Report of a Multi-Departmental Review of Competitive Tendering and Contracting for Services in Government Departments*, London: HMSO

—— (1988) *The Government's Expenditure Plans 1988–89 to 1990–91*, CM. 288–1, London: HMSO

—— (1989) *Financial Statement and Budget Report 1989–90*, London: HMSO

Treasury (1991) *Competing for Quality: Buying Better Public Services*, CM. 1730, London: HMSO

Treasury (1992) *The Government's Expenditure Plans 1992–93 to 1994–95, Departmental Report, Department of Health*, CM. 1913, London: HMSO

—— (1995) *Financial Statement and Budget Report 1996–97*, London: HMSO

—— (1996) *Financial Statement and Budget Report 1997–98*, London: HMSO

Universities Statistical Record (1994) *University Statistics Volume 1: Staff and Students*, Cheltenham: Universities Statistical Record

University Funding Council (1989) *Report on the 1989 Research Assessment Exercise*, London: University Funding Council

Waine, B. (1991) *The Rhetoric of Independence: The Ideology and Practice of Social Policy in Thatcher's Britain*, Oxford: Berg

Walby, S. and Greenwell, J. (1994) 'Managing the National Health Service', in J. Clarke, A. Cochrane and E. McLaughlin (eds), *Managing Social Policy*, London: Sage

Walford, G. (1990) *Privatization and Privilege in Education*, London: Routledge

Walsh, K. (1989) 'Competition and Service in Local Government', in J. Stewart and P. Stoker (eds), *The Future of Local Government*, London: Macmillan

—— (1995) 'Competition for White-Collar Services in Local Government', *Public Money and Management*, April–June, pp. 11–18

—— and Davies, H. (1993) *Competition and Service: The Impact of the*

−275−

Local Government Act 1988, London: HMSO

Warburton, W. (1993) 'Performance Indicators: What Was All the Fuss About?', *Community Care Management and Planning*, 1:4, 100–5

Warde, A. (1994) 'Consumers, Consumption and Post-Fordism', in R. Burrows and B. Loader (eds), *Towards a Post-Fordist Welfare State*, London: Routledge

Webb, S. (1901) 'Lord Roseberry's Escape From Houndsditch', *The Nineteenth Century and After*, 50, pp. 366–86

Wedderburn, W. (1986) *The Worker and the Law* (3rd Edition), Harmondsworth: Penguin

Wedderburn, W. (1989) 'Freedom of Association and Philosophies of Labour Law', *Industrial Law Journal*, 18:1, pp. 1–38

White, G. (1996) 'Public Sector Pay Bargaining: Comparability, Decentralisation and Control', *Public Administration*, 74:1, pp. 89–111

Williams, K., Cutler, T., Haslam, C. and Williams, J. (1987) 'The End of Mass Production', *Economy and Society*, 16:3, pp. 404–37

—— Haslam, C., Johal, S. and Williams, J. (1994) *Cars: Analysis, History, Cases*, Providence: Berghahn Books

—— Williams, J., Cutler, T. and Haslam, C. (1992) *From National Autarky To European Integration? Labour's Policies in the 1980s and 1990s*, Paper presented at the Conference on 'Labour: The Party of Industrial Modernisation', London School of Economics, April

Wistow, G. (1995) 'Crunch Time for Community Care?', *Focus on Community Care: News from Nuffield*, Issue 3, p. 1

Wood, S. (1989) 'New Wave Management', *Work, Employment and Society*, 3:3, pp. 379–402

Index

Association of London Authorities, 49, 198–201
Audit Commission 1, 30–2, 35–6, 43, 47–50, 89, 91, 188–98, 201
  audit role, 30–1, 49, 188–9, 191, 193
  community care and, 62–3, 66, 69, 206–10
  compulsory competitive tendering and, 87, 96, 115, 225–7
  Labour Party and, 150
  pay and, 137–8
  political role, 30–1, 35, 43, 47–51, 189–90, 192–201

Blair, Tony, 149
Bottomley, Virginia, 57, 63
British Social Attitudes Survey, 23–4
Brown, Gordon, 147–8, 149, 159

Callaghan, James, 36
Caring for People, 62–3, 65, 69, 211–14
Care Manager, 63, 209–10
Citizens' Charter, 5, 30, 34, 46, 178, 179, 182–3
  performance measurement and, 30, 34, 46, 178–9, 182–3
  producer groups and, 5
Command economy, 11
Community Care, 62–9; *see also* quasi-markets
Community Care Plans, 63
Competition, *see* compulsory competitive tendering, quasi-markets
Competitiveness, 19, 79, 84, 147, 173–4, 223
Competitive Tendering, 87–115, 225–31
  Acquired Rights Directive and, 93
  'anti-competitive' notices, 92–4
  central government departments and, 95, 107
  competition and, 92, 95–104, 226, 228–30

compulsory competitive tendering 87, 89–90, 97, 227–31
  contracting out, 88–9, 97, 225–6
  direct service organisations, 88, 92, 96–101, 103, 114
  employment effects, 91, 93–5, 100, 105, 107–15, 229–31
  gender employment effects, 108–9, 114–15
  local government services, 87–8, 90, 92, 97–100, 104–5, 109–10, 112, 226–30
  NHS ancillary services, 89–91, 95, 97, 100, 105–7
  political implications, 87, 91, 94, 98, 101–2
  privatization and, 88
  procurement and, 89, 226
  quality of service and, 104–5
  regulation, 89–94, 97, 114, 226–31
  'savings' and, 103–7
  Trade Union Reform and Employment Rights Act 1993, 93, 230–1
  trade unions and, 91–2, 94, 113–14
  Transfer of Undertakings (Protection of Employment) Regulations, 93, 230
  US experience of, 103, 106–7, 110–11, 113
  white collar services, 102–3
  see also District Health Authorities, 'Efficiency'
Comprehensive schools, 75
Confidential Enquiry on Perioperative Deaths, 33
Conservative Party
  electoral performance, 22
  employment policy and, 118–19
  financing of welfare state, 19–20, 145
  flexible labour markets and, 142–5, 232
  inflation and, 141–12
  labour law and, 16–19
  New Right and, 16–20

NHS, 54
professions and, 14–16
public expenditure and, 116–17
public sector managerialism and, 20–2,
28
public sector pay and, 118–21, 137–40
supporters' attitude to welfare state, 23
unemployement and, 143–5
Consumer choice, 54, 63–4, 68, 71–4, 85,
154
see also, quasi-markets

Decentralisation, 155–6
see also, quasi-markets, public sector
pay
Department for Education and
Employment, 83–5, 223–5
Department of Employment, 118
Department of Health, 56, 166
Directly Managed Units, 55, 58
District Health Authorities, 55
compulsory competitive tendering,
89–91, 95, 97, 100, 105–7
purchaser role, 55, 89–91, 204

'Economy' 30, 35, 53, 191, 197
Education Act 1944, 69, 217
Education Act 1980, 41, 69, 71, 217–18,
222
Education (Scotland) Act 1980, 74
Education Reform Act, 1, 54, 69–71,
74–6, 218–22
'Effectiveness', 30, 35, 39, 48, 50–2, 191,
201
'Efficiency'
compulsory competitive tendering and,
109–10, 112–13, 177–8, 180, 191
performance measurement and, 29–30,
34, 39–40, 45, 48, 52–3 103,
Efficiency Unit, 2–6, 21–2, 33, 50
Employment Department, 118–20, 232–4
Employment protection legislation, *see*
labour law
Empowerment, 156, 165
Enthoven, A., 55
'Excellence' approach, 162–6
Executive Agencies, 127

Family Health Service Authorities, 60,
205

Financial Management Initiative, 2
Fordism and Post-Fordism
critique of, 154–8
definitions, 151–2
production processes, 152–4
public sector and, 154–9
Fowler, Norman, 2, 62
Full employment, 118, 147
see also, Hayek, Friedrich von
Further and Higher Education Act
(England and Wales) 1992, 1, 54, 76

General Practitioner Fundholding, 56, 59,
60–1, 205–6
General Practitioners, 5
Government Expenditure, *see* Public
expenditure
Green, D., 21
Griffiths, Roy, 2–6, 21–2, 33, 50, 63,
210–11

Hayek, Friedrich von, 9–14, 16, 112
freedom, concept of, 10–11
full employment, 13–14
inflation, 13
Keynesianism critique of, 12–14
Law, Liberty and Legislation, 16
managerialism and, 21
markets, 9, 10, 21
NHS, 9
price controls, 20
producer groups, critique of, 14, 112
rationalism, critique of, 10, 13
social insurance, 9
social justice, critique of, 10–12
state monopoly provision, 9
taxation, view of, 10
trade unions, critique of, 14
Health Authorities, 1, 58
Higher Education Funding Council
(England), 7, 76–7, 81, 225

Inflation, 141–2, 147
see also Conservative Party, Hayek,
Friedrich von
Informal carers, 40, 50, 166
Institute of Economic Affairs, 24

Jenkin, P., 62

Index

Job-Seekers' Allowance, 146
Joseph, Sir Keith, 10, 16, 116

Keynesianism, 12–14, 142
see also, Hayek, Friedrich von
Keynesian Welfare State, 152, 159

Labour Law, 16–19
see also, Conservative Party
Labour Party
  'Alternative Economic Strategy', 146–7
  consumerism and, 51
  electoral performance, 22
  Exchange Rate Mechanism, attitude to,
    147
  education policy, 148, 150, 166–7
  NHS and, 51, 148, 150
  public sector managerialism and,
    148–50, 166–7
  social welfare policy, 146, 149–51
  supporters' attitude to the welfare state,
    24
  unemployment, 147
Laming, H., 64
Local Authorities (Goods and Services)
  Act 1970, 96
Local Government Act 1988, 1, 54, 90–2,
  95–6, 100, 228–30
Local Government Finance Act 1982, 30,
  188–9
Local Government and Land Act 1980, 90
London Implementation Group, 57
London Speciality Reviews, 57

Macmillan, Harold, 8–9, 15
Major, John, 19, 36, 74, 154–5
Managerialism, *see* public sector
  managerialism
Making a Reality of Community Care, see
  Audit Commission, community care
  62–3 and 206–10
Making London Better, 57
Managing the New NHS, 59–60, 203–4
Mandelson, Peter, 149–50
'Middle Way', 8, 15–16
multi-divisional organisation, 3–6

National Audit Office, 30, 189
National Health Service

capital charges, 55–7
decentralisation, 59
general management, 2–6
London hospitals, 56–8
priorities, 61–2
public expenditure, 148
public opinion and, 24
trusts, 55, 58–9, 127, 131–4, 135,
  202–3
see also compulsory competitive
  tendering, Conservative Party,
  Hayek, Friedrich von, Labour Party,
  performance measurement, quasi-
  markets
National Health Service Executive, 33, 56,
  59, 60–1, 134
National Health Service Management
  Executive, 59–60, 203–4
New Right
  Conservative Party and, 16–19
  consumers and, 15
  NHS and, 15, 21
  privatisation, approach to, 20
  producer groups, critique of, 14
  professionals and, 14–16
  public sector managerialism, 20–2
  public spending and, 25
  state monopoly and, 9, 15
  trade unions and, 18
  see also Conservative Party
'New Wave' Management, 161–6
'Next Steps', 2–3, 5, 127, 169, 234
NHS and Community Care Act 1990, 1,
  54, 58–9

Organisation for Economic Cooperation
  and Development, 12, 117, 143–4

Performance measurement, 29–53,
  174–201
  accountability rationale for, 30–1,
    47–53
  causality, 44–5, 191–2, 198–201
  central government and, 32–3, 35, 39,
    45, 51, 175–81
  'cheating', 46–7
  comparison, 29–30, 36, 40–2, 47,
    174–81, 184–7, 189, 191–2,
    196–201

consumers and, 34, 43–4, 51–3, 182–3
expenditure control and, 36, 48–9
growth of, 29–30
higher education, 30, 34–6, 38, 51–2,
    181
housing, 45–6, 50–1, 191–2, 197–200
inputs, 35–6, 39
league tables, 34, 36, 42
local government, 30–1, 35, 45, 49,
    188–201
NHS, 30, 32–4, 36–41, 45–7, 53,
    174–87
'outcomes', 37
'outputs', 37, 39
performance indicators, 31–2, 53
performance-related pay and, 50
personal social services, 30–2, 37, 42,
    45, 53, 199
private sector comparisons, 45
professionals and, 33–4, 38, 190
public sector managerialism and, 36
resource allocation and, 46
secondary education, 33–4, 40–1, 43–6,
    52, 190
social security, 34, 45, 200
value-added measures, 33, 41, 52, 150
poll tax, 23
Polytechnic and Colleges Funding
    Council, 78, 82–3
Post-Fordism, see Fordism and Post-
    Fordism
Prior, James, 17, 171
Privatisation, 19–20, 23–4, 63, 85, 107
professions, 14–15
provider/purchaser division, 20, 56, 63,
    204
public expenditure, 25–8, 116–17, 139,
    149, 231–2
public sector managerialism, 1, 2–7,
    20–3, 145–6, 166–7
    central government and, 1
    definitions of, 2–7
    producer groups and, 14–15
    see also Conservative Party, Labour
        Party, New Right
public sector pay, 116–40, 231–59
    ad hoc pay inquiries, 121–2
    Burnham, 121, 127
    civil service, 122, 124, 127–8, 134,

234–6, 245–6
Clegg commission, 122–4, 127
collective bargaining and, 123
comparability principle of, 119, 122–5,
    128–30, 238–9
decentralised pay, 120, 125–7, 130–4,
    138–9, 239–43, 245–6, 253–7
Department of Employment and, 118
Edmund Davies report, 122
Employment Department and, 118–20,
    232–4
external comparisons and, 128–30,
    246–9
'fair comparison', 122–5, 235–6, 249
Halsbury report, 122
Houghton report, 122
incentive allowances,
incomes policy, 119–20, 138
indexation, 122–3, 130
Interim Advisory Committee
    (Teachers), 118, 125, 127–30, 134,
    251–3
internal relativities 122, 124, 236–7
local authority employees, 117, 135
Megaw Inquiry, 118, 122, 124–7,
    130–1, 134, 236–40, 243–4, 249–51,
    253–4, 258
National Board for Prices and Incomes,
    122–3
national pay bargaining, 119
'Next Steps' and, 127
pay determination, 123, 139, 232–3
Pay Research Unit, 122
performance-related pay, 119–20,
    126–7, 134–7, 234, 243–5, 258–9
police, 122, 130
Priestley inquiry, 122, 124, 234–8
regional pay, 125, 131, 249–53
Remuneration of Teachers Act, 121
Review Bodies, 118, 121, 138, 234
Review Body (Nursing Staff,
    Midwives, Health Visitors), 118, 125,
    128–34, 135, 137
Review Body (Doctors and Dentists),
    118, 126, 128–9, 132, 135, 137, 239,
    246–8
School Teachers' Review Body, 118,
    127–8, 130, 135–6, 258–9
Social Contract, 123

Index

social justice and, 119
Teachers Pay Act 1991, 131, 139
Tomlin Committee, 122, 124
Wages Councils, 119, 233
Whitley Councils, 121

Quasi-markets
  community care
    choice and, 63–4, 214–17
    eligibility criteria, 65–9
    funding of, 62, 64–5
    social security and, 62–5
    Standard Spending Assessment and,
      65
  education (higher)
    expansion of, 76–7, 79–80, 83, 85,
      223
    funding of, 77–8, 81–3
    research and, 78, 81–2
    teaching quality assessment, 77,
      83–5, 225
    standards of provision, 79–80, 83–5,
      223
  education (secondary)
    age-weighted pupil numbers, 70–2,
      219
    choice and, 71–6, 217–18
    City Technology Colleges, 73
    'effectiveness' and, 71–2, 74
    'efficiency' and, 69, 71–4, 217–18
    grant-maintained schools, 70–1,
      73–4, 127, 131, 140, 219–20
    local education authorities and,
      69–71, 73, 75
    local management of schools, 70,
      127–8, 156, 222
    national curriculum, 71–2, 74, 76,
      220–2
    open enrolment, 69–70
    Parents charter, 72
    special educational needs and, 75,
      219
  NHS
    centralisation and, 58–9
    contracts and, 58

decentralisation and, 58–62
regulation of, 59–62
trusts, 58–9, 202–3

Rationing, 65–9
Research Assessment Exercise, 78, 81–3
Reagan, Ronald, 8
Regional Health Authorities, 60
Regulation Theory, 159–61
Resource Allocation Working Party, 4
Ring Fencing, 63, 65, 215–16

Schumpeterian Workfare State, 152, 159
Smith, John, 147
Social Services Inspectorate, 30–3, 63
Social Services Committee, 63
Stakeholder, 53, 166

Taxation, 24, 149
  see also, Hayek, Friedrich von
Teaching Quality Assessment, 77, 83–5,
  225
Thatcher, Margaret, 8–9, 16, 19, 36, 54,
  141, 154–5
throughput, *see* performance
  measurement, output
Tomlinson Committee, 57
Trade Unions, 11, 16–19, 119
  see also, compulsory competitive
    tendering, Hayek, Friedrich von
Treasury, 231–2

University Funding Council, 38, 78, 81–2

Vouchers, 15, 19–20, 62, 155

Webb, Sidney, 29
Weighted Capitation, 55
Welfare State
  public opinion and, 23–5
  universalist concept of, 150
Winterton, N., 171
Women, 140,
  see also, compulsory competitive
    tendering, gender employment effects
Working for Patients, 55, 201–2